A History of Western Art

A History of
Western Art

Michael Levey

PRAEGER PUBLISHERS
NEW YORK · WASHINGTON

To CHARLES

BOOKS THAT MATTER

PUBLISHED IN THE UNITED STATES OF AMERICA IN 1968
BY PRAEGER PUBLISHERS INC.
111 FOURTH AVENUE, NEW YORK, N.Y. 10003

© 1968 IN LONDON, ENGLAND, BY MICHAEL LEVEY
THIRD PRINTING, 1974
ALL RIGHTS RESERVED
LIBRARY OF CONGRESS CATALOG CARD NUMBER: 68-54496

ISBN 0-275-70820-9

PRINTED IN GREAT BRITAIN

Contents

Art never expresses anything but itself. . . . So far from being the creation of its time, it is usually in direct opposition to it, and the only history it preserves for us is the history of its own progress.

OSCAR WILDE

Introduction

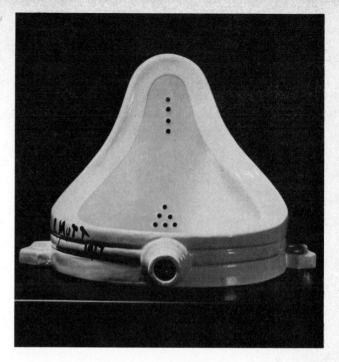

1 DUCHAMP *Fountain*
1917

Art is not something which has ceased to be created. It is more important for a history of art to begin with that fact than to offer any theory of what art is – still less to try and guess what art will be.

It is important to begin with that fact partly because the art that is sealed off by belonging in the past has often lost its power to shock, startle or annoy. History has made it all dreadfully palatable. We smile to read how disconcerted were contemporary spectators when they first saw the art of, for example, Tintoretto, or Borromini or Cézanne. But few people have worked out their own estimate of these artists' creations; history seems to have done it for them.

Not only is there no credit in mindlessly subscribing to the cult of 'old masters', but there is a positive danger in this waiting for the anaesthetist, history, to turn art drowsy before one dares inspect it. Such an attitude comes from fear. It is nothing to do with 'modern' art as such but is connected with ordinary human reaction to novelty of any sort.

Art is always novel. It all aspires to the condition of Duchamp's *Fountain (Ill. 1)*, in so far as it means to be something

7

different from what art has been before, and the difference is always in some degree unforeseen. Duchamp has said that he restricted the production of such 'ready-mades', knowing that 'art is a habit-forming drug'. Ultimately there is no *explanation* of any work of art, whenever it was executed, but history is largely concerned with explanations. The phenomenon of the 'Wars of the Roses' is susceptible of this treatment; a painting of the Madonna of the Rose-hedge will remain inexplicable, even when every fact of iconography of the Virgin, ecclesiastical patronage, and the development of altarpieces in the fifteenth century, has been investigated.

This means that individual judgment is as necessary in estimating the art of the past as in estimating that of the present. Or rather, it means that greater independence needs to be exercised over the past because that comes with an impressive accumulation of history which may bring us emotionally to our knees without waiting to see the object. Dealing with the prestige of antiquity in the eighteenth century, the sculptor Falconet pertinently pleaded, 'that we may be allowed, before genuflecting, to consider the god'. And this scrutiny is the only method by which finally we can appreciate art of any sort of any date, ancient or modern. The best tribute we can pay it is to take it seriously, even if this leads eventually to taking some of it away and putting it in the cellar. The result is better than impossibly crowded, overstocked rooms where everything is present but nothing is really cared for.

Art is the furniture which man will go on creating in his attempts to make the physical universe more pleasant and endurable. In whatever form it exists, art remains some sort of barrier or bulwark, however temporary, against the particular physical fact of death. Life's brevity and art's longevity, the immortality of art contrasted with the mortality of both those who create it and those who enjoy it: such typical, long-established clichés pay tribute to the super-vitality which is felt to be art's secret. Something of that may rub off on to us – if only for a few moments – and help us forget that in reality we are doomed. The awareness is there in the Egyptian tomb or in the sculpted porch of a Gothic cathedral. It is no accident that so much art has always found itself connected with death, erecting tombs and propagating myths of immortality. Art offers its own illusion not only in the teeth of death but just because of that. It is the only constructive alternative to a life-time of death-like inactivity. Our one chance lies, as Pater said, 'in getting as many pulsations as possible into the given time'. The furniture that is art was originally constructed by the artist to mitigate his own sentence, but in some way or other it can be of service to us, his fellow prisoners.

It is not surprising that art has always been enlisted in the service of myths, whether religious or profane. Indeed, it might be said that art is equally in need of myths to propagate and when it can do no better is glad to seize on Superman or Batman or the miracle of modern canned goods. It is magic – a magic most apparent to us perhaps not in any visual art (unless the cinema) but in the act of reading. The intense spell which a book can usually cast on anyone is less easily cast by the visual arts. Conversely, there is less demand for explanations *about* books. A novel by Simenon needs no explanation of its function or purpose. It is not necessary to urge the reader to work his imagination and try and take some interest in fictional characters in lace-curtained Liège on a foggy afternoon. The reader perfectly understands and responds to the novel's convention. The spectator in a gallery of pictures (even when they are all old masters) is perpetually asking questions which extend from the works of art and which reveal how little he can instinctively sink himself in them.

To such an extent is this so that, ironically, he may well find himself disorientated when confronting modern works of art where the very questions he is used to asking have no application. The spectator looks for the myth rather than the art. Trained to believe that there are extra-artistic reasons why a Romanesque crucifix looks as it does, he expects to be given an explanation of Rauschenberg's work beyond the fact that it looks as it does because that is how the artist made it. History's explanations may have their validity, but they are dangerous if relied on too much. We may appreciate an object better for comprehending its original purpose, but many works of art have always been created for no purpose except to be art; and, further, no amount of interesting historical explanation will turn a non-work of art into art. As we approach closer to the art of our own time, historical explanations become less convincing and coherent. A. J. P. Taylor's *From Sarajevo to Potsdam* is not intended to, and will not prove to, illuminate either the architecture of Frank Lloyd Wright or the paintings of Matisse, though it spans effectively much of their active lifetimes.

There is, of course, a good, and indeed historical, reason for this. The purpose and powers of art have actually become less certain as it has developed out of its social context. During the nineteenth century it lost much of its myth material. Religious belief declined; autocratic monarchies declined – Napoleon being probably the last ruler whose propaganda became art. At first it seemed that art would throw its energies into propagating a new religion of factual realism and scientific observation. And there it encountered a new rival, the camera. Well into the present century, there were aspirations for art to be *true* in an almost evangelical sense of the word. Degas is as usual alone, honourably alone, in stating quite flatly, 'Art is deceit.' Failure to understand the paradox of art led to the quintessentially nineteenth-century disaster of Holman Hunt's *The Light of the World (Ill. 235)*. The least embarrassed art form of the nineteenth century was, significantly, architecture which retains its primary functional purpose. Two new types of building required by the nineteenth century's own progress were the railway station and the office building: triumphant solutions were found to both, involving new concepts and new materials. A confident excitement is apparent in the lyric prose in which the American architect, Louis Sullivan, wrote about the 'tall office building', and his buildings were finer than his prose.

When art, of all kinds, has most effectively served a religious system, that system has itself usually been more than a pillar – a positive colonnade – of society. At such periods there are naturally no debates about art's role in the community. Its purpose gives it a definite utilitarian basis – one that has gradually been pulled away from under it until today it need support nothing, but also runs the risk of being unsupported. Religious pictures and portraits are the two ends of painting according to Dürer, and it is remarkable how much great Western art up to 1800 is subsumed in those two categories, especially when one adds works of art that, though not overtly religious, are didactic in intent.

Today the problem may seem at first to be that art has lost its social purpose. And it is only apparently given one by the polite commissioning of sculpture for new buildings and schemes of decoration for some university or satellite town which often attract more attention at the planning stage than when the work is finally executed. We are basically uncertain what to do with art. Certainly our squares and our cemeteries are not the place for it. Even when modern monuments do exist, they may be as free from all 'programme' reference as is Barbara Hepworth's monument in memory of Hammerskjöld

10

(Ill. 2). This simply exists in its own right as a soaring form in bronze. That it would anyway be free of cemetery associations might be expected, but it is particularly interesting that the sculptor has spoken of the liberating effect a visit to Brancusi's studio had on her, after living in a Northern climate, 'where the approach to sculpture has appeared fettered by the gravity of monuments to the dead'.

Rodin's *Balzac (Ill. 239)*, executed at the end of the nineteenth century and rejected by its commissioners, offers us, as well as its form to appreciate, an image we can recognize as human. But its rejection was probably inevitable, because it insists on being not a factual representation so much as Rodin's reaction to, his impression of, Balzac's personality. If to us it now appears devoid of all shocking quality, we can perhaps recover some of its original disconcerting novelty by seeing it against the tradition expressed by an eighteenth-century monument, Pigalle's to Marshal Saxe, *(Ill. 198)*, with its elaborate iconographic programme. Pigalle's is in fact the triumphant culmination of a tradition – the last, and one of the greatest, of Baroque tombs. Its imagery is easy to read at the most essential level: man confronts death. This is obvious, and made very effective, without our needing to know anything about Saxe. Rodin's *Balzac* is private by comparison. Whereas the more one learns about Saxe the more one can 'read' his monument, with the *Balzac* it was the very knowledge of the writer that made Rodin's sculpture so shocking to the Société des Gens de Lettres who had commissioned it. Hepworth's monument is free of any such problem. It need not symbolize anything, still less represent anything connected with the real person Hammerskjöld. It does not prompt one to ask questions about him. It is simply a shape which the sculptor has associated with him.

The only question it may, accidentally, prompt is: do we have any place for art that has no purpose except to be art? While it is not worth pretending that we can use art in the way it was once used, it is perhaps significant that we nowadays find art in things that are utilitarian. What were once called minor arts – or not even arts at all – now have their opportunity to be taken as seriously as a painting or piece of sculpture. The very word 'art' may immediately give the wrong connotation, suggestive of stuffiness, and bourgeois respect for the museum. This is no longer such a modern idea, for it is over fifty years since Duchamp thought up the idea of 'ready-mades', of which his *Fountain* is a good example.

The idea of art's immortality is itself brought into doubt by the ephemeral poster, the window display or the *collage* which quickly grows dusty and may even be intended to drop to bits. The magic of the creator, and awe at what he has created, can be disposed of best either by setting up the *objet trouvé* as art or by positively destroying art, in ridicule or by a physical act. The idea of attacking 'art' is something that, once again, goes back to Duchamp: not only for his witty gesture of putting a moustache on the *Mona Lisa* but also for the hinted destruction in his remark, 'use a Rembrandt as an ironing-board'.

In such ways art proclaims its freedom to be anything it likes. It keeps trying to be exciting and topical, thinks up new ways to astonish and amuse us, and yet increasingly seems unable to be needed. Perhaps most people have frankly lost their interest in art of any sort. If that is so, art cannot help it and the way back to an audience certainly does not lie in appealing for one. Even the loss of social purpose is something partly more apparent than real, because we persuade ourselves into seeing the past peopled with connoisseurs, every Renaissance man a fine judge of merit in a building, a statue or a painting. But it is simply untrue that there ever was a climate of universal appreciation. When art was most closely tied to social uses, probably most people could hardly see the art for the use: they went to the temple or church as a religious duty, not for an aesthetic experience. Probably half the citizens of Florence were quite uncaring about Cellini's *Perseus (Ill. 134)* when it was first put up – or, if they liked it, did so for the wrong reasons.

Today we are actually much better placed, to respond to art of our own period as well as to survey that of the past. Artists have encouraged the autonomy of the spectator to the point where we may each be our own artist, picking up our own *objets trouvés*, making our own assemblages of junk. If that achieves nothing else, it may at least encourage our confidence and help us exercise discrimination over art of all periods. Just as not everything produced today is necessarily good, great, or even authentic, so what has survived from the past is not necessarily great – however historically important it may be. There is really no secret about appreciating art, except to have a belief that art – whatever it is – is essential. It is not just a pastime or an amusement, but a deadly serious activity which must be taken seriously.

Nevertheless, art does not speak one international, universal language easily comprehended by everyone. It is more a Babel than Esperanto. Works of art into which artists put all their technique and energies are not going to yield their secrets at a glance. Assimilation is slow – and with the visual arts there is always a difficulty in preventing too hasty a survey. Books and music take time to read and hear. Visual works of art require time just as much, but the spectator has there to apply the discipline for himself. Temples, tombs, cathedrals, monuments, built and planned and decorated all over Western Europe during the course of centuries, do not necessarily make plain immediately their functions or their artistic effect. It is not true that Giotto and Picasso are really the same sort of artist, because no two artists are ever the same. Even when two artists seem to set out to be rather similar, in a little moment out of whole centuries of art, they diverge to become quite different. Style makes them each individual and we learn to recognize, for example, that Fragonard is utterly distinct from Boucher – just as we learn to distinguish a German Gothic cathedral from a French one.

It is this sense of individuality that has become the chief characteristic of Western artists and Western styles of art. Even if one were to begin only at AD 1500, the shifts and changes, the crowd of conflicting individualities and contrasting creations are themselves bewildering enough to justify some attempt at a guide. To go right back to the origins of art makes the attempt much more hazardous, but perhaps all the more worth trying.

CHAPTER ONE

From the Cave
to the City

3 Arch of Titus, Rome.
    First century AD

The story of man's progress from living in caves to building
cities is also the story of art's evolution – an evolution that does
not by any means throughout imply artistic progress – from the
long-hidden paintings of Lascaux and Altamira to the never-
neglected monuments of imperial Rome. Between intervenes
a huge period of time. But myths and a sense of magic lie behind
much of the resulting works of art. Art has a definite ritual use,
whether it suggests vitality or positively aims at giving an
individual immortality. Magically, it extends the limits of
ordinary experience: making appear on the cave walls creatures
that are not present, and giving posthumous life for ever to the
Divine Titus, son of the Divine Vespasian, on an arch inscribed
with his name and dedicated to him by the Senate and People
of Rome (*Ill. 3*).

   That was put up nearly nineteen hundred years ago, but may
be claimed as a very recent artifact when we start to descend to
the murky prehistorical times of cave art to seek the origins of

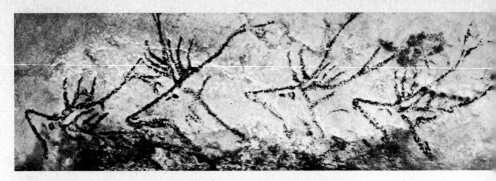

4 Stags, Lascaux
cave, Dordogne

5 Standing bison,
Altamira cave,
Santander

6 The 'Venus' of Willendorf

Western art. These origins are themselves isolated, a largely Northern European prologue which gives us art without civilization long before there took place the main Mediterranean drama of art *and* civilization which culminates in Greece. We need expect no architecture from a shadowy era when the land-mass was covered largely by ice, but painting and sculpture were already practised by primitive man – with surprisingly accomplished results, far in advance of any social development. The emphasis of this art lies not on mankind but on animals which retain their impressive vitality even when man – in the shape of stick-like hunting figures – begins to include himself in the images. Some *mana* was perhaps thought to reside in the animal, powerful and huge, whose flesh and blood will renew one's own. Indeed, it is possible that *mana* resided not so much in the living animal as in the image of it painted on the rock. The idea of animal-derived virility is not merely a naïve pre-historical concept, but something that lingers on in our steak-obsessed age. The Altamira bison *(Ill. 5)* can be seen almost in the terms of those large-scale diagrams often appearing on the menu of steak-houses where dotted lines and arrows indicate the most succulent portions.

Though their actual means of expression may be cruder, the cave paintings reveal equal, if not greater, observation. Telling us little about the hunter, they vividly convey – in outline or in blended tones – the hunted. At Lascaux a frieze of stags *(Ill. 4)*, each with its muzzle at slightly different angle, passes over the rock wall like some slowed-down image from a film. There is a developing, deliberate naturalism which leads from these, the earliest images, traced with an unvarying outline, to the coloured, even textured effects represented by the Altamira animals. Yet even over this great period of time, there seems little temptation to enlarge subject-matter. The artists continue to concentrate on what perhaps they were most conscious of: other living creatures which existed but which were different from mankind. They were more worth recording than man's appearance or his environment. Yet, given the means at the command of the creators of Altamira, they would have been fully capable of producing images of themselves as economical and effective as their portraits of animals.

When the human body appears, it is in sculpture. It appears without any concern with the face, made up of a series of tactile bulges which suggest buttocks and breasts – for it is the female body that is preferred in these small amulet-like objects *(Ill. 6)*.

17

More patently than the cave paintings, these reveal a concern with form and suggest an ability to stylize quite consciously, anticipating Brancusi by many thousands of years. The so-called 'Venus' found at Willendorf is naturalistic by comparison with other more geometrically-stylized statuettes in which the head may shrink to a small blank ovoid. And though the Willendorf 'Venus' has no face, her hair is noticeably elaborate and the pose of the head tilted forward avoids the problem of a featureless face. The result is, perhaps accidentally, a self-regarding figure: among the very first of navel-gazing nudes (the Willendorf 'Venus' has a clearly-marked navel) and a tight little nut of sexual potency.

Although we do not know whether such sculpture preceded cave painting, both are products of an early, shifting, tribal world where buildings were probably no more than reed or mud huts. Not until long after the Western European cave paintings had been produced did there begin to be monuments in stone set up by men, connected with ritual, either in worship of some god or in honour of the dead (if the two were distinctly separated). These suggest ideas of permanence which probably never occurred to the cave artists, who certainly cannot have guessed how well preserved, though concealed, their art would prove to be. Some three thousand years or more seem to separate the naturalism of the Upper Palaeolithic cave paintings from the Neolithic Age (around 7500 B C) when man emerges on the earth's surface to build such large-scale monuments as Stonehenge, one of the earliest surviving magic circles (Ill. 7). This retains an atmosphere at once impressive and oppressive. Its stones are like dragon's teeth, sprung up in a circle which appears more threatening than holy, but they mark a new achievement and suggest some definitely organized society.

It is an indication of man's imaginative powers that it was for the needs not of the living but the dead that stones were first set up. Whatever type of primitive hut he lived in, he built more enduringly when he made tombs, by the construction of the dolmen, two upright stone slabs roofed with a horizontal slab. This is the principle extended to make at Stonehenge a complete circle, or rather, two concentric circles within which stood other dolmen-like groups of stones. And it is the same simple principle that, literally, underlies the construction of the Lion Gate at Mycenae (Ill. 19).

In some way or another it is probable that Stonehenge is connected with the sun, serving either as some kind of temple or

7 Stonehenge, Wiltshire. Late Neolithic between 1900 and 1700 B C
to Bronze Age *c.* 1500

even as a giant sun-dial. Nor does sun-worship cease with this
Neolithic monument. The solar myths of Egyptian culture are
a fairly familiar idea, but it is more unexpected to find Plato
naming the sun-god, Helios, as joint leader in his concept of a
new state cult (in the *Laws*), in which Helios and Apollo are
joined. Stonehenge may be taken to mark the end of the pre-
historic prologue to the development of Western art. The scene
shifts to the Mediterranean. Even though magic still rules the
universe, it is now magic that seems a controllable force, that
can be manipulated by a whole elaborate code of rules. It is as
if man had at last dared to look at other men, and discovered
that nature, the gods (and man's own secret urge) were all
placated by images of himself and his environment. The family
groups of Egyptian sculpture are sympathetic as sculpture and
also for their suggestions of a more homely and less death-
obsessed environment than is usually supposed. Above all, in
moving to the different climate – in every sense – of the Mediterranean cultures, we encounter not merely works we can
recognize as art but the activity of art for its own sake.

19

As an introduction to this world, therefore, the small ivory hippopotamus *(Ill. 8)* is perhaps better than a pyramid. This is old indeed, produced by the Badarian culture which preceded the First Dynasty in Egypt, and thus from before 3100 BC. No cult object, it is an unguent jar that happens also to be a miniature work of art. It pays tribute to the artist's power of observation, and it evokes a sophisticated, positive civilization where such an object might be as useful in life as in death: useful by delighting the eye in addition to serving as a receptacle for ointment or scent. Its creator was not content with providing simply the most utilitarian form but amusingly worked the shape into that of a common animal to be seen along the Nile.

Although it is true that Egyptian culture revolved round the fact of death, and much of its art was produced with a view to providing for death, all this thought and activity had exorcized its terror. Whereas the Greeks were too restlessly inquiring ever to settle on a satisfactory myth of an after-life, and seem always hovering on scepticism about their entire religion, the Egyptians evolved a clear, calm and fundamentally naïve system which really mirrored as closely as possible the life they knew. The gods lived in their temples as houses – and their temples were built on the plan of the Egyptian house. In death each spirit inhabited his tomb on the same domestic principle; his daily life was reproduced there in painting or sculpture, along with models of objects of ordinary use, and an image of himself, often with his family. Eternity consisted in hunting *(Ill. 9)* or doing nothing, just existing, content within the comfort of a religious

8 Ivory hippopotamus jar. Before 3100 BC

9 Ti hunting, relief from the tomb of Ti, Saqqara. V Dynasty *c.* 2500–2350 B C

system well summed up by one hieroglyphic text which reads: 'I have given thee all good things and all offerings which are in the South, for thou hast appeared as King of Upper and Lower Egypt for ever.'

Like the Egyptian climate, its art hardly changed. Centuries passed in a fertile land that needed little effort at cultivation by its inhabitants. The vital act of irrigation was performed by the Nile, conveniently flooding its banks once a year. And the river is in some ways the real subject in that relief in the tomb of Ti, for if he is taller than his servants, the long, level stems of the background papyrus, growing beside the river, are taller still. The fish and the hippopotami in the water below, and the flapping birds amid the papyrus buds, are all part of the Nile bank scenery – here skilfully laid out to cover a wall like a great animated screen.

21

It is usual to express surprise that Egyptian art retained its conventions for so long (going on drawing the eye frontally in profiles, for example) without further attempts at naturalism, but there was wisdom in this conservatism as long as it preserved its artistic vitality. An early admirer of Egyptian art was Van Gogh; writing to his brother about it he said: '... when the thing represented and the manner of representing agree, the thing has style and quality'. This serves to remind us that there must always be some convention in art; and thus paradoxically we may more easily be able to appreciate a head such as that carved in yellow quartzite *(Ill. 10)* rather than the fully naturalistic portrait busts of Greece or Rome *(Ill. 44)*. The Egyptian head is a portrait also, of an unidentified queen, done about 1360 BC, but its appeal is not connected with lifelikeness so much as with its combination of bulk and delicacy. On the hard shape of head are scooped out the deep winged eye-sockets, shapes pleasing in themselves and echoed by the curved heavy lips. While recognizably a human head, it keeps an aura of remoteness and strangeness which is part of its beauty. It stands for a person rather than is concerned with minute particularization of a person, and yet it is completely art. Any absence of the lifelike is not the artist's failure but the pursuit of a conscious convention. Already art tacitly poses the question for us of why should it pursue merely natural appearances. Its task is to create not imitate.

10 Head of an unidentified queen from Amarna. Late XVIII Dynasty *c.* 1360 BC

11 Frieze of King
Smenkhkare and
Queen Meryt-Aten.
Late XVIII Dynasty
c. 1365 BC

Only once during the course of thirty centuries were
Egyptian politics, culture, religion – and hence art – drastically
changed. The king Akhenaten (1378–1360 BC) moved his
capital from Thebes to a newly-built city, broke the domination
of the priests of the god Amon, and introduced a less rigid and
immobile style of art. His revolution did not outlast his reign,
and under his weak son-in-law Tutankhamen (disproportion-
ately famous to us, because of the intactness of his tomb) the old
religious and artistic forms were re-established. The naturalism
encouraged by Akhenaten's reforms is shown by such relief
portraits as that of his successor, Smenkhkare, and his Queen
(Ill. 11), where the thin King positively lounges in casual pose,
legs crossed, body relaxed – man rather than god, simply gazing
at his wife who brandishes a bouquet of flowers. Yet even
though this frank domesticity is new, a domestic vein is deep in

23

all Egyptian art. Women are shown equal, not subordinated to men. If death has dictated the reliefs and the statues, at least man and woman face it together, often with interlinked hands, in a homely harmony quite foreign to Greek art – and, indeed, to Greek culture.

Egyptian art is neither intellectual nor aggressive. It does not glorify the human body (and is mercifully unaware of the glamour of being an athlete) but is quite conscious of physical appearance and able to record it *(Ill. 12),* even when it is not conventionally beautiful. There is a human air to the architecture of Egyptian temples, their pylons heavily decorated with figures in sunk relief, approached through an avenue of human-headed sphinxes, or with a façade where giant statues act like pillars. The pillars themselves in these comparatively simple structures, where the curved arch was hardly used, are worked into shapes derived from papyrus and lotus plants, suggesting again the fertile Nile which made living easy in a climate that hardly encouraged thought. It cannot be said, however, to have discouraged work if we reflect that the Egyptians built the largest surviving mass of man-built stone in the pyramid of

13 The Sphinx and ▶
Pyramid of Chephren,
Giza. IV Dynasty
c. 2615–2500 BC

12 Statuette of
Meyrehastel.
VI Dynasty
c. 2350–2130 BC

Chephren *(Ill. 13)* which, together with the near-by Sphinx, remains the most potent symbol of their civilization. Against the achievement of the Parthenon *(Ill. 25)* it seems almost irrational, absurdly unsubtle, exercising the power less of art than of the picturesque.

Within pyramids like that of Chephren was once treasure, accumulations of objects of every kind, presumably comparable to the piled treasure found in the uniquely intact tomb of Tutankhamen. In some ways it is all Egyptian art that was sealed in there: from the life-sized statues flanking the entrance, to the elaborately jewelled bracelets on the mummified arms of the king. There is a sophistication and sensuousness about the painted alabaster and gilded wood creations which, like fabulous toys, littered the tomb, and a delicacy as well as moving strangeness in those gold goddesses *(Ill. 15)* who stood guard over the king's viscera. Once again, they are not totally lifelike nor perfectly proportioned. At first glance they may all look alike, though their head-dresses are carefully differentiated. They may seem expressionless, and yet the gesture of their open arms and the alert pose of their heads together combine to suggest graceful guardianship. For all their bodies' apparent rigidity, there is a nervous fluidity in the modelling of their fine, many-pleated, clinging dresses, and it communicates itself to their long thin feet, with toes almost like extended pleats of drapery.

The lack of prestige from which Egyptian art has always suffered is partly a matter of history rather than aesthetics. Although climate and sand were to preserve an extraordinary amount of its art, sand long concealed a great deal; the body of the Sphinx at Giza was in this way hidden more than once in ancient times, and was not exposed again until the nineteenth century. Egyptian civilization was a dead one, without the apparent continuity which was to lead from Greece to Rome and then to Christianity. It did not conquer, in either a military or an artistic way. It left no proper literature, and barely left any writing – for the system of hieroglyphics is typically a matter of pictorial images not abstract symbols. Even its cities were always lifeless cities, where the major monuments were not palaces but tombs and temples. As a system of civilization, it has nothing to teach us; but that should leave us only the more free to appreciate the considerable achievements of its often austere art *(Ill. 14)*.

14 Ramesses II and his son lassoing a steer. XIX Dynasty *c.* 1304–1237 BC

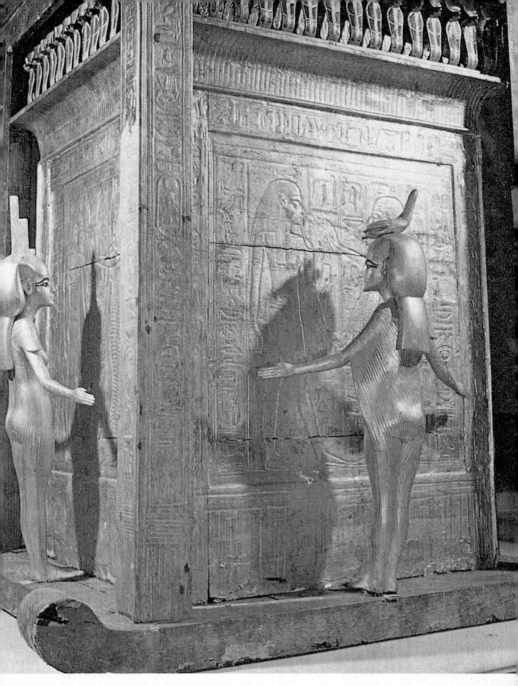

15 Guardian goddesses of Tutankhamen's viscera. XVIII Dynasty
c. 1360 BC

A considerable move west, psychologically as well as geographically, is required to encounter the next, the most relevant civilization, that of the Aegean, which begins with the Minoan culture of Crete. In strict archaeological accuracy, it begins with a Neolithic period that is to be set at least as far back as 5000 B C but artistically Crete will probably always mean the culture of the Minoan Bronze Age, centring on the complex palace which grew up at Knossos, associated with the legendary king Minos. Much about that world still remains controversial and mysterious, and equally mysterious is the catastrophe which around 1400 B C destroyed the civilization – not many years before the reign of Akhenaten in Egypt. Not surprisingly, there are some tenuous links between Minoan art and both Egyptian and Mesopotamian, but the Cretan products are very different. They appear remarkably undominated, to begin with, by religious preoccupations. The agglomeration at Knossos was not a temple but a palace, meant to be lived in and well equipped with civilized appurtenances. Cretan art seems equally free from dynastic obsessions, commemorating no monarchs or rulers, and leaving no very clear evidence at all about the island's political and religious organization. There was apparently no monumental sculpture – in marked contrast to Egypt – and no grandiose concept of tombs. Eternity, an after-life, even the future, seem to have raised no very urgent problems. Art no longer aims to impress posterity, but seems much more eager to catch vitality and thus in some, highly sophisticated, ways becomes closer to Altamira than to Egyptian art.

There is a sense of action and movement which is startlingly new and quite obvious in the statuette of a girl athlete vaulting over a bull's horns *(Ill. 16)*. It is typical of Minoan culture that this practice seems to have been as much sport as religious ritual. Highly popular as a theme in Cretan frescoes and statuettes, the bull was perhaps a sacred animal but it appears as sheerly animal, a creature against whom men and women pit their wits in a game of, apparently, bloodless skill. In the statuette movement and athletic – almost balletic – grace are prized for their own sake. Cult objects, frescoes in the palace at Knossos, and the distinctive decorative spirals on Minoan pottery all extend these ideas of movement.

Where Ti in his tomb *(Ill. 9)* hunted for ever, as solemn as if engaged in a sacred ceremony, acrobats at Knossos are depicted positively dancing as they sport with a bull hardly less elegant, slender and nimble-footed than themselves *(Ill. 17)*.

28

16 Cretan bull-jumping statuette. Sixteenth century B C

There is such wit and refinement in this admittedly restored fresco that one might hesitate to accept it as representative of Cretan culture – and there is an element of false chic as well as false history in giving the name 'la Parisienne' to a woman's profile in another fresco from Knossos. But the vitality, and the wit too, genuinely are present in the naturalistic ornaments of the pottery which developed out of vigorous geometrical designs into the recognizable marine creatures *(Ill. 18)* spread so convincingly over often aptly bulbous surfaces that they seem writhing within the jar. It was particularly in categories like pottery, now usually termed a minor art, that the Minoans displayed their sophistication and their artistic abilities. At its height, their culture was very prosperous and Crete peaceful. Everything in their art encourages the idea of a luxury-loving, ingenious, social people, fond of games rather than hunting, and particularly keen on dancing. Like an echo of all those interests sound the lines where Homer describes the gold and silver shield of Achilles, wrought with a dancing-place, 'such as Daedalus made for Ariadne in broad Knossos'.

That is an echo from the already distant, increasingly mythical, past. Shifting west again, we encounter the earliest culture on the Greek mainland, in that Mycenaean one which is so closely

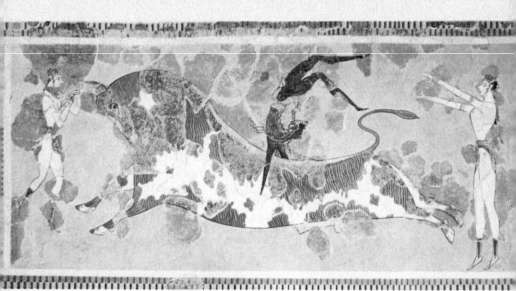

17 Bull-jumping,
fresco from the Royal
Palace, Knossos *c.*
1500 BC

18 Octopus jar from
Palaikastro *c.* 1500–
1450 BC

19 Lion Gate, Mycenae. Fourteenth century BC

and mysteriously bound up with the Minoan. We do not know whether it was a natural disaster, quite possibly a series of volcanic eruptions, or a foreign invasion which destroyed not only Knossos but the whole Cretan culture. And while Crete continued to decline, Mycenae rose to power in the Mediterranean. Crete itself was colonized and a Mycenaean–Minoan style grew up, fostered perhaps by Achaean princes who had settled on the island. On the mainland, a much tougher, monumental rather than miniaturistic world is evoked by the most famous relic, the Lion Gate at Mycenae *(Ill. 19),* which is

20 Geometric vase
c. 750 BC

defensive as well as summarily, heraldically, decorative. Mycenae and the other chief Aegean city of the period, Tiryns, were really fortified citadels, surrounded by massive walls which to the Greeks of later, classical times seemed to have been built by giants.

It might well seem to them that the Mycenaean Empire had been the creation of a mythical race, giants or heroes, because it too fell and its cities became ruins. The Greeks themselves did not have any clear idea of what had happened or who exactly were the invaders who disturbed the whole of the pre-classical Mediterranean world. There were invasions and counter-invasions; the Trojan War was fought, and Troy fell to the mixed bands of Achaeans, Dorians, Argives. The collapse of old cities was not immediately followed by the creation of new. It is almost suitable that there should be a pause, a period of confused darkness, out of which gradually came some simply patterned vases whose austere ornament is called Proto-geometric, and which are the first signs of a quite fresh centre of artistic activity, Athens.

Greek art begins with these. They, and especially the large-scale partly Geometric vases *(Ill. 20)* which follow them, can be seen to embody to a surprising degree the principles of an art and a civilization which was more than just harmonious or classically balanced. If lack of evidence prevents us getting a

21 Achilles slaying the Amazon queen Penthesilea at Troy, on an amphora by Exekias *c.* 540 BC

complete idea of the Minoan and Mycenaean cultures (scarcely having any existence in history before the archaeological explorations of the nineteenth century), it is through the mist of a two-thousand-year-old reputation that we gaze at Greece – and mist can be as much of a nuisance as missing evidence. With Athens we encounter the first city that has remained a city, dominated still by the Parthenon on the Acropolis (or upper city), but which has become also a symbol in European consciousness. It is almost easier to talk about our debt to Greece than about Greece itself.

The decoration on the large mixing-bowl *(Ill. 20)*, placed for libation on an Athenian grave about 750 B C, is a useful reminder that Greek art was a beginning all over again. It did not evolve directly from Mesopotamian or Egyptian, though it was to

22 *Antiope and Theseus* from the Temple of Apollo at Eretria *c.* 510 B C

23 *Zeus and Ganymede,* ▶ terracotta modelled by a Peloponnesian artist, from Olympia *c.* 480 B C

borrow from Egyptian art for its own ultimately very different purposes. Partly perhaps as a result of performing its own evolution, impetus carried it in sculpture and architecture far beyond anything dreamt of by the Egyptians – not in terms of engineering but of sheer art. To some extent, the Greeks began with nothing. They had not got a rich fertile land, but one stony and rugged. There is some aptness in the fact that the Acropolis is not even now a grassy hill but a hard slippery sea of stone, like a mixture of volcanic lava and marble. Greek daily life was fairly rugged too, at least austere; nor was death accompanied by the luxury objects which accompanied any Egyptian who could afford them. The somewhat drone-like palace existence suggested by Knossos was equally alien to the Greeks, as was the Minoan interest in small-scale *objets d'art*.

Instead, the Greeks had imagination. It is more usual to lay stress on their intellect (which is perhaps only the imagination active in a purely mental sphere) but even Socrates survives for us largely thanks to a series of literary works of art. We have come almost to assume that his death actually happened as Plato describes the scene; were that so, still Plato is its artistic creator, as Thucydides is the creator of the Pericles who makes his famous speech to the Athenians. Plato and Thucydides confirm something that already finds expression, however crudely, on the eighth-century mixing-bowl: a concern with human action and narrative. Greek pottery was not long to be content with either geometric patterns or lifelike animals as decoration; it was to develop a subtle accomplished language for painted scenes on vases *(Ill. 21)*, vivid as scenes from Greek plays and, like them, ranging from high tragedy to low, clowning comedy.

As Greek sculpture evolved, it too was animated by concepts of humanity and action, quickly resulting in something much more lively than any culture had previously created. Apart from vase-painting, not much Greek painting survives. In architecture some great buildings were produced, but the style was condemned to a basic lack of variety and inability to design beyond the needs of the temple and the open-air theatre. It was in sculpture that the Greeks found the fullest imaginative freedom, first in the belief that man is what matters. Their myth was one not really about gods or goddesses in the sense of beings different from men (for they are quarrelling in sculpture often enough, as they quarrel in the *Iliad*) but about how marvellous it is to be men. The statues are confident, not doubting, serene even when struggling, bodies in which physical well-being has itself become a religion. For all the brilliant mental qualities exemplified in their literature, the Greeks sculpted figures that seem almost shockingly brainless and incapable of thought.

Today, after experiencing so many dusty white plaster casts in museums, and so much talk of idealization and classicism, it is easy to think of Greek sculpture as always colourless in surface and frozen in attitude, Olympian in the sense of superior aloofness. Yet in many ways it was warmer and more essentially human than any sculpture before or since. Its gods – and much Greek sculpture was concerned with them – were entirely human figures, expressing divinity not by bizarre costume, still less by animal attributes, but by their physical power, beauty and, often, nudity which displayed this divinity to advantage. Sculpture was often literally colourful. Instead of those chalky masses with blank eyes which words like 'classical sculpture' evoke, we encounter the non-Olympian (though from Olympia) group *Zeus and Ganymede (Ill. 23),* probably once a temple pediment, inevitably damaged but still retaining a good deal of its original colour. When this was executed, around 480 B C, Greek sculpture had fully emerged from its primitive, Egyptian-style beginnings. After some tentative movement, a mere shift in statuesque pose of a single body, a slight turn to the head, it had gone on to tackle the problem of several figures, often engaged in violent actions like fights and rapes (like, indeed, that by Zeus of Ganymede). But archaic conventions still kept it from complete naturalism, and within their restriction marble could be carved to achieve the beauty and inner calm of another, more graceful-seeming rape – that of Antiope by Theseus *(Ill. 22),* executed some thirty years before the *Zeus and Ganymede.*

The *Antiope and Theseus* is also a portion of sculpture from a temple pediment, and the delicacy of its carving must have been less easy to appreciate in its original position high up in the air. Yet that location helps to emphasize the public quality of most Greek sculpture – indeed, most Greek art – and a good deal of Greek life. It is directed less towards individuals than to the community of citizens. The focal point of it all becomes not the palace or the tomb, but the city. Where Egyptian art seems hermetic, with its splendours largely hidden from profane eyes, Greek art is open or open-seeming, suggesting communal participation, in the temple or at the theatre. In some ways the sculptured pediments are comparable to Greek plays, which were also publicly acted-out religious ritual in origin. Like sculpture, these plays evolved from the stiffness of archaic tragedy with a single actor to the flexible naturalism of Euripides' tragi-comedies. The final manifestations of Greek sculpture in the last two centuries BC are frankly theatrical in their dramatic effects. If the *Laocoön* group is the most famous example, other groups better reveal the extremes of human agony and pathos which were to be sculpted in fully realistic terms. The *Gaul killing himself and his wife (Ill. 27)* represents supreme virtuosity in the pursuit of emotional and physical realism in stone: a complete drama in itself, at once heroic and human, it was probably to exercise influence over Bernini in the seventeenth century.

The language of groups like the *Zeus and Ganymede* seems somewhat homely; certainly it is not heroic. Zeus strides along with rustic vigour – like a farmer carrying home his son, rather than a god suddenly infatuated with a mortal. The *Antiope* group is perhaps harder to judge, being so fragmentary; but its restrained air is quite deliberate, made patent in those few beautiful pleats of Antiope's short tunic – a musical and almost

24 Temple of Hera, Paestum. Mid-sixth century

25 The Parthenon, Athens 447–433 B C

trill-like effect against the barely articulated corselet. Its poised grace, and graceful balance between extremes of stiffness and complete naturalism, are typical of a stage of artistic evolution which was not to be prolonged. The Greek political world too was changing, sharpening into new awareness under the constant challenge of invasion by the barbarian Persians. It cannot quite be claimed as a national consciousness, because even at times of greatest common danger individual city-states remained jealously unhelpful to each other, but it culminated in the transformation of Athens from a city into the centre of an empire – its dominant position visually expressed in the splendour of its temples and their sculpture.

The earliest Greek architecture has much of the restraint of archaic sculpture, but with greater massiveness. Temples were built in the early Doric style, surviving most impressively in the temple of Hera at Paestum *(Ill. 24)*, elemental and even elementary beside the refined Doric of the Parthenon *(Ill. 25)* a century later. The Paestum site is a reminder that Greek art

39

26 *Apollo* from the
west pediment,
Olympia *c.* 460 BC

spread with Greek colonies; and the temples themselves there
have become almost natural shrines, on flat ground, between
the sea and the mountains, thrusting up their powerful columns
amid thick grass and wild oleanders. Standing within the
precincts, we can appreciate all the better the giant bones of the
plan – bones which have not whitened, only grown more deeply
honey-coloured under exposure to the sun – still satisfyingly
harmonious in its simplicity. There is more than massiveness in
this architecture. Each sturdy column, springing without
individual base to a plain cushion-like capital, has a fluted,
tapered shaft that introduces delicacy and relief into the monumental general effect. These columns are strong blocks of
masonry, but beautifully spaced so that they and the intervals
between them *are* the building, which, though roofless and
without sculpture, remain not just a picturesque ruin but fully
architecture.

From another huge Doric temple, that of Zeus at Olympia,
comes the clay group *Zeus and Ganymede (Ill. 23)*. Before the

40

Parthenon this was the largest temple on the Greek mainland, and one of the Seven Wonders of the ancient world. At Olympia the rudiments of Greek architecture could once be seen, for the temple of Hera there was built with wooden columns, only gradually replaced by stone ones as they decayed; some wooden columns were still standing when the traveller Pausanias visited the temple in the second century A D. Olympia was one of the two great religious sanctuaries of Greece, the other being Delphi. Although the seat of worship of Apollo was Delphi, it was at Olympia that Apollo triumphed at the centre of one of the pediments *(Ill. 26)*. This figure, majestic without effort, relaxed amid a battle of drunken Centaurs and struggling Lapiths, marks the final achievement of Greek sculpture before the full 'classical' naturalism of the Parthenon sculpture. This Apollo recalls a pillar, for all the articulation of his muscles; his lips are slightly parted to suggest breathing, but the planes of his face are stylized, not realistic. The few folds of drapery over his arm are as formal as the fluting on a column. He is still a Dorian figure, vigorously vertical, in movement but not in violent action. He embodies *rappel à l'ordre*, a triumph of reason over irrationality,

27 *Gaul killing himself and his wife.* Original bronze of third century B C

and the defeat of brute instinct by intellect and courage – qualities of the Greek mind which we like to think most typical. Apollo here has apparently been purged of his mysterious Asiatic origin; before the clarity and command of this figure, it is easy also to forget the Apolline oracle at Delphi, with its prophetic hysteria and cloudy prophecies.

Apollo's monumental calm at Olympia is the product of art. The statue dates from around 460 B C, by which time dramatic political events had shaken the Greek world, all its scattered city-states threatened by invasion from the great kings of Persia, first Darius and then his son Xerxes. The defeat of the Persians at Marathon in 490 was a moral as well as military victory for Athens, one consolidated ten years later when the Athenians, having evacuated the city, won the naval battle of Salamis. But Athens itself had been virtually destroyed by the Persians; the sacred edifices of the Acropolis were levelled to the ground, statues were overthrown and buried, and the remnant of the garrison slain in the temple of Pallas Athene before the building too perished. Rebuilding of the city offered an opportunity to express new pride in it as the heart of an empire. The removal from Delos to Athens of the treasury of those Greek states who had united against Persia is a symbol of the new concentration on this city – and it is rather typical of Athenian ways that money from the treasury was soon financing private Athenian concerns, including the new buildings on the Acropolis. This diversion, like the initiative in the reconstruction of the city, was due to Pericles; and Periclean Athens has become a by-word for an ideal of civilization.

The reality was full of disconcerting events, not least the imprisonment and death in prison of the great sculptor Phidias who was judged guilty of impiety when a charge of defrauding the state could not be upheld. The achievements of Phidias can scarcely be judged by us, but he represents the emergence of the individual, named artist on to the Western scene – taking his place in history with rulers and generals and writers on the strength of his achievements in the visual arts. And though the sculpture of the Parthenon can hardly all be his in execution, it was probably planned by him under his friend, Pericles. What was built on the Acropolis in the middle years of the fifth century B C did not differ in kind from earlier Greek monuments. It was simply a more intense idea of corporate homage to the gods which set up there temples and public buildings at once beautiful, functional and didactic. There were to be no triumphal arches to Pericles, no statues of actual great men, or palaces to house a ruling class. What was honoured was an idea: of democracy or patriotism or virtue. It was art to impress the stranger and encourage the citizen. At the heart of the Parthenon was the barbaric splendour of Phidias' huge gold and ivory statue of Pallas Athene – an idol which might have served to be worshipped in Assyria or Egypt. But the long frieze which ran round the inside of the outer colonnade *(Ill. 28),* showing a procession of ordinary people coming to honour the goddess, represents the quintessence of Greek art.

It takes an actual, secular event, the Panathenaic four-yearly ceremony, and depicts this in terms of recognizable humanity, calmly riding or walking, masters of themselves and their animals, yet scarcely individuals. Nothing could be less like portraiture; these are types of young man, older citizen, or girl. Part of the sculptor's skill has gone into rigorous control of reality and casual appearances. These people are elevated into an unlocalized, timeless sphere. Perhaps they are a little too

28 Waterbearers from the Parthenon north frieze. Mid fifth century BC

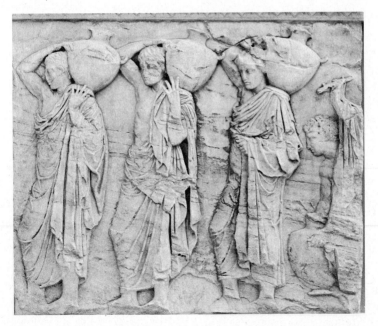

balanced, a little too bland. The consciously graceful folds of their drapery have become almost too insistent and fussy in the group of goddesses *(Ill. 29)* from the east pediment. It is usual to call this a 'progress' from the sculpture at Olympia, although the aesthetic reasons for that judgment seem unclear, and in terms of evolution it might suggest rather a decline. Marble here certainly wonderfully suggests the thinnest of creased and ruffled drapery, clinging to breasts and limbs; in terms of imitation it has gone further than any art we have previously encountered. Yet the idea of divinity is already here perhaps rather commonplace; the moving magic of the imagination which had made Apollo so truly a god *(Ill. 26)* seems in this group to have grown less bold. To some extent, it is this Phidian classical style that is the transitional one: it has modified archaic vigour by a good dose of harmonious naturalism.

Something of the same modification of sterner styles of architecture is seen in the variety of buildings put up during the fifth century on the Acropolis, and in the mingling of Doric with Ionic columns in the entrance portico there, the Propylaea. Damaged and restored though this is, the Propylaea still conveys a convincing sensation of what it was like to climb up and enter the Acropolis. And here the façades of outer columns in Doric style gave way in the central passage to more slender Ionic pillars with their convoluted, more expressive capitals *(Ill. 30)*. Other buildings, like the Erectheum, were built in this comparatively new style which introduced a fresh rhythm into Greek architecture, particularly necessary since the units of

29 Group of three goddesses from the Parthenon east pediment *c.* 435 BC

30 The Propylaea, Athens 437–432 B C

pillar and pediment remained constant. Against the austerity
and regularity of the near-by Parthenon, the Erectheum stands
out all the more because of its asymmetry, its highly decorated
capitals with patterned bands, and its famous Caryatid porch
where the archaic derivation of figures from columns is finally
reversed by having columns turn into women – strong but
effortless supporters of the roof *(Ill. 31)*.

They serve, accidentally, to forecast the inevitable shift of
Greek art towards more patently human themes. The caryatids
of the Erectheum are fully-clad maidens who have the severity
of priestesses; but as a novel subject to display its virtuosity
sculpture was soon to strip off the garments and – after centuries
of the male nude – reveal the female nude. The most famous
statue of this kind was the *Venus* of Cnidus by Praxiteles, who
worked as a sculptor in the fourth century and who was
inspired not by the goddess but by his mistress.

45

31 Caryatid Porch of the Erectheum, Athens 421–405 BC

Praxiteles is perhaps the first mannerist artist in Western art. To this extent, his style represents a phenomenon which later occurs again at other periods when a convention of elevated naturalism has been fully grasped, and art then sets out to become more patently artful. The high polish on Praxiteles' marble flesh, his use of painters to tint his sculpture, the elaboration of surface detail (a whole simulated tree-trunk with a climbing lizard in his *Apollo Sauroctonus*; a patterned water-pitcher in the Cnidian *Venus*) all point to new sophistication. The *Hermes (Ill. 32)* is so familiar and 'classical' in its mutilated state, that we easily forget what must have been the original effect of the god's graceful upraised right arm – a pose of asymmetrical elegance and deliberate virtuosity. The idea of a statue carved out of a single block of stone is immediately destroyed by this extension into the air above the head, in a gesture that suggests new freedom. The statue stirs and stretches into a further dimension, not with strained effort but with a lazy, teasing mastery which is more impressive. The subject of Hermes with the infant Dionysus – one comparatively novel in

46

32 PRAXITELES
*Hermes with
the Infant
Dionysus*
c. 340 BC

introducing sheer charm and childhood appeal into large-scale Greek sculpture – did not of itself require Praxiteles' virtuoso design. This is, as it were, an additional conceit by the sculptor who carries off with fluent ease a difficult task, presenting us with an unexpected, highly accomplished treatment of such a theme.

It is wrong to try and make such art as this symptomatic of decline because it is less severe and bracing than earlier work. Art will not obey public school rules, though they have continued naïvely to be applied; one writer of a history of Greece has expressed doubt whether Praxiteles' *Hermes* 'could stay a long cross-country run'. It may be true that the whole fabric of Greek civilization was itself beginning to decline during the lifetime of Praxiteles, but art is not governed by national and political laws. A society at a particular nadir may well witness an exotic peak of flourishing art. The last centuries of the pre-Christian world experienced a collapse of the city-state and its replacement by gigantic empire concepts – most splendidly displayed by Alexander the Great's ambitions, but most permanently achieved by the Roman Empire. The result was a new level of civilization, richer and more sophisticated than anything produced before, in which almost every object of use could be one of beauty and rarity too. Not even in the Renaissance would art find itself so fully and consistently required as in these years of Hellenistic activity, when Greece included large parts of Asia Minor.

There was an internationalism in the arts which suited the internationalism of Alexander, as he conquered Egypt, entered Babylon, overthrew the Persian Empire and adopted Persian dress and customs. Art had come a long way from its magical beginnings. It possessed nearly perfect technical accomplishment, able to serve with new expression the old requirements of tomb or palace, and able also to create the exquisitely wrought, miniature object which is to serve only art's sake. The new cities were not completely Greek ones, but those like Antioch, Pergamum and Alexandria, Alexander's own foundation, where Asiatic influences mingled with Greek. In the colossal Pergamum altar *(Ill. 33)* the architecture virtually *is* the sculpture, with figures writhing and sprawling in forceful poses which threaten to pull them out of the frieze, in a new type of almost theatrical assault on the spectator. Obviously, if moderation and balance are one's standards for art, this will not seem art; in place of Praxiteles' mannered fluidity, it offers

48

33 The Pergamum altar, north wing of Great Altar of Zeus
c. 180 BC

Baroque vigour and extreme emotional involvement. Not accidentally does it seem to recall the group of the *Gaul killing himself and his wife (Ill. 27),* for that too, in the original bronze, was Pergamene work, commissioned by King Attalus I (died 197 BC), whose successor erected the altar at Pergamum.

Desire for new expressiveness made popular the third architectural order, the Corinthian, suitably though accidentally named as the richest, since the city of Corinth was famous for its luxury. Literally more florid possibilities were introduced by use of this capital, with its springing, carved acanthus leaves curling around an inverted bell shape, which was particularly to be used by the Romans. It represents a more opulently decorative style, reaching its popular peak not in Greece but at Rome, with architecture that no longer needed the pillar as an essential unit. Opulence and a patent richness of material appear in many of the artifacts produced by the minor arts – cameos, gems, coins and blown glass – all evoking a much more frankly colourful and luxury-loving world than that of fifth-century Athens. Yet it still continues the Mediterranean tradition of artistic concentration on the human body. Although clay figures had been made earlier, it was in a new mood of charming genre that there appear the elegant figurines *(Ill. 34)* associated with Tanagra. In one way they are a gossipy, plebeian-seeming art compared with the heroic statue, but even that was to be scaled down, becoming half-table-ornament, half-toy, in bronze statuettes which often had the additional refinement of eyes inlaid in silver or enamel, with lips and nipples of copper *(Ill. 35).*

Alexander the Great's own patronage points to concepts very different from those of Pericles with his public concern but private withdrawal and unostentation. Not even Alexander has managed to come down to posterity with the effortless ability of King Mausolus whose widow built the Mausoleum at Halicarnassus which has become a synonym for an imposing tomb. It is the living Alexander who was to be so well reflected in the busts of Lysippus, the sculptor most prized by Alexander for combining observation of the set of his head with expression of his determined character. The Tanagra figurines are one testimony to an interest in how people look and what clothes they wear. Lifelike portrait busts, with emphasis on the character of the face, begin to be popular in the Hellenistic period: significantly, it was in this category of the not too wildly imaginative, that Roman sculptors were to make their finest

50

35 Statuette of a god,
   probably Poseidon.
   Second century BC

34 Tanagra figurine,
woman with a fan and
sun-hat. Third century
BC

36 *Alexander mosaic*, from an original Greek painting of *c.* 330 BC.
Before AD 79

contribution. While at times Alexander appeared as a god, or
the companion of gods, at others it was as ordinary man that
he was depicted. Little Greek painting of any period survives,
but an echo of pictorial style at Alexander's Court is apparent
in a Roman mosaic copy, the 'Alexander mosaic', showing his
victory over the Persians at the Battle of Issus in 333 BC *(Ill.
36)*. There is nothing conventionally 'classical' about this
scene. Its pantingly vivid characterization includes not only
Alexander but his highly-spirited horse, as wild-eyed and
nervously resolute as its rider. Alexander is shown not naked,
nor in timeless cloak and stylized breastplate, but in highly
particularized armour – recorded down to the laces which
partly hold it in place, and the knotted belt. Against that detail,
the King's bare head is all the more effective: an individualized
portrait which is convincingly human, heroic and yet unideal-
ized. That this mosaic comes from Pompeii is one small
indication of the permanent debt of Roman art to Greece.

52

It is too sweeping to say that the Romans did not have imagination. But unlike their written and spoken language, their artistic language was not completely their own. Physically, they had conquered Greece; artistically, it had conquered them. Guilt perhaps mingled with their admiration, while a certain pride in their superior practical achievement made them able to enjoy the quiet of Athens after the noisy bustle of Rome.

Greek artifacts had for long been imported into Italy and were much prized, as well as imitated, by the Etruscans – those people more famous than they quite deserve to be. Perhaps there is something which still seems intriguing and mysterious about them, partly because they became a 'lost' race, absorbed by the power of Rome. There remains something very shadowy altogether in the reconstruction of their civilization – in much the same way that Minoan Crete is still shadowy; and what has been conjectured is not always convincing. The Etruscan emphasis on the tomb as a sort of house returns us to

37 The ambush of the Trojan prince Troilus, wall-painting from the Tomba dei Tori at Tarquinia c. 530 BC

Egyptian concepts, and the whole idea of their decorated tomb interiors *(Ill. 37)* is in opposition to the Greeks'. Just as there is something niggling about their goldsmiths' work, so there is a rather straggling, slack style to these painted decorations. They do not seem to have settled for a single completely realized convention. At times, the wriggling, linear beasts and stunted trees could almost be mistaken for Anglo-Saxon work, which is perhaps only to say that an endemic Eastern fondness for calligraphic pattern lies behind them both.

Because they had no marble for sculpture, the Etruscans evolved – especially from clay – their most impressive contribution in vivid statues which are quite unlike anything produced elsewhere. Clay sculpture was used on sarcophagi, as well as on temples, and in both cases with striking narrative effect; the man and woman from a sarcophagus lid of about 520 BC *(Ill. 38)* might be reclining at a banquet, with their lively expressions and busy, gesticulating hands. Other comparable clay pairs of men and women show the same relaxed air of intimacy, and even more individualized portraiture. What is additionally remarkable about these groups is the place accorded to women – again very different from Greek social ideas, and anticipatory of Roman standards. Etruscan concern both with painted wall decoration (albeit for tombs) and with portrait sculpture links its art strongly with Rome. And though Roman sculpture was largely content to copy and pastiche Greek work, usually with heavy, uninspired results, Roman portrait busts speak their own novel idiom. Swelling to greater size as the Empire evolved, they could be sometimes forceful, imperial, hewn from multicoloured marble, at other times surprisingly delicate – and always intensely realistic.

It is realism, in another sense, that was the animating principle behind the Romans' most considerable artistic achievement: their architecture. 'And pompous buildings once were things of use', is Pope's crisp summing up of that essentially practical urge which laid out the Roman public places, the *fora,* designed the great arches of aqueducts that still stand, made use of concrete for building purposes, and roofed in large structures with vaults and domes. The result is a triumph of the city – not in the rather showplace sense of Periclean Athens, where the outstanding buildings were sacred edifices up on the Acropolis, but as a utilitarian environment for citizens. It is their needs, rather than those of the gods, that are catered for by amphitheatres, public baths, basilicas (law courts) and libraries.

38 Etruscan tomb
sculpture, terra-
cotta figures of
man and woman
c. 520 B C

All is physical and material in comparison with Greek intellect –
sometimes grossly material, imposing rather than beautiful
– but it is profound recognition of what people want, even
down to its comparative indifference to canons of beauty.

The transformation of Rome itself began under Julius
Caesar, in a typically practical project to employ surplus
labour as well as improve the city. The activity was still going
on in the fourth century A D when the Basilica of Maxentius
(*Ill.* 39) was completed by Constantine. Even in ruins, it
reveals not only a vast scale but its quite un-Greek sense of
volume and space. In place of the pillar and flat roof, it is constructed in terms of wall and arch – the wall pierced with
windows and the arches coffered. Whereas the Greek temple
is to be appreciated essentially as an exterior, buildings like the
Basilica of Maxentius are planned not merely to accommodate
a crowd of people but to be appreciated from within. They are
spacious – in a way that no Greek building had aimed to be. The
Basilica of Maxentius, completed by an emperor who had been
converted to Christianity, may seem in some ways more

39 Basilica of Maxentius, Rome, begun by Maxentius and finished by Constantine. Completed soon after AD 313

Romanesque than Roman. In fact, its solution to the problem of roofing a large space by a series of vaults is a basic solution of Western architecture.

But the Basilica is also fully in the tradition of the Empire, itself to be dated from the assumption of the title Augustus by Octavian in 27 BC and which was technically to live on in the West until Romulus Augustulus, the last – ironically named – Emperor, was deposed in AD 476. It was perhaps from Asia Minor that the Romans had learnt the principles of arch and vault. In terms of strict invention they possibly invented nothing, but they dug determinedly into space and contained volume. Their architecture is physically experienced by the spectator who becomes involved with his relationship to the arch, triumphal or ʹotherwise, under which he passes, and the vault that soars over him. Where, for example, the Greek theatre began as a natural depression, using a hillside for the half-circle of tiered seats, the Romans built up the complete

56

40 Colosseum, Rome, begun by Vespasian, finished A D 80
by Titus

ring of amphitheatre on open ground, rising in row upon row
of arches, to reach the monumental grandeur of the Colosseum.

Pierced outside by arches, it was also circumscribed at each
level by corridor tunnels *(Ill. 40)*. While standing almost aggressively huge and high, it was also planned to accommodate
hundreds of spectators, facilitating their passage to the different
levels of the seats through the network of corridors which were
reached from no less than eighty entrance archways. What it
accommodated spectators for is equally typical of the Romans as
opposed to the Greeks; it is hard to connect the word civilization with people who inaugurated their amphitheatre with the
slaughter of five thousand animals in a single day – a mere
beginning to their barbaric use of the Colosseum.

Yet these people achieved more than feats of engineering, or
cruelty. That concern of theirs with architecture which is a
containing of space within an interior created the Pantheon,
typically Roman in its great porch of free-standing Corinthian

57

41 The Pantheon, Rome, started A D 118/119, consecrated between
A D 125 and 128

42 Mosaic pavement with head of Medusa. First century A D

columns, and more typical in its perfect domed interior
(Ill. 41). This remains today still luminous, uncluttered and
serene. It seems to symbolize an absolute, ordered cosmos in
which space does not frighten man but surrounds him, without
diminishing his stature. In a dramatically simple way light is
introduced into the interior, and at the same time concentrated,
by the single, circular opening at the centre of the beautifully
coffered dome. As either temple or church the Pantheon is
without vagueness or mystery. Completely coherent and
harmoniously planned, it expresses the almost magic power of
the circle – here become perceivable, solid, architectural form –
which is a shape continually haunting mankind. The concept
of the Pantheon, so irrelevant to Gothic thought, returns with
new relevance in the Renaissance obsession with centrally
planned churches and in the Baroque triumph of the dome.

Some Roman mosaics play with space in eye-deceiving ways
which give almost the illusion of looking up into a dome – or
down into a whirlpool *(Ill. 42)*. The flat walls of Roman

villas constantly dissolve in decorative schemes, whether executed in paint or mosaic, which enliven the surface with swags of fruit or arabesques, and once even simulate a complete orchard, as in the frescoes from the villa of Livia, the wife of Augustus *(Ill. 43)*. The mosaic pavement illustrated takes the eye on a more dazzling optical journey, achieved by the careful arrangement in pure geometrical pattern of diminishing black and white cubes – now seeming to radiate outwards from the central opening with the Medusa head, and now apparently drawing one rapidly into its vortex with the effect of a whirling disc. Spinning discs by Duchamp, and the further modern developments of Optical artists, are already anticipated by this ingenious challenge to the eye.

43 Fresco from the Villa of Livia, Rome. Late first century B C

44 *Head of a Young Girl*, probably Minatia Polla

The solid, actual people of Roman portrait busts were not very likely to feel deceived about reality. In those busts aesthetics again seem to matter less than psychology and truth to physical appearance; and the result is an extraordinary gallery of many quite brutal, decadent and sinister faces which seem only too familiar as the people described in the pages of Tacitus or Suetonius. When idealized and heroicized, they are both less interesting and less convincing. More fascinating, and sometimes equally frightening, are the female portrait busts where elaborate hair-dressing gives regal effect even to women who did not rule. But their variety cannot easily be summed up. The *Head of a Young Girl (Ill. 44),* whose coiffure suggests the period of Tiberius and Claudius, has an impressive candour and simplicity which seem not idealization but fact. She lives as a convincing yet quite ordinary human being, girl not goddess, recognizably a person although we cannot be sure of her name.

45 *Head of a Man c.* A D 450

The emphasis on personality and the calm, proto-Victorian air of much Roman portraiture were to change – as so much changed – with the collapse of the antique world and the challenge of the new Christian religion. It is from a strange climate, half-pagan still but at a date well after the official establishment of Christianity, that one of the very last Roman portrait busts comes *(Ill. 45)*. This man with huge, haunting eyes – eyes no longer naturalistic but windows of the soul – might stand as saint on some cathedral façade. Already he looks towards the future.

CHAPTER TWO

The Impact of Christianity

The challenge which Christianity deliberately offered to the antique pagan world might seem to reverse nearly all that world's established artistic ideals and return art temporarily to the cave. It was there that Christianity had been born, there its adherents took shelter (adorning the Catacombs with pictorial religious symbols) and there, rather than in palaces or triumphal arches, its victorious humility might best be exemplified. Its deity was attractive through his sufferings and meekness; a deliberate paradox is enshrined in the god who may be represented by a lamb. The final achievement of antiquity had been the creation, in the East as well as in the West, of great cities. Christianity's early achievements were rather in the number of its churches and monasteries. Even the most famous Christian creation – Constantine's foundation of the capital called after him Constantinople – was in fact a re-foundation of ancient Byzantium, once protected not by the Virgin Mary but by Hecate. A Christian was the citizen of a kingdom not of this world. Whatever splendour was created by art, be believed that there is here no abiding city. Even the sacking of Rome in AD 410 by Alaric, which might appear an appalling blow to civilization, was seen by St Augustine in a different perspective. Man's city is nothing compared with the universal, non-material city, that City of God which is the subject of *De Civitate Dei*, a book which we shall later hear of as delighting Charlemagne.

While it is true that the new religion everywhere brought a dramatic revolution which gradually changed every aspect of life as well as art, its emphasis on the transcendental was not new. Late pagan antiquity had already undergone the crises which fostered mystery religions, like Christianity coming from the East, concerned like it with the immortality of the soul, and worshipping sometimes in temples which (to judge from that of Mithras excavated in London) were close in form to the Christian basilica. Perhaps we shall never know exactly how much Christianity and Christian art were indebted to such cults as Mithraism – itself popular enough to have a temple erected to it at Rome by the Emperor Marcus Aurelius.

Yet, though Christianity had not originally had any monopoly of the spiritual, its triumph put on it the onus of breaking an old Mediterranean tradition. In the early Renaissance, men like the sculptor Ghiberti were to look back on the victorious establishment of Christianity as a period when the noble arts of antiquity were destroyed. Events were actually a good deal more subtle – so subtle in fact that they still remain rather baffling. It is not just that pagan ideals lived on even after Constantine had officially established Christianity as the religion of the Roman Empire. Many antique pagan motifs lent themselves to Christian adaptation; and Christ would appear not only as a shepherd but as a Roman centurion. Yet the whole ethos was slowly changing, and art changed with it. Concentration on the affairs of the soul meant a dwindling of interest in the body: once solidly realized, physically studied for its own sake, it is no longer a proper subject in early Christian art. There no longer seemed space for it – and this was almost literally true. Against eternity everything shrank and grew cramped. The gesture and pose of Anastasius in the ivory diptych (*Ill. 47*), carved to celebrate his proconsulship in AD 517, are stiff and restricted. There is here no sense of depth, little sense of proportion, and a preference for decorative symbols (rather too many of them) to cover every inch of space. Apart from sarcophagi (*Ill. 46*), sculpture as such virtually disappears from art altogether in these years; small carved ivories remain typical. Mosaic is first preferred to painting, and painting comes to mean the illustration of religious texts. Throughout, religious purposes dominate all other ones. Architecturally speaking, there are virtually no private houses between late Roman villas and fifteenth-century Florentine palaces. For centuries the ordinary person could be forgiven for assuming that art's sole function was to serve religion.

The most fascinating period of Christian art is not perhaps its finest, unimpeded years of Romanesque style, but the earliest one when it was still humble, co-existing with pagan art in a strange climate of old and new. Two private Roman citizens, Secundus and Projecta, were married towards the end of the fourth century AD, and the silver marriage casket made for their wedding (*Ill. 48*) evokes this world more effectively than any words. Perhaps it looks rather clumsy against fully

64

46 Jonah sarcophagus. Late third century

47 Diptych of the Consul Anastasius AD 517

48 Marriage casket of Secundus and Projecta. End of fourth century AD

antique artifacts, with its stumpy pillars and its rather lumpish bodies. Nereids, peacocks and sea-monsters cover it with pagan imagery, while Venus floats across the lid, shell-borne on a wavy sea. These scenes exude a last poignant breath of antique mythology, the visual equivalent of some late Latin love poem, the *Pervigilium Veneris* perhaps, where wave-borne Venus, 'undantem Dionem', is still a ruling goddess. A different deity has left its mark on this marriage casket, inscribed with a quite new sentiment: 'Secundus and Projecta, may you live in Christ.' Two cultures are blended without conflict. Wisely preserving Venus – for she stands as a primal force in human beings – Christianity incorporates her into its scheme, turning love into charity and then into divine longing. Ultimately, it is with Christ that Secundus and Projecta must hope to be united.

Such hope was in differing ways to lie behind so much of the art produced in the years that followed. Silver marriage caskets themselves seem to disappear not merely under the pressure of Christianity (not surprisingly, though, in an increasingly monastic climate, and considering some of St Paul's advice to the Corinthians) but in a Europe which was often swept by Barbarian invasions and struggling to keep some flicker of culture alight in a dark, uncertain world. It constantly seemed that Antichrist's coming was imminent. Piety, rather than art, might delay him. Cultural chaos and darkness gave in fact a period of gestation out of which were to come brief renascences and finally the Renaissance. Five hundred confused years elapse between the Age of Constantine and that of Charlemagne. It was the Emperor Constantine who had recognized the Christian faith and given it official existence. In the shape of Pope Leo III, that faith recognized Charlemagne and gave him official existence when he was crowned Emperor at Rome on Christmas Day 800.

These events have their relevance for the centuries when art had to cling to whatever culture and literacy there might be. It could hardly dispense with serving religion – even had it wished to. At Rome, at Ravenna and at Milan – a particularly important artistic centre – it was actively working to give visual expression to Christianity. In the person of St Ambrose at Milan this was a religion now able to challenge the Emperor himself when necessary; and it was the Emperor who yielded. The collapse of the Roman Empire in the West threw into relief the Byzantine civilization which centred on Constantinople and which artistically, legally, theologically, is particularly associated with the achievements and the failings of Justinian. The mosaics at Ravenna, especially those of S. Vitale *(Ill. 52),* best reveal the flavour of this exotic Court art – less hieratic and monotonous than it is usually said to be. And although the mosaic portraits there of Justinian and his Empress, with their retinues, are so famous, they are subordinated in the overall scheme to the commanding figure of the youthful Christ, seated on a globe, in the centre of the apse. Even the Western renascence under Charlemagne was really a religious movement, concerned with Biblical scholarship and proper conduct of church services, pious and literary rather than consciously artistic in most of its manifestations. Few or no works of art can be shown as having personally belonged to him. He owned swords, jewelled reliquaries and – perhaps most prized of all – a live white elephant, presented to him by the Caliph Haroun al-Raschid.

But Charlemagne stood for civilization, literacy and order. When he stopped travelling and settled at Aix-la-Chapelle, it was to construct a physical expression of his aims in a complex of buildings which was significantly called 'nova Roma'. At last, it might seem, culture had been fully re-established in Europe with a splendour and a certainty which recalled imperial Rome. But it remained a culture so deeply tinctured with Christianity that the two had become virtually the same thing. Throughout those confused centuries between Constantine and Charlemagne, the Christian religion had been the real bulwark of Western civilization. Even if, as seems likely, Charlemagne did not welcome his unexpected coronation by the Pope, he himself remained deeply religious; and a courtier-cum-biographer tells how much he delighted in the writings of St Augustine, 'especially that one which is entitled *De Civitate Dei*'. It is merely chance perhaps that of all his buildings at Aix, only the palace chapel now survives – but this is no bad symbol of the enduring purpose behind all art in these years. Whether creating monasteries and churches, carving ivories or illustrating books, artistic activity is closely connected with propagating a definite spiritual message. Until the Renaissance this continued to be its primary concern. 'We pressed the completion of the work . . .', Abbot Suger wrote in the twelfth century, of his rebuilding at Saint-Denis, 'lest God have just cause to complain of us.'

The earliest specifically Christian attempt to avoid God's complaints inevitably concerned the actual place of worship,

49 S. Sabina, Rome (interior). Begun 425

50 S. Vitale, Ravenna (interior). Consecrated 547

the church. The nearest antique parallel for such buildings lay less in temples than in Roman meeting-halls or basilicas (like that of Maxentius, *Ill. 39*). Constantine built a huge basilica of St Peter's at Rome, a wonder of the Western world until it was demolished and replaced during the Renaissance. Despite their antique name, such basilicas changed many of the previous ideas of a place of worship. They are built almost as an allegory of the Christian world-view: unadorned brick outside, all mosaic and marble within, buildings experienced like the soul's pilgrimage, as the worshipper moved first through an arcaded courtyard, then into the porch or narthex (where penitents and the uninitiated catechumens assembled) and finally into the pillared nave of the church itself, with its pronounced longitudinal rhythm leading the eye and mind to the altar where during the Mass would be manifested God himself. Behind the

51 S. Sophia, Istanbul (interior). Built by Justinian 532–7

altar curved the apse with its half-dome suggestive of eternity – an effect increased by its usual gold mosaic decoration, a heavenly, space-dissolving shimmer as background to some scene stressing the merciful divinity of Christ the Saviour. Secundus and Projecta could still have been alive and able to worship, perhaps in S. Sabina *(Ill. 49)*, a typical Roman basilica, begun in 425. Here the apse mosaics are later, but the building's dominant effect is the rhythmic progression down the nave, marked by Corinthian columns, with arcades and simple clerestory above. Such interiors, even at their most splendid, remain straightforward and uncluttered.

There already existed an altogether alternative construction, used chiefly for baptisteries, derived from circular Roman mausoleums, and culminating in the centrally planned church and the dome. If the basilican church is ancestor of the Gothic cathedral, the early Christian baptistery already looks forward to the Baroque church. What amounts to a combination of the two plans, resulting in a basilica with a dome, was a design more popular in the East than the West. However, one outstanding example, Sancta Sophia at Constantinople *(Ill. 51)*, is too vast to be neglected. Better than any other surviving monument, it symbolizes the grandiose concepts of Justinian and shows him to have been an Emperor completely in the imperial Roman tradition. The exterior of the huge church is huddled and undistinguished – redeemed, indeed, only by the four tall minarets, a Turkish addition which positively improves its appearance. The interior is bewildering in its spaciousness, annihilating the spectator's consciousness in a way not attempted by the Pantheon. Space seems hardly to be contained at all in Sancta Sophia, so colossal are its proportions; its ground-plan is that of a three-aisled church, but one is scarcely aware of this when standing in the actual building. The mosaics in Sancta Sophia are remarkably disappointing and apparently all date from later than Justinian's reign. Whereas no building in his Western capital of Ravenna can equal the scale and effect of Sancta Sophia, it is the mosaics at Ravenna which now best convey not only the jewelled splendour of the Byzantine Court but a good deal about personalities at his Court.

The centrally planned church of S. Vitale *(Ill. 50)* represents a sophisticated richness which takes on yet brighter lustre since it is one of the last beacons in a rapidly darkening Italy. Justinian's Western capital was more artistically splendid than politically stable. His whole huge empire, barely held together by battle during his lifetime, disintegrated at his death. A last wave of Barbarian invaders, the Lombards, swept over Italy. Their coming and their establishment is – in artistic terms – a sign of the new, powerful, non-Mediterranean tradition which had its own contribution to make to art. Northern Europe was about to take the initiative. The revival of Roman tradition and Roman imperial power took place outside the Mediterranean altogether, with the cultural and political achievements of Charlemagne. In more ways than one, he is the heir of Justinian. It is fitting that at the 'nova Roma' of Aix-la-Chapelle, his chapel was itself nothing but a plainer, less colourful, somewhat cruder version of Justinian's S. Vitale.

S. Vitale was intended as a palace chapel, very much the Emperor's personal foundation and consecrated by him in 547. An octagon crowned by a dome, its interior is almost confusing at the point where one enters it today. The first impression is of archways and galleries curving like theatre-boxes about a central space and billowing outwards to the surrounding ambulatory. Everything seems pierced and worked. Such flat surfaces as exist appear undulating, covered by veined marble or the glittering, unquiet texture of mosaic.

Hints of illusionism and the theatre are even more relevant in looking at the famous mosaic of the Empress Theodora and her retinue *(Ill. 52)*. Despite the usual application to it of adjectives like hieratic, we see – as doubtless the first spectators saw – a vivid, eye-deceiving assembly of varied human beings, brought into the church as dramatically as if a curtain had suddenly been lifted. These people look out with real curiosity and vitality – one woman, at the extreme right, positively peering round the corner, anxious not to be squeezed out. Despite the restriction of mosaic, every effort has been made to suggest varied physiognomies and indeed different reactions to the moment of the Empress seeming to advance with her golden offering, while on the opposite wall the Emperor advances with his. The background of his mosaic is quite plain; but the whole setting of the Empress's is illusionistic. At the right a swag of boldly striped awning suggests a raised curtain and gives a sense of depth. Around and behind the Empress is an elegant, decorated niche, once again curving the flat wall with its shell-like half-dome. More remarkable is the casual action at the left, where an attendant stretches out to push aside a curtain at a doorway – thus relating himself to his setting in a way that was not to be caught by art again for centuries.

71

52 Empress Theodora and her suite, mosaic at S. Vitale, Ravenna *c.* 540

Far from being hieratic, timeless images (a cliché idea prob-ably derived from hazy associations of Byzantium and icons), these figures are among the most vivid beings, in virtually human scale, that we shall encounter, at least in Italy, before Giotto. It is true that they evoke a Court world – but not an unreal one – and even a *mondain* atmosphere: no accident, one might feel, that the Empress had been a witty comedian, as well as a prostitute, before she married Justinian. Yet her very presence on the wall at S. Vitale in splendour equal to his is a tribute to her personality, symbolizing the importance assigned to her in government as well as in private life. Not for a long time afterwards in the Western world is an ordinary woman (certainly in this case positively no virgin and no saint) to be so effectively treated by art.

Such an image would certainly not have been possible in Northern Europe. There the arts were altogether on a more miniature scale, and their aims were scarcely representational. If the S. Vitale mosaics are in essence courtly art (confirming a tradition that extends from Alexander up to Ingres' portraits of Napoleon), there existed already a tradition of monastic art. Monasticism had spread to the West originally from Egypt as a form of ill-organized asceticism. It became a power-house as well as lighthouse in Barbarian-ravaged Europe, consolidated by the spread of the rule of St Benedict, founder of the great monastery of Monte Cassino, who died a very few years before Justinian consecrated S. Vitale. Yet in the North, Barbarian delight in abstract ornament and pattern influenced the chief art fostered by monasticism: the writing and illumination of books. The monasteries of Ireland and Northumbria produced a whole series of such works in which complete pages were given to an elaborate fretwork of interwoven patterns. Even when human figures were represented, it was with conscious abstraction and a distinct indifference to the appearance of objects. A miniature of St John the Evangelist from the Lindis-farne Gospels, probably influenced by Mediterranean example, might superficially seem in the same convention as the Ravenna mosaics; but the illuminator cannot help making abstract patterns of the face, the zigzag folds of drapery and the strange open-work chair with its cushion that in reality would fall through if anyone sat on it. The very placing of the writing on the page denies any sense of depth; like St John's eagle, it is planned for its linear, decorative effect *(Ill. 53)*. Other pages of these Gospels, executed about 700 on the island of Lindisfarne, retreat from all representation. The four lines that here enclose St John become elsewhere the frame for an intricate embroidery whose serpentine knots and ribbons are all woven into the overall pattern of a cross. However barbaric the style, that is the significant symbol.

The triumphant emergence of the monastery as such is nowhere better expressed than in the 'ideal' plan for the build-ings at Saint Gall *(Ill. 55)* – a project drawn up about 820 within the Carolingian circle, though by then Charlemagne himself was dead. It is remarkable for its careful planning and elaborate complex of structures which range from lavatories to a special enclosure for geese; but its core is the twin-towered church. Everything is provided for: prayer, work, illness, food, and visitors, who have their own accommodation. The result is more than a plan for a monastery; it is a cosmic blueprint for the conduct of Christian life. It symbolizes too the feudal medieval world, where each object or person has an appointed place in the hierarchy. Its scale and extent well suggest the

53 *St John*, Lindisfarne Gospels *c.* 700

54 *St Matthew*, manuscript illustration of *c.* 800

palatial air of a great monastery. The abbot of such a community must inevitably become a prince, an administrator and a powerful landlord. Such dominance was to be assumed by the famous abbey of Cluny, and is expressed in the spread throughout Europe of the Cluniac Order. Artistically, the greatest achievement of monasticism was its fostering of the Romanesque style – the first and perhaps the last truly international architectural style. Against the heaven-scaling bravura of high Gothic, the style of Romanesque architecture-cum-sculpture may look rather heavily earthbound – a sort of Christian Doric – but the steps it took were solid through a sense of confidence and cohesion which was excitingly novel in Europe.

Something of that is already hinted at least in Charlemagne's intentions. The basis of the art – never to become quite a single style – centred on his Court was more monastic than secular.

55 'Ideal' plan for St Gall *c.* 820 (redrawn)

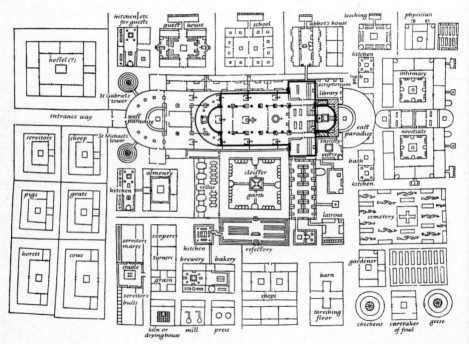

There seems to have been no urge for portraits, not even votive ones, of the Emperor in his lifetime, and thus nothing to equal the vivid portrayal of Justinian and Theodora at S. Vitale. It was from the monastery at York that Charlemagne brought the scholar Alcuin ('your Virgil', he called himself, but he was a tonsured Virgil who died virtually an abbot). A place is found on the 'ideal' plan of Saint Gall for the typical scriptorium where the monks would work at painted illumination of the Gospels – while Alcuin, it might be said, had worked for Charlemagne in illuminating them metaphorically. What both achieved was a fresh grasp on significance and narrative, resulting in manuscript illustrations which contrast with the patterned linear conventions of the Lindisfarne Gospels. In place of the flat calligraphic St John there, we now see an articulated St Matthew engaged in writing, seated on a more solid-looking chair, in a setting of curtained room *(Ill. 54)*. Obviously, this more realistic image of an evangelist is not artistically superior by reason of that reality – itself easily made to look stereotyped and conventional if compared with some figure by Giotto. But it is certainly much more descriptive of reality: making a continuous action out of what it illustrates. The saint is seen at his task, grasping his book, his body propped in a position like that of someone writing. Above all, there is ordered narrative, in which humanity is more striking than sanctity – or, rather, through vivid observation the religious message is enhanced.

It is perhaps not altogether an accident that those curtains twisted about the pillars which frame St Matthew should recall the looped-up curtains in the Ravenna mosaic of the Empress Theodora. Byzantine art had certainly influenced such sophisticated illumination as this. Byzantium had, however, already undergone one religious crisis in which angry iconoclasticism rejected the idea of sacred images of any kind. When that movement subsided, Byzantium restored the concept of such images, but to some extent sealed them off in an unchanging convention of gold backgrounds, and truly hieratic poses and features. It was Eastern timelessness against Western change. The Byzantine icon continues down the centuries – still present in much the same form in nineteenth-century Russia.

In the West, Byzantine influences were to die gradually away. Far from there being a European iconoclastic controversy, a steady fostering of the visual arts in the service of religion culminated in the Romanesque achievement. What under Charlemagne and Alcuin had been primarily a literary movement now became sculptural and architectural. The saints and Christs in glory who, on a small scale, had decorated Gospel-books were now carved in the porches of churches. As for the churches themselves, they were becoming architecturally more articulate, eliminating the plain and temporary aspects of the old-style basilica. Their roofs were vaulted stone; a whole cluster of chapels would radiate out where before there had been a plain apse; and the church exteriors would be enriched not only by elaborate sculpted porches but by dominating groups of towers marking out the plan (Ill. 57).

Articulate as architecture had become – capable too of variations which range over France, Spain, England, Germany and Italy – it is in sculpture that the Romanesque style expressed itself most boldly. This was the very art form that Christianity had previously neglected, as if inhibited by pagan achievement. Quite suddenly, it seems, sculpture was seen to offer a strikingly new channel for the telling of the Christian story. What had perhaps happened, no doubt much more gradually than now appears, was a shifting away from the symbolic and transcendental aspects of religion to emphasis on the more actual, realistic ones. The Bible could be illustrated – not in the sense of decorating pages of a manuscript with ornament, but in showing its dramatic scenes in dramatic terms. There is another shift too, connected with the impact of religion on a wider public. The illuminated Carolingian books are essentially reserved for a cultivated, usually monastic, clientele: individual treasures to be owned by a great individual, an abbot or abbess. The same must largely be true of ivories and reliquaries – things which certainly can make no strong single visual effect on a congregation.

But if the doorway of the church is itself a Bible in stone or bronze, with vivid, clear, intensely dramatic scenes carved on it (Ill. 56), the scriptural story will make its impact on even the most unlearned worshipper. The doors of some earlier churches had been similarly carved, but the masterpiece of such work was achieved in the doors, of which a detail is reproduced here, commissioned for his church at Hildesheim by Bishop Bernward in the very early eleventh century. The church itself is one of the earliest examples of a grand Romanesque exterior, a proclamation as it were of Germany's sympathy for this style in which great churches were soon to be built all over the country – notably at Cologne. Bishop Bernward was said to

78

56 *The Expulsion of Adam and Eve*, from the doors of St Michael's, Hildesheim. Early eleventh century

be experienced and knowledgeable about the arts; he had also been tutor to the Emperor Otto III, last of three emperors who have given their name to this period – the Ottonian. Politically and artistically, it represents the main European development after the collapse of Charlemagne's huge empire at his death.

Germany's long tradition of superbly eloquent sculpture is already established in the Hildesheim doors where the figures seem scarcely content to remain in the flat plane of bronze relief, so forceful and expressive are their animated bodies. Bare of scenery other than essential properties of a tree or a cloud, each composition is animated by a dramatic force conveyed through the figures – with marvellous use of gestures. God stalks forward to point accusingly at Adam who bends, naked and ashamed, pointing at Eve; she crouches lower still in shame, in turn pointing at the serpent. Abel seems positively to spin as he falls to the ground, felled by Cain's club – and the huge hand of God thrusts itself dramatically from a cloud overhead. It is in intensely human terms that the risen Christ appears – almost brutally remonstrating, it might seem, with the gesticulating Magdalen who expostulates even while she adores.

79

This art seems perfectly attuned to its purpose. The stress is not on the mysterious elements of Christianity but rather on its ethical, practical ones. At Hildesheim, Old and New Testament subjects are ranged in analogy. It is as a warning with regard to this life that Christ appears carved in porches as Judge of the World – and he appears not floating in a heaven of gold mosaic but with exemplary scenes of the blessed and the damned. The emphasis is again on narrative. The very capitals of pillars, especially in French churches, are often not abstract ornament or leaf patterns but alive with complete miniature scenes of compressed action. It is a sign of the developed importance of the sculptor that several of the greatest Romanesque achievements, especially the sculpture on cathedral façades, are signed work by individual artists who thus emerge from dark age anonymity. We know that Guglielmus worked on the cathedral at Modena. The famous tympanum of the cathedral at Autun is signed under Christ's feet by Gislebertus. The lavishly carved, almost Gothic Puerta de la Gloria of the cathedral of Santiago at Compostela is by Master Mateo.

Although it is usual to say that subordination of sculpture to architecture is a typical feature of the Romanesque style, this is

57 Church of the Apostles, Cologne 1035–1220

partly a hindsight judgment. Not only were façades, capitals, pulpits and fonts sculpted with figures, in quite revolutionary proliferation, but free-standing sculpture – often in painted wood – was evolved. The whole style might be said to be imbued with a feeling for modelling as well as carving; there is something moulded and soft about the arched interiors of most Romanesque churches, and about their gentle, rather agglomerated exteriors, with rows of round windows and arcades. Sculpture and architecture are perfectly married in the rich yet somehow intimate exterior of Notre-Dame at Poitiers *(Ill. 58),* a church that might seem to have reversed the original basilica principle of plain exterior and elaborate interior. At Poitiers the nave is a series of tall arches which support a simple barrel-vault. The façade is carved and shaped with a screen for sculpture within arches, niches, recesses, and even the two towers might be sculpted features, almost refusing to assume architectural domination, and remaining more turrets than towers.

Perhaps it is true that there lingers something artistically rather haphazard and not always accurately calculated about some effects in Romanesque architecture. Yet it was a monumental style capable of considerable variations, increasingly

58 Notre-Dame,
      Poitiers.
Eleventh century

expressive of the confident power of established Christianity. It is well summed up by the cathedral at Durham *(Ill. 59)*, an artistic product of the Norman Conquest, planted triumphantly on its hill site like a fortress as much as a church. At the period it was begun, Christendom was expressing its sense of unity and divine purpose by the First Crusade: the Western world had set out to do battle against the East, carrying the cross but trusting even more in the sword, and at first seeming to be successful in its devastating mission.

The religion which had begun so tentatively and humbly now appeared to have become the literal driving force of Europe. Even if it had somehow abruptly vanished from Romanesque Europe, it would have left not just traces but the whole Continent one artistic monument to its empire. In every country great churches and cathedrals testified to its ubiquitous power. Pilgrims crossed Europe to worship at shrines like that of St James at Compostela, and not only there but along the pilgrim route churches had arisen on a huge and imposing scale – part of that public sense of religion providing for great masses of people. Indeed, from a religious point of view the Romanesque style served most beautifully. There would seem no reason for art to evolve any further, but already its vitality refused to be constrained by purely religious purposes. In the twelfth century St Bernard of Clairvaux shrewdly detected the dangerous symptom of sheer beauty – art for its own sake –even in the very churches and cloisters. He wrote a strongly worded letter about the dangers of marvelling over the products of art when instead one should be meditating on the law of God.

Of course, some secular works of art had been created in the years between Charlemagne and St Bernard. Especially in Norman-occupied territory, and therefore notably in England, there had been castles built which represent more than just fortresses for defence; the sheer engineering achievement too of roofing over a large space was expressed not only in the stone-vaulted Romanesque churches but in William Rufus' Westminster Hall, which remained for over a century the largest room in Europe. One of the rare objects which can actually be shown to have had a personal commissioner, and presumably owner, is the 'Alfred Jewel' *(Ill. 61)* which presents a highly stylized, typically Northern, linear image of the King and is inscribed 'Alfred had me made'. Although religious associations certainly enter into the Bayeux tapestry *(Ill. 60)*, which was probably intended from the first as adornment for

59 Durham Cathedral. Not later than the twelfth century

the nave of Bayeux cathedral, the subject-matter is fully secular and historical – a picture chronicle which has something of the gesticulating vigour of the earlier Hildesheim doors. What is there conveyed in strongly three-dimensional, tactile terms, is expressed by once again linear ones in the Bayeux embroidery: in a rhythm which rises to the agitated effects of the actual battle, including the extraordinarily memorable image of a horse completely perpendicular, its head on the ground and its hind legs kicking wildly in the air.

Yet over these years religious purpose and religious imagery continued to be the primary concern of art. Christianity had evolved out of the early basilica a totally new sort of building, conditioned by Christianity's own needs, and exemplified so well by Durham cathedral. What had begun as no more than a new message scratched on the old-style marriage casket of Secundus and Projecta, had taken tangible shape in buildings and sculpture which might artistically challenge the greatest achievements of antiquity.

Durham itself is a building which more than consolidates the Romanesque – and this not merely because of its later Gothic western towers. Despite what its massive circular pillars might suggest, the roof they support has an unexpected lightness of effect and, owing to the clerestory, the interior is light-filled. In place of the long tunnel-vault there is now – almost certainly

60 Bayeux tapestry (detail).
Late eleventh century

61 'Alfred Jewel'.
Late ninth century

for the first time in Europe – the criss-cross pattern of a rib-vault which introduces new aesthetic as well as technical possibilities. Art and knowledge – a conjunction that sounds worthy of Leonardo and the Renaissance – is in fact a medieval formulation concerned to produce a style which, though once sentimentally thought of as profoundly religious, was really urged on more by aesthetic and secular considerations. Gothic creativity springs from a soil already rich in cathedrals, in a united Christendom that might seem – briefly – a vision of St Augustine's come true. In fact, Christendom would become disunited long before the final expiry of the Gothic style. The Crusades were ultimately to prove a spiritual disaster. Monastic ideals were to be replaced by university-inspired, intellectual ones. Power rather than piety is what is represented by a Gothic cathedral, and it becomes the focal point not of some monastery complex but of a rising town, often itself a commercial centre.

For long art had been tolerated and employed for religion's sake. The Gothic world is one where, gradually but definitely, art can be employed for its own sake. It needed the solid, established Romanesque pillar from which to take flight. From that basis it soared into sophisticated fantasy, exulting in sheer artistic freedom which was to be curtailed, rather than encouraged, when the Renaissance came to take a more sober look at things.

85

62 Freiburg-im-Breisgau, openwork interior of spire *c.* 1340

CHAPTER THREE

The Gothic World

It is more than a convenience of chapter-heading to speak of a world created by the Gothic style because it is perhaps the first fully pervasive, homogeneous style in Western art, marking clearly quite minor objects as much as great cathedrals, and manifesting itself in secular as well as religious artifacts. Even if this should be claimed as already partly true of the Romanesque, Gothic makes a sharper stylistic impression not only because of a greater range of surviving evidence but because it is a much more consciously stylish style. It is the product of refinement, thinned constantly to yet more brilliant exiguousness until its success seems to depend not only on what we see but on what we are aware has been suppressed. After the achievement of building solid towers and spires comes the achievement – as at Freiburg *(Ill. 62)* – of making tower and spire all open-work. The minster of Freiburg is a paradox of monumental fragility which is to demonstrate how art can surprise us, defying the natural laws.

Indeed, as a way of expression Gothic may be said to have never totally died out. This certainly seems true historically, for some of its later but still valid manifestations are of the seventeenth century (like the wonderful Gothic fan-vaulting of the staircase to Christ Church hall at Oxford, executed in 1640), while by the eighteenth and nineteenth centuries it was being – more artificially – revived. And although the term 'Gothic' is ridiculously inappropriate in its literal sense to the high refinement of thirteenth- and fourteenth-century art, the adjective has come to take on a significant validity. It is hard to think how one could apply the adjective 'Romanesque' to anything other than the strict products or imitations of that period, but 'Gothic' can be used as apt stylistic shorthand to define something in the art of Botticelli, Cranach or Bernard Buffet.

Not surprisingly, there is really no clear-cut close to the Gothic style. The Renaissance, whatever that is, did not brusquely reverse all its concepts at one blow; Gothic

63 Saint-Denis, Paris (interior). Begun 1140

coexisted with new styles, and an artist like Ghiberti evolved, without any sense of revolution, from an early Gothic style into one that is apparently more 'Renaissance' – is certainly very different. But if there is no end to Gothic, there is a conveniently clear beginning in the new choir *(Ill. 63)* built under Abbot Suger for the abbey of Saint-Denis, outside Paris. Begun in 1140, this was dedicated four years later. It is a consciously new addition to a Romanesque church, using rib-vaults and windows with pointed arches, so that in Suger's own words, 'the church shines with its middle part brightened'. And this concept of the shining church is more relevant for Gothic art than any of the actual motifs used – the pointed arch, the rib-vault or the flying buttress – none of them strictly the invention of Gothic architects. Suger's desire for lightness and brightness is a haunting idea which finds fulfillment a century later in the Sainte-Chapelle *(Ill. 64)*, which really might be the architectural realization of that fantasy 'chapel of glass' occurring in some medieval romances. One of these tells of a glass chapel which magically contracts and expands, and such playing with space is more than a conceit of Gothic buildings: where the visitor is drawn, dazzled, uncertain of what is real and what is not, along high aisles with fragile, fretted roofs and walls that are almost

88

64 Upper church of Sainte-Chapelle, Paris (interior) *c.* 1243–8

entirely translucent – constantly glimpsing eternity, which yet always lies one elusive step ahead.

It is certainly convenient that Saint-Denis should be the place of birth of the Gothic style. The exact origins of the style are not beyond dispute, but the pointed arch as such perhaps came to Europe from Eastern buildings – and it is tempting to suppose that the Crusades may have played some part in this. However it actually originated, it remained basically the creation of France. Although it crossed to England it was never properly established in Italy, and only gradually in Germany. Saint-Denis is itself a crystallization of French consciousness, dedicated to the patron saint of France, directly associated with the monarchy – especially under Suger, who was the King's chief minister as well as the abbot – and once the home of marvellous treasures of goldsmiths' work which equally reflect the new Gothic refinement. Just about the same time as he had the new choir constructed, Suger had an antique porphyry flagon, which he had found neglected in a chest, converted into an ingenious symbol of St John the Evangelist's eagle *(Ill. 66)*, with vivid, almost witty use of the vase as the bird's body. So vivid is the final *objet d'art* that it looks like a clockwork automaton. One might almost imagine the eagle's head swivelling and its sharp, blade-like wings beginning to beat. Such ideas are very close to the Gothic reality, not just as written about in poems but as executed. The architect and master mason, Villard de Honnecourt, working in the thirteenth century, left a book of drawings which record not only buildings, sculpture, methods of design and some tips on lion-taming, but also gives instructions for the making of such automata ('engiens', he calls them) as an eagle lectern which turns its head when the Gospel is read, and a bowl with a semi-mechanical, drinking dove *(Ill. 65)*.

So much of this aspect of the Gothic world has been destroyed that it easy to forget that it was not all sublime cathedral porches and church vessels. The painted metal flowers which at one palace splashed unsuspecting spectators, and other comparable ingenious toys, have proved as ephemeral as the wonderful architectural puddings and the often fantastic, plumage-like clothes. These are things which have to be read about or seen in the pages of illuminated manuscripts, but that testimony is sufficient to show how the artfulness of art was being appreciated. Even where it continued to serve religion, art was now recognized as a power in its own right and the artist (whether

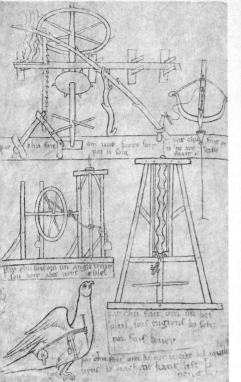

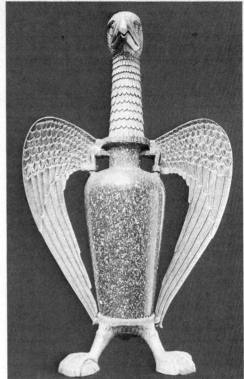

65 (*left*) Page from album of designs for various machines, including mechanical eagle, by Villard de Honnecourt *c.* 1235

66 (*right*) Eagle flagon made for Abbot Suger, mount *c.* 1140

architect, engineer, sculptor or painter) began to be recorded as an actual, and important, person. It is true that Abbot Suger, who wrote at length of his improvements at Saint-Denis, did not bother to mention who had designed or built the new additions there. Elsewhere a few years later we hear several names of architects and even hints of their personalities.

Villard de Honnecourt's wide-ranging interests are one reflection of the increasingly multifarious Gothic world where individual judgments begin to matter in a quite new way. 'I drew this, because I liked it best', he wrote beside his drawing of the choir windows at Rheims, and this aesthetic concern is perhaps the keynote of all Gothic art. What is sketched by Villard is positively enshrined in the finest Gothic cathedrals, mirrors of the restless range of art which is always ambitious for change and elaboration. It cannot be said that the architecture in these centuries radically changed the basic concepts established by the early Christian basilica and consolidated by the Romanesque church, but it elaborated these to the point of exhaustion. When the final stone was twisted and cut to make the undulating, filigree effect of late Gothic architecture there remained nothing left except to conceive the Rococo style. And in Germany particularly the affinities between late Gothic and Rococo – notably in sculpture – are almost bewildering; the Renaissance call for sober, scientific truth is strangled amid writhing foliage and gilt gesticulating figures poised in emotional extremes.

The Gothic cathedral already points to these extremes. Its very art is responsible for a feeling of alienation in comparison with the calm and simple ordering of a Romanesque cathedral. The incredibly rich façade of a cathedral such as that of Amiens *(Ill. 67)* has passed beyond anything which might have seemed its Romanesque forerunner, even the church at Poitiers *(Ill. 58)* that is comparable in its general idea. But Robert de Luzarches, the architect at Amiens, has out-soared that until it is no longer recognizable as the germ from which this tremendous plant has grown and proliferated. And Amiens is not even now completed, because spires were intended to crown the pierced and fretted towers, a final extension of that vertical movement which begins in ascending the steps before the building. It is hard to see how any ordinary worshipper could grasp the significance of the visual richness which is here carved and sculpted on such a huge scale into row upon row of figures, crockets, pinnacles, on a wall that has virtually ceased to have solidity. It is all false entrances and blind, statue-inhabited arcades, at a level so far above that of human beings that whatever the sculpture's exact significance, it can hardly be analyzed without prolonged scrutiny and considerable scholarship.

The usual explanation of such elaborately sculpted façades is that they served as the bibles of the illiterate – but at Amiens the language used is scarcely more easily comprehensible than would be a theological textbook. And in one way, despite the giant scale of this façade, the effect is an extension of the extreme sophistication and private ethos of illuminated manuscripts. Like those, its first impact is of extreme richness (deep relief and play of light and shadow serving as background instead of burnished gold) presenting a vision which amazes rather than communicates to the spectator any specific single message. As

92

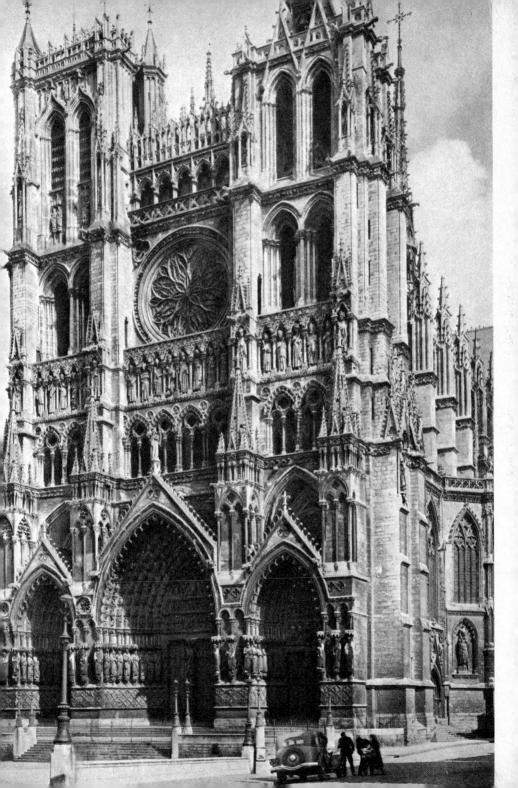

well as a church, it is intended to be a scarcely rational temple of sheer art. In the seventeenth century the engineer Vauban was to refer to the sublime madman who had conceived the cathedral at Coutances, but a member of the Chapter of Seville cathedral in 1401 already thought in these terms for the huge Gothic building planned there, 'so great and of such a kind that those who see it finished shall think we are mad'.

Nor is the interior of a Gothic cathedral a place where the worshipper should immediately feel at home. Wonder and excitement are more likely to be provoked by the mysteriously high nave, linked by slender, stalk-like columns which begin at human level but finally flower far overhead in the sinewy, thin shoots that trace out patterns on the distant vault. Looked up at from the ground, these vault-patterns are abstractly beautiful *(Ill. 68)*, triumphs of geometry that need no other adornment. At first they may seem more intellectual and less florid than the exteriors, but gradually they too assumed almost their own life – no longer pretending to serve a serious structural purpose. The vault of Suger's Saint-Denis is a very uncomplicated affair compared with what was to grow up especially in England. Here the almost rushing verticality and thrust of a French cathedral like Amiens was exchanged for lower and more longitudinal effects. Even the most elaborate façades of English cathedrals were conceived as strongly horizontal screens – like those of Salisbury or Wells. There was nothing comparable to that obsession with height which reached a positive height of folly in the choir of Beauvais cathedral – the highest ever achieved until it collapsed within a few years of being built. Yet the vaults of English cathedrals show an equal addiction to extremes, not of height but complexity. The architects seem to delight in constructing a web of ribs, now fanning out, now clustering in star-shapes, sometimes growing elaborate bosses where they intersect. Increasing virtuosity of effect turned what was originally something which marvellously defied gravity by soaring upwards into something no less gravity-defying and marvellous: a pendant-vault, like that at Christ Church *(Ill. 69)*, where the miracle seems to consist in the whole structure being suspended in space – forever dropping, and forever held like a canopy over the choir. That was built in 1478, when the Gothic style in England had gone through the permutation hoops set up by architectural historians – Early English, Decorated, Perpendicular – and even then had not reached the firework brilliance of Henry VII's chapel in Westminster Abbey.

94

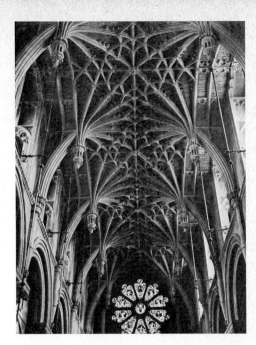

58 Chapter-house vault, Wells Cathedral 1295–1319

69 Choir ceiling, Christ Church, Oxford Cathedral c. 1478

Within the Gothic cathedral, where art is always busy paring away solidity, altering the property of stone, teasing the eye by deception, the perfect art form was not sculpture, still less painting, but the stained-glass window. This was the final paradox of visible and invisible – one that it is easy to understand, for the human fascination with glass is something exploited again by modern architecture. Seen from outside, the elaborate tracery of some cathedral's wheel-like rose-window already dissolves a portion of wall; but looked at from inside, where the actual amount of light available is controlled by the deep colouring of the glass itself, there is no wall at all. It is out of a shadowy penumbra that a giant, translucent kaleidoscope assembles itself – in sheer colour and pattern, before any 'subject' can be deciphered. Close-up details of stained-glass windows may show their stylistic affinities to manuscripts, but it is the glowing total effect, and even subordination of detail, that matters most as a visual impression.

The artist (and there were individual artists in glass, for Clément, 'verrier de Chartres', signed a window at Rouen) was

95

free to obey decorative laws. To achieve the final harmony of colour, he might make haloes red or blue or yellow *(Ill. 70)* and garments that change colour quite arbitrarily. The convention of lead strips increased the pattern-making effect and set off the different shapes of each piece of coloured glass like a more exciting, and much more translucent, form of mosaic. In early Gothic windows, the colours have a real gem-like intensity and in themselves are mystic, like fragments of those gems which had haunted the medieval imagination, stimulated by the New Jerusalem described in St John's Revelation.

Such visions are hardly the experiences of every day. Medieval men did not automatically become mystics by virtue of living when the cathedrals were being built and decorated. Like Abbot Suger, they might be practical administrators as well as contemplators of jewels. Suger himself certainly marvelled over the precious stones that he was given or acquired for Saint-Denis, and an interesting passage in his book on his work there tells how the beauty of 'many-coloured gems' sometimes called him from external cares, encouraging him to meditate. The material objects led to immaterial concepts; as he pondered, he felt himself transported from the inferior to the higher, spiritual world. Consciously or unconsciously, he here seems to be answering the fears expressed by St Bernard.

Nevertheless, within a few years, the tendencies of art would really be the other way about – bringing the spiritual world closer to man by expressing it in more 'realistic' and less symbolic forms. This 'realism' is partly a matter of psychological truth as well as the copying of natural appearances. For this reason, there is often a sharp stylistic distinction between the apparently bourgeois, even brutal, realism of some art (true to what we might see) and the extremes of courtly refinement and emotion (true to what we might feel). Architecture was inevitably free from this particular problem of realism, but it is useful to note that the problem was not brought into existence through the rise of secular patronage. In so far as it is a problem, it is one for the spectator perhaps rather than for the artist. The artist was, in fact, gaining an autonomy whereby he could develop a personal style. Giotto and Duccio are contemporaries working in patently opposed styles. Exactly at the close of the fourteenth century when Claus Sluter was sculpting in Burgundy his intensely solid, almost stubbornly realistic figures, there developed the most affectedly graceful, sinuously swaying images – usually of the Madonna or female saints – which were

96

popular all over Europe. Sluter's work was for a great aristocratic patron, the Duke of Burgundy; many of the small Madonna images must have prettified private, bourgeois homes.

For this sculptural variety to exist there had first to be a considerable evolution of technique: the image needed to be released from the stone where, in Romanesque sculpture, it had lain in fairly flat relief or partly been imprisoned in pillars. It is the same evolution towards the freestanding figure which had taken place in Greece in antiquity; and the same law applies. The later work is not of itself better for this freedom. Comparable conventions to those which govern the *Apollo* from Olympia *(Ill. 26)* govern the Old Testament figures, executed in the mid-twelfth century, for the west porch at Chartres cathedral *(Ill. 71)*. Their very proportions reveal their difference from ourselves; like enough to be recognizably human, they are otherwise almost oriental in their delicate remoteness, with beautifully cut, thin drapery that not only clings to their bodies but virtually is those bodies: tunics of minutely-pleated material topped by solid, yet still remote and absorbed heads. There is scarcely any movement in terms of realism.

Thus, in their own terms, they stand like guardians rather than prisoners. Yet it was certainly one of the major achievements of the Gothic world – with its love of automata and magic objects – to make statues step forward from cathedral façades, moving now with revolutionary ease, experiencing emotions, positively mirroring human beings with a lifelikeness that had been lost to Western art since antiquity. The graceful, almost Phidian *Visitation* group at Rheims *(Ill. 72)* –

◀ 71 Old Testament figures, Chartres *c.* 1150

72 *The Visitation*, Rheims Cathedral *c.* 1230

73 *The Foolish Virgins*, Magdeburg Cathedral *c.* 1234

74 Equestrian statue of Otto II, Magdeburg *c.* 1240–50

probably of about 1230 – is a very familiar, typical illustration of what could be achieved, but it is perhaps rather too bland in its conscious gracefulness.

The emotional assault which new technique had also made possible is seen in the row of Foolish Virgins *(Ill. 73)* on the cathedral of Magdeburg, in Germany, executed only a few years after the Rheims *Visitation*. Extremes of raging grief and chagrin shake these figures out of rhetoric into a quite extraordinary humanity – and art makes them the plastic equivalent of a disturbing cry which might well halt anybody approaching the cathedral porch. This is art which achieves a mimesis that had not been experienced before in the West. It perturbs rather than elevates (though it is fair to add that the Wise Virgins are sculpted on the opposite side of the porch). Few things are more misleading than equations of art and national temperament; but in sculpture at least a distinction can early be established between Germany and France – and by the eighteenth century it will be seen to be quite patent. Meanwhile, the technical command which is revealed by Rheims and Magdeburg makes it possible for sculpture to be utilized in new ways, serving purposes other than purely religious ones.

The Foolish Virgins are, for all their freedom of movement, still conceived as attached to a supporting wall. But also at Magdeburg, standing under a stone canopy in the market place, is the equestrian statue of the Emperor Otto *(Ill. 74)*, which was probably done at the same period as the sculpture on the cathedral porch. It marks the emancipation of sculpture from architectural support, quite literally. An earlier equestrian statue in the cathedral at Bamberg (the 'Bamberg rider') may have inspired the Magdeburg concept, but does not have the free-standing, fully modelled effect which makes the latter so public and remarkable. The Emperor had been dead for some two hundred and fifty years, but he lives vividly again in this – one of the earliest of such secular monuments, and one of the most elaborate. It is not an idealized image of royalty, but an individualized, lively and almost coarsely vigorous depiction. Nor was it set up at Magdeburg in any mood of obsequiousness – rather the opposite. Otto II is there because of the civic rights he had granted to the city, and the statue is the result of a new source of patronage, neither religious nor royal, but civic. Beside the cathedral and the palace in the Gothic city, there would soon be architectural expression of the commune in an equally large and dominant building, the town hall.

The Magdeburg equestrian statue shows that sculpture could now ably commemorate an actual man – giving a sense of keen portraiture even where the sculptor had not seen the living original. The artist's power to commemorate combines with his power to create. On tombs the figures are no longer flattened impersonal images whose attributes of kingship or clerical status have to serve instead of character, but take on new depth and weight – both emotionally and literally. Their faces

75 Tomb of Henry III, Westminster Abbey, London. Late thirteenth century

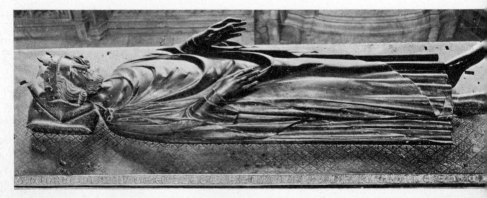

76 Hunting Lodge of Frederick II, Castel del Monte, Apulia *c.* 1240

become individualized portraits, sometimes characterized to convey too the impact of a death-mask, in smiling repose or grimly rigid. A distinct personality is already suggested by the bronze effigy of Henry III of England *(Ill. 75),* who died, after a disastrous reign, in 1272. Perhaps the quivering, empty-handed effect – as of one who has strained himself in vain – is partly an accident, but at least some impression of character is conveyed. The fourteenth-century monuments of English kings – like those of Richard II and Edward III – undoubtedly aim at exact portraiture: recording each individual curve of eyebrow and wrinkle of forehead.

   The splendid abbey where they are all buried was Henry III's creation, but he was also the builder of an adjoining palace at Westminster. He was in fact one of the first of those cultivated royal patrons who prove markedly more successful in artistic than in political affairs. It is something of an irony that his palace has been absorbed and lost in the present structure of the

Houses of Parliament, because they represent the power of Parliament to which politically he lost as well. What best survives of his palace and its decoration is entry after entry in the royal accounts, showing that he had whole rooms painted with allegorical figures and battle scenes (perhaps rather as Uccello was to paint for the Medici some two hundred years later). With Henry III there can be no doubt that his patronage was direct and personal – keeping architects, sculptors and painters very busy. The King's personal wishes and his memoranda can be detected or positively read: 'We remember' – runs one of these latter – 'that you said it would be much grander to make the two leopards, to be placed on either side of our new chair at Westminster, of bronze rather than of marble. . . .' This has a positively Renaissance ring to it. It serves to show the secular patron offering an alternative to ecclesiastical patronage, and Henry III's painted rooms in his palace sustain the secular note. Rooms now begin to exist for decoration and furnishing, to provide an agreeable atmosphere in which people can relax.

Just about the period Henry III began his palace of Westminster, the Emperor Frederick II built the Castel del Monte *(Ill. 76)* in Apulia, which was not intended to be a defensive building but a hunting-lodge. No haphazard affair, this is built with a deliberate and typical symmetry (echoed all over Europe with carefully planned castles and manor-houses) and also includes a conscious classical antique motif – remarkable enough in the largely Gothic Europe of 1240 – in the pedimental gateway. By the fourteenth century castles, palaces and palatial city halls could architecturally challenge the dominance of the cathedral. Great commercial centres like Venice and Bruges expressed a sense of their own civic pride in buildings *(Ills. 78, 79)* which are graceful as well as imposing, secular churches raised to the religion of trade and to the greater glory of the state. Art is lavished on such buildings no less than on cathedrals. The high town hall at Bruges might easily be mistaken for a church, with its spire and pinnacled façade pierced by tall windows; at Venice, the Doge's palace stretches its vast pink flanks along sea and land, reducing the near-by basilica of S. Marco to its original status as the Doge's chapel. As for the princely castle, it had become the fragile-looking but actually quite firm cluster of white towers and chimneys, blue roofs and gilt fleur-de-lis weather-vanes which the Limbourg brothers set against a perfect sky of deeper blue *(Ill. 77)*. This is not an enchanted fairy-tale vision but an autumnal view of the castle

77 *September* (detail) from the Limbourg brothers' *Très riche Heures de Duc de Berry* 1413–1

of Saumur, owned in the late fourteenth century by the Duc de Berry, brother of the King of France.

This prince is himself the quintessence of Gothic man, superb patron of the arts, inquisitive, acquisitive, intoxicated by visual splendour, fond of exotic objects which ranged from a dromedary and an ostrich to a prize collector's piece of jewellery – St Joseph's wedding-ring. Saumur was only one of his many castles, several of them recorded in the background to the Calendar pages of the months painted for his sumptuous book of hours, *Les très Riches Heures*. This book was outstanding even among his treasures: so elaborately conceived that it was not quite finished at the Duc de Berry's death in 1416, though he had encouraged the illuminators by pledging them a valuable ruby from his store of such treasure. Inside castles like Saumur, there would be splendid, heraldic tapestries, marvellous gold plate, and objects which almost defy description, fantasy works positively challenging the achievements of a Fabergé.

For New Year's Day 1404, the Duc de Berry's nephew – Charles VI of France – received from his wife the 'Little Gold Horse' *(Ill. 81),* basically a religious tabernacle but remarkable for its secular feeling and virtuosity – no accident that it should be called by a name emphasizing not the Virgin and Child group but the white-enamelled gold horse which stands below. That and its fashionable groom, equally brilliantly enamelled with particoloured hose and patterned sleeves, are tribute enough to the Gothic artist's awareness of reality. Aware of it, able as here to capture it well enough, the artist is not bounded by it. Just as the late antique world had delighted in bronze statuettes where eyes were enamel and lips were copper *(Ill. 35),* so the high sophistication of the late Gothic world could enjoy the Virgin's bower of gold leaves and huge pearls, varied by other larger stones, set up on a dais of gold approached by twin golden staircases, and where, setting the whole object's courtly cheerful mood, the King's horse finds its prominent place – a reminder of the secular world which waits when prayer is over.

As for the Calendar pages illuminated by Pol de Limbourg and his brothers for the Duc de Berry, while these represent a supreme achievement in the long tradition of illuminating manuscripts (the culmination of what had been done at Lindisfarne seven hundred years before, *Ill. 53),* they also proclaim the end of that tradition. The pages have become complete pictures, atmospherically vivid, yet elegant and controlled. It was not necessary to wait for the invention of

78 The Doges'
Palace, Venice
1309–1424

79 Town Hall,
Bruges.
From 1376

printing to realize that beyond these marvellous pages there can be no progress. The illuminated manuscript as such could barely contain what painters now wished to do. Despite the linear technique, and only faint colour washes, there is a Chaucerian vigour and forcefulness about the dedicatory page *(Ill. 80)* which John Siferwas executed for the Lovell Lectionary (before 1408), showing him presenting his illuminated manuscript to the patron, Lord Lovell. The most famous painter to begin with such work is Jan van Eyck full in the fifteenth century; but he moved beyond it, never to return, becoming instead a European 'prince of painters' in the new technique of oil painting.

Just as the Gothic style had developed and made more expressive the potentiality of architecture and sculpture, so it touched with quite new and sophisticated articulateness the

80 *John Siferwas with Lord Lovell*, frontispiece of the Lovell Lectionary. Before 1408

81 'Little Gold Horse' altar tabernacle. Before 1404

82 GIOTTO
*Annunciation to
St Anne*
c. 1306–12

83 DUCCIO *The
Annunciation*
c. 1311

110

previously rather humble art of painting. The taste which had manifested itself in Southern Europe largely through mosaic, and in the North through stained glass and illuminated manuscripts, now encouraged in both South and North an art that held up a fresh sort of mirror to the imagination: a picture. The word itself is an addition to the vocabulary in late Middle English and in the modern sense of a painting does not apparently occur before 1484.

Churches had certainly been decorated with frescoes, but it was perhaps the creation of actual panel pictures – first in painted altar frontals and crucifixes – which raised the status of painting. More directly than any other art it could also reflect the visible world. How men would see this reality naturally varied, as much as how they would choose to express it. As expressed by Giotto *(Ill. 82)* there was a revolutionary illusionism in the actual depiction which traditionally sets Western painting on a course which would falter only in the nineteenth century.

That fresco was painted about 1306 – an accidental manifesto of the 'modern' style which would largely triumph over the Gothic. That world where splendour of colour, linear grace, a conscious quest for beauty, all matter more than truth to natural appearances, is perfectly expressed in Duccio's small, exquisitely wrought panel of the Annunciation *(Ill. 83)* of some five years later. It is also in a house that the Virgin here receives the angel, but a house that obeys purely artistic laws: set against

84 SIMONE MARTINI *The Annunciation* 1333

a flat gold background, it is really only the symbol of a building, a structure that might be of coloured cardboard, no more suggesting substance than the delicate figures, graceful yet hesitant, that do not quite stand but quiver rather in linear tension. The full blaze of Gothic intensity is exposed in the complete work of art that is made up by painting and frame in Simone Martini's *Annunciation (Ill. 84)*, painted in 1333, and itself an artistic defiance of all Giotto's realism. The frame burns upwards with its tongues of flickering gold; and it is against a great sheet of gold and simulated marble that the Virgin almost affectedly shrinks before the angel-apparition with its leaf-crowned head from which shoot further fiery rays of gold. This is pure vision, lyrical in its linear insistence and blaze of colour.

The pictorial equivalent of some complex vault tracery or sinuously graceful statue, this style became international. Simone Martini himself was a famous artist at the period; he worked at Avignon as well as in his native Siena. A whole knot of influences and effects is tied together in the *Glatz Madonna (Ill. 85)* which breathes an echo of Byzantium mingled with the half French-half Italian courtly richness of Martini, a suitable altarpiece to have been produced in the international centre of Prague in the mid-fourteenth century. The throne alone is a Gothic triumph, with its pinnacles, roofed niches for lions to crouch in, opening windows whence angels peer, all fragile but finely carved, in a heaven of gold-embroidered drapery suspended by the topmost angels. Although the commissioner of the altarpiece is only a small kneeling figure, his presence is significant. All this splendour is, as it were, his personal vision; it is his crozier and his gloves which lie on the steps in front of the Virgin, and he himself – Ernst von Pardubitz – is portrayed in his new rank of archbishop, going down to posterity within the work of art.

It is true that Giotto's revolution might seem to doom this style to look old-fashioned, but art is not *haute-couture*. Not only does the *Glatz Madonna* retain its validity, but the Gothic style in painting retained its vitality in different artists long after Masaccio in the fifteenth century appeared to consolidate Giotto's achievement. Indeed, although Italy is conventionally the home of the Renaissance, the centre of scientific naturalism, the least Gothically-inclined of countries, it was there that Gothic painting bloomed longest. In Pisanello, who did not die until 1455, all its supreme stylishness is summed up. His *Vision*

85 BOHEMIAN
MASTER *Glatz
Madonna*
c. 1350

86 PISANELLO *Vision of Sts Anthony Abbot and George*

of Sts Anthony Abbot and George (Ill. 86) is an exotic encounter
of chivalry and old age near a dark wood, where the two saints
seem oblivious of that celestial sizzling aurora borealis in the
sky which contains within it the embracing Virgin and Child.
This is the country of enchantment; and it is a final fantasy touch,
yet somehow not surprising, that the foreground grasses have
twisted themselves into forming the painter's name.

CHAPTER FOUR

In a New Perspective

The house that Giotto had built in the *Annunciation to St Anne* *(Ill. 82)* proved a significant and prophetic structure in architecture, sculpture and painting.

Such harmony and coherence – achieved through a conscious, rational organization of space – were to be sought by all the arts during the fifteenth century. Instead of bewildering the spectator by sheer visual splendour, they would attempt an intellectual, even scientific brilliance. The untidy actual world would not be merely reflected but re-ordered, in those interests of art and knowledge which achieve finally a new fusion in the personality of Leonardo da Vinci. His life span, as well as his artistic contribution, makes him the culmination of Renaissance endeavours, the most gifted offspring of the fifteenth and father of the sixteenth century. The medieval formula which found expression in the sentence 'Ars sine scientia nihil est' (used during the discussions about the building of the Gothic cathedral at Milan towards the end of the fourteenth century), now became applicable in a quite different sense. In whatever medium he works, an artist is expected to display not only skill and craftsmanship but his intellectual knowledge, incorporating some general or particular truths about the universe.

If we turn back to Giotto's fresco and look at it in the light of these Renaissance requirements, it conforms remarkably well and makes one easily understand the constant fifteenth-century Italian praise of Giotto. He was the founder-figure needed too when Italian art-history came to be written. In Vasari's *Lives*, Duccio receives a very brief biography – and part of that is devoted to someone else; but pages are given to the work, and also the personality, of Giotto. It was Vasari who first printed Petrarch's reference to a painting by his friend Giotto, 'the beauty of which is not understood by the ignorant, but the knowledgeable marvel. . . .' The *Annunciation to St Anne* is equally for such connoisseurs.

It brings us down from the Gothic gold heaven to earth. The wall on which the composition is projected becomes like a transparent window – not of visionary stained glass but totally colourless – through which we look into a box-like, delimited space. Both outside and inside of the house are plotted with geometrical precision. This architecture is austerely classical; and a positive antique classical reference – an early hint of renascent interest in antiquity – is provided by the sarcophagus-derived relief carved on the roof. Far from everything being covered by decoration, each object is stripped to reveal its essential form. To Giotto it is more marvellous to depict the event within a firmly human framework of life (one realized as firmly as is the cube of house) than to emphasize the super-natural. It is a feat of the intellect to have created the illusion of a three-dimensional building; and a feat of the imagination to have created the simultaneous effect of the girl outside in the porch carding wool while within St Anne kneels before the angel. It is typical, too, of the practical aspect of Giotto's art that this angel makes use of the window to appear at – thus obeying, as far as possible, ordinary physical laws. Everywhere rationality has been at work.

But in its concern with a reasonable, harmonious universe, art was bound to encounter, and respond to with new intensity, the relics of that antique civilization which had been apparently buried by Christianity. Out of that misty past, which the Gothic had typically seen in magical, mythical terms, there now emerged buildings and statues which took on new significance and reality. It was the Gothic cathedral which would appear the alien edifice, while the domed containment of space which is the Pantheon became an ideal to be carefully studied and copied. What antique sculpture happened to survive would equally be studied.

It was inevitable that the theatre of this sort of re-discovery must primarily be Italy, since everything bound Italians (as it still does) to the tradition and prestige of their Roman ancestors. Indeed, so strong and enduring was that tradition that it had never really died out. Negatively, it offered resistance to dis-semination of the alien Gothic style; positively, it offered possibilities of imitation and continuation which are associated with the concept of 'the Renaissance'. One of the many difficulties about this concept – which was not truly a style, and certainly never a single-minded artistic movement – is that it declines to have a date of origin. In Italy the Romanesque style

87 Cathedral, Civita Castellana, Umbria 1210

was deeply Roman in feeling. All the balanced architectural harmony which it used to be thought was created by Brunelleschi in fifteenth-century Florence as a result of rediscovering antiquity is apparent in Romanesque works, some of which Brunelleschi must have very carefully studied. Whether or not he went to see the cathedral at Civita Castellana, near Rome, this building *(Ill. 87)* already in 1210 revives classical forms in an impressively majestic way, incorporating the Roman triumphal arch motif for the entrance. The complexity of different styles, which is the history of Western art, can hardly be more effectively conveyed at that period than by comparing this cathedral façade with that at Amiens *(Ill. 67)*, begun only ten years later.

The aura of antiquity which hovers around Civita Castellana was actively fostered by one of the most gifted and eccentric figures of the Middle Ages, truly the 'Wonder of the World', the Emperor Frederick II (died 1250), whose Castel del Monte *(Ill. 76)* sufficiently reveals his deliberately classicizing tastes. The fact that he revived antique forms – including the triumphal arch – to create an ethos in which he could become a veritable Roman emperor, a second Augustus, is more significant than that other influences inevitably mingled with the classical in

117

much of the art produced in his kingdom of Norman Sicily and Southern Italy. Frederick certainly challenged the perspective of affairs as sketched by the Papacy, and Dante perhaps unwittingly paid him a great compliment by singling him out – alone of Roman Emperors – for a place in Hell.

It was from Frederick's Apulia that there came the sculptor Nicola Pisano. The *Crucifixion (Ill. 88)* is one carved relief on his pulpit at Pisa, dated 1260. This gravely beautiful work is clearly influenced by antique prototypes, sarcophagi above all. Its almost stubborn sense of monumentality, with heads still proportionately too big for bodies but making impressive masks of dignity, declares a new mastery of the human figure in Italian sculpture. It is more natural-seeming than what had gone before; and yet almost more remarkable is its restraint. In another relief from the same pulpit, the Virgin stands at the Presentation like Juno, wearing a diadem and clasping her toga-like cloak in great noble folds. Antique reminiscence is combined with a keen perception of individual faces, expressive

of varied emotions, characterized at various ages. Above all, the compositions are held in a harmony that is timelessly classic as well as classical. Even in the *Crucifixion* the violent swoon of the Virgin is checked by the supporting figures of steady, simply draped women, like Roman matrons, who have much of the organic toughness of Giotto's people, while the extended arms of the crucified Christ seem to embrace all humanity – the mockers as well as the mourners.

It is true that in Nicola's distinguished son, Giovanni Pisano, there is some veering towards French Gothic grace, a quickening of rhythm which has moved away from the classical antique tradition towards the more elegant, international standards which were to be represented in painting by Simone Martini. But another great pupil of Nicola's, Arnolfo di Cambio, responded to his sense of gravity and monumental form, to produce the tremendous block of *Virgin and Child (Ill. 89)* destined for the façade of the Duomo at Florence, itself projected and begun by Arnolfo in his capacity as architect. The Virgin

◀ 88 NICOLA PISANO
Crucifixion, pulpit of
the Duomo, Pisa 1260

89 ARNOLFO DI
CAMBIO *Virgin and
Child c.* 1296

and Child group is probably from only a few years before Giotto's *Annunciation to St Anne*, and it fits well into that power-fully plastic world. Neither Virgin nor Child is conventionally beautiful, but they are invested with a power which is more impressive than beauty. These boulder-like forms suggest endurance; the heavy spheres of their massive heads, the jutting rock of the Virgin's knee, are not realistic but natural-seeming shapes that might have been evolved by weathering rather than by the sculptor's skill. Arnolfo's Virgin seems to enshrine maternity, beyond the associations of the Christian religion, going back to tap the roots of humanity and being Demeter, Cybele, Mater Matuta whom the Roman women worshipped by bringing children in their arms, and yet ultimately Mary seated with her blessing Child on the cathedral of S. Maria della Fiore.

It is like a proclamation of the specifically Florentine contribution to the 'new' art – anti-Gothic and derived from the antique past which lay so close to the ground on which Italians walked. Established in Giotto's work, the tradition passes down from him to Masaccio and thence to Michelangelo. The Arena chapel frescoes, of which the *Annunciation to St Anne* is one, consistently unfold the Christian story on the solid, even chill, earth of actuality where monumental human beings move the more effectively for their very economy of emotion and gesture. It is all a cosmic drama, but Giotto keeps his stage free from trivial genre touches – so that the moment of Joachim's sorrowful return to his sheep in the hill country *(Ill. 90)* is made poignant by the still figure of Joachim, oblivious of the dog that hastens to greet him, and to the patent embarrassment of his shepherds.

Giotto's truth seems to pierce to the heart of the human condition, and in that neither Masaccio nor Michelangelo rivalled him. It is difficult not to make him virtually the founder of Western painting, because in him its potentialities are fully revealed – indeed, in one way are fully realized. Never before had painting managed to organize a completely spatial world in which recognizably human figures could act out intensely human emotions. In the Joachim fresco, it is not just the protagonist's feelings which matter, but those of the shepherds – and the dog's – so that, as he savours the situation, the spectator experiences a positive miniature drama. This is something very different from the effect of straightforward images of Christ crucified or the Virgin and Child, or even the vivid humanity of the Hildesheim doors *(Ill. 56)*. Yet in some ways it is a dangerous power; less artistically concentrated than it is in Giotto's work, it can easily dwindle into being illustration. Giotto's own followers could not sustain his concentration, and thence onwards Western art would keep lapsing into trivial illusions of realism until frightened off finally by the invention of photography.

By the fifteenth century the achievements of Nicola Pisano and Giotto assumed a new meaning. Their empirical results – achieved in a largely Gothic Europe – were inspiring particularly to Italian artists trying to incorporate into art standards of the natural and the truthful. Yet these standards were not the prerogative of Italy. The sculpture of Claus Sluter *(Ill. 91)* in Burgundy shows that before 1400 a Northern artist could think in anti-Gothic, monumental terms, and with a powerful sense not merely of realism but of portraiture. Here Duke Philip the

Bold kneels with impressive effect in the doorway of the monastery he had founded at Dijon – projecting fully from the architecture, with bulky, heavily-carved robes and lifelike features, a statue originally made still more living probably by painted naturalistic colour. This type of realism was to pervade Northern sculpture, and especially its painting, to an extent which first astonished Italy and then came to seem rather prosaic. But it too is part of the new feeling for humanity, expressed in human terms. Its basis remains empiric rather than intellectual; yet it was for 'art et science' that a later Duke Philip, the Good, of Burgundy, was to praise his well-beloved painter and equerry, Jan van Eyck.

Van Eyck's spatial world is no less crisply constructed than Giotto's, but it is intimate rather than epic, its quintessence the interior where man is not noble but homely, positively at home in a personal environment which had never been so exactly mirrored before until Van Eyck painted the double portrait of the Arnolfini *(Ill. 92)*. This still astonishes us by its revolutionary technique and revolutionary concept. In itself it almost justifies all that used to be written about the Renaissance triumph of the individual, because it exudes a sense of man emancipated and standing proudly in his own right.

92 VAN EYCK *The* ▶ *Marriage of Giovanni(?) Arnolfini and Giovanna Cenami(?)* 1434

91 SLUTER *Philip the Bold and St John the Baptist*

This scene of the betrothal of Giovanni Arnolfini is painted with almost legal minuteness and accuracy. It opens for us a window on no ideal but a positively eye-deceivingly real world where we encounter not sacred personages, no historically important episode, but a private ceremony between two quite private people. On that Van Eyck has worked with all his 'art et science', to convey the cube of their fully-furnished room with its central mirror – significant object – that reflects even the wall which is behind the spectator. In the mirror figures can be seen entering the room – just as the spectator seems to enter it, his eye drawn up the line of floorboards. Without a knowledge of perspective, this almost peep-show effect would not be achieved: so much is 'science'. Art is yet more, one may feel, for the grasp of atmosphere is instinctive, a delicate response to light falling on a whole gamut of textures, moulding to a glowing velvety surface the hard mathematical framework. Like Giotto, Van Eyck anticipated the course of naturalistic Western painting; certainly he unwittingly created 'the interior' as a subject for pictures, and left Dutch seventeenth-century genre painters little to do except duplicate his effects, rarely with such rigorous control.

Although it is wrong to divide fifteenth-century, still less sixteenth-century, Europe too neatly into North and South – for there was a constant exchange of influence, and Jan Van Eyck, for example, was highly esteemed in Italy – it yet remains valid that Northern art tended to emphasize, with Aristotelian concern, natural man in his natural environment, while in Italy more elevated, transcendental obsessions lifted him into Platonic spheres. Before Dürer, few Northern artists showed much interest in artistic theory or would have claimed a deep intellectual basis for their art.

Interest in man himself encouraged the most personal of mirrors – the portrait – which nearly every Northern painter produced. Marvellously plotted as are Van Eyck's, it is the portraits by Rogier van der Weyden *(Ill. 93)* which best capture the living, emotional impact of sheer humanity, with some elusive sense of the fragility as well as the beauty of human existence. Rogier's religious pictures show that this sense is not subjective, for there the pathos is quite apparent. Superbly lifelike in surface realism, his people are more intensely real for being vessels of interior emotion – themselves men, and women, of sorrows 'and acquainted with grief'. It was no mere illusionistic trick when Rogier painted a crystal teardrop on the Virgin's face. And though for long Northern art notoriously showed little interest in the nude as such, it was always conscious of the naked, exposed human condition. The greatest fifteenth-century sculptor in the North, Nikolaus Gerhaert, shared Rogier's intensity; his almost shockingly realistic portrait bust *(Ill. 94)*

93 ROGIER VAN DER
WEYDEN *Philippe de Croy*

94 NIKOLAUS GERHAERT
Portrait Bust 1467

125

95 House of Jacques Cœur, Bourges, Mid fifteenth century

has inevitably been called a self-portrait. Despite the solidity of stone, it too conveys fragility, with a palpitating sense of skin creased by the hand's pressure – and the hand a marvel of weight and texture, suggesting sinew, knuckle and fingernails. The hunched pose is a pose of actual life, at once brooding and relaxed, so that we seem to encounter another person at a private moment when he is unaware of scrutiny.

The new illusionistic power of art to reflect back man and his environment is seen on a monumental scale and yet in domestic context on the façade of the house of Jacques Cœur at Bourges *(Ill. 95)*, a private dwelling for a great mid-fifteenth-century financier, one of the rising middle class. That Cœur was quite conscious of aspiring is made clear by his motto, *A vaillans cœurs rien impossible*, which is carved in the well-designed, elaborately decorated rooms of his house. A citizen's home has now become palace and church combined (Cœur's chapel is incorporated within his house); and the guardian saints from cathedral porches have become the lifelike servants – forever

96 VAN DER
GOES *Portinari
altarpiece*
(right wing)

97 LEONARDO *Adoration of the Kings* ?1481

waiting for their master – carved to peer inquisitively out of
simulated windows on the façade.

No less monumental was the scale in which, before the end
of the fifteenth century, painting mirrored actual people. In
Hugo van der Goes' Portinari altarpiece *(Ill. 96),* atmosphere,
buildings, water, hills, trees and people – the whole range of
the visible world – are contained with astonishing verisimilitude. It challenges painted sculpture by its powerful forms with
full-length, actual-size portraiture and every refinement of
texture from heavy, brocaded, fur-lined robe to the silky half-
transparent strands of the kneeling girl's hair. But that is only
the beginning. Thanks to the luminous property of oil paint, it
can eclipse all other arts in conveying in the same composition

the very tang of a winter day, in a countryside of bare, brownish hills, where a few birds perch in tall, leafless trees, and a cold light gleams on the steely surface of a lake.

Commissioned by a Florentine, Tommaso Portinari, agent of the Medici bank in Bruges, the altarpiece probably really was a revelation when it arrived in Florence about 1476. As a picture to convey the sense of what it might have been like to be present at the Nativity – or rather, if the Nativity had taken place in the fifteenth-century – the impact of the whole huge altarpiece is as immediate as a miracle play. In other pictures Van der Goes aims at almost disturbed, highly emotional assaults on the spectator, to impress scenes on him with eye-witness effect in a way that anticipates Grünewald *(Ill. 154)* in the following century. As for the wonderful winter landscape, this has almost gained autonomy; it is by no means the first of such sensitively observed landscapes embedded in Northern pictures, but on this scale, and with its integration of figures into the landscape, it becomes a prototype for Bruegel *(Ill.156)*. Some Florentine painters too certainly responded to the total impact of the altarpiece, which is indeed a quintessence of Northern achievement.

Yet, within five years of its arrival in Florence, Leonardo da Vinci was to begin his *Adoration of the Kings (Ill. 97)*, more ideal than naturalistic, in a setting utterly unlike any ordinary environment, ruled by intellect as much as by observation. Mystery has replaced clarity – and this would probably always have been so, even had the picture been completed. Not astonishingly lifelike portrait figures but shadowy, graceful types of youth and old age, dressed in timeless robes, ebb and flow with elemental vitality about the graceful still centre that is the Virgin. After Van der Goes' vigorous miracle play, we are witnessing a classic drama: one that crystallizes Italian achievement, marvelled over by Leonardo's contemporaries and to inspire the young Raphael, born two years after it was begun.

Leonardo is a culmination of those Italian interests which from the early fifteenth century had been attempting in effect a combination of *ars* and *scientia* which would produce ambitiously new and more truthful art. They are particularly associated with Florence through the triumvirate of friends Donatello, Brunelleschi and Masaccio, by far the youngest and shortest-lived. To these must be added another Florentine, Alberti, also their friend but more obviously learned, literate and more theoretically-inclined. The very prestige of Florence,

98 DELLA QUERCIA *Creation of Adam* 1425–38

asserted by Florentines like Alberti and codified in the *Lives* of that Florentine by adoption, Vasari, perhaps blinds us to the attempts sporadically made elsewhere in Italy. Although it is customary to explain nearly every Renaissance manifestation as engendered by Brunelleschi's architecture or by his discovery of a method of visual perspective, by Donatello's sculpture and by Masaccio's paintings, this is too neat an explanation. Thus, somewhat older probably than any of these famous artists was a Sienese sculptor, Jacopo della Quercia, who is increasingly recognized as an independently great figure. He brought to sculpture his own remarkable feeling for organization and monumentality – achieving in the Genesis reliefs *(Ill. 98)* for the church of S. Petronio at Bologna massively eloquent effects which were to be admired by Michelangelo. The strongly muscular body of Adam, naked and newly stirring under God the Father's gaze, is itself no bad Renaissance symbol, showing a quickening concern with anatomy, and expressive too of art's confident power to re-create the moment of first human creation. Quercia's vital, alert Adam, gazing up directly at his Creator, seems to offer inspiration for the heroic Adam of Michelangelo's electric, cosmic vision *(Ill. 127)* where God the Father creates not man but a demi-god.

Jacopo della Quercia is probably the most distinguished non-Florentine artist of the early fifteenth century, serving as a reminder that Renaissance concepts might be embodied in any genius and did not require a specifically Florentine climate in which to bloom. Indeed, it was at Florence that della Quercia was signally defeated, when in 1401 a competition was organized for a new pair of bronze doors for the Baptistery. Brunelleschi also was ultimately defeated, and turned from sculpture to architecture. Donatello was too young to compete, but he was soon to be employed in the studio of the victorious contestant, Lorenzo Ghiberti.

What is remarkable about Florence in these years is the diversity of talents, sometimes interacting, sometimes opposing each other, yet always sharing some intellectual quality, and over-spilling from one category of art into another – not surprisingly when most of the exponents were proficient in several media. Ghiberti is, in many ways, the father of them all. Himself trained as a painter and goldsmith, involved in the project for the dome of Florence cathedral, as well as responsible eventually for a second pair of bronze doors for the Baptistery, he inevitably had a busy workshop through which passed many young artists over a period of some forty years. To his other activities, Ghiberti in old age added writing; he is the first artist to produce, in effect, an autobiography. Whereas he fairly speedily described his first pair of bronze doors, he lingered lovingly in detail over the second pair, not only describing each scene but stating what his guiding principles had been in executing them: close imitation of nature, observation of proportions and use of perspective.

The result of these clearly formulated aims is seen in the story of Isaac *(Ill. 99),* one of the ten large gilded-bronze panels that make up these later Baptistery doors, placed in position in 1452, 'the Gates of Paradise', as Michelangelo called them. Although three episodes are combined in the scene, the effect is of total, overall harmony – a quite consciously organized effect which comes from the precise calculation of space into, as well as across, the composition. Ghiberti has made explicit his concern with much more than just telling the story. Indeed, his 'nature' is a very different concept from the natural effects achieved by Jan van Eyck, Hugo van der Goes, or even by Giotto. It is much more artful and artificial. One can hardly call the beautiful series of interlocked, palatial arcades, receding in ever-thinner relief into the bronze panel, merely the setting, because they – and the space they adumbrate – are virtually the subject.

They are part of that almost programmatic determination to explore space in art, to organize in real architecture too – as well as in sculpture and pictures – lucid buildings in which spatial relationships would be defined with new clarity. Ghiberti has here built his own temple of this new art, rising gracefully but firmly from the elaborately chequered pavement which itself forms a geometrical grid, demonstrating command of perspective. In fact it is perspective which is the secret subject of the composition. Everything within it obeys this intellectual law, where all the lines of pavement and architecture, and the disposition of the figures, are calculated to lead the eye to a single vanishing-point, beyond the last arcade, in the centre of the composition. Ghiberti lays over disparate phenomena the cool scheme of his own intellectual vision which presents us with an order that underlies the merely visible. Order rather than beauty is his aim, though inevitably a sense of beauty comes from such an ordering.

That Ghiberti had been trained as a painter is probably relevant, and his square reliefs with their thick, plain frames are like so many individual pictures inserted into the elaborately

99 GHIBERTI *The Story of Isaac* 1425–38. Relief from the Baptistery doors, Florence

sculpted outer framework of the doors. Painters rather than sculptors seem to take up the theme of organized, architecturally-defined space in which figures can move with calm assurance. It is a theme continually worked on and refined throughout the fifteenth century, and then subsequently stated in one final, definitive masterpiece – Raphael's *School of Athens (Ill. 129)* – beyond which there could be no progress. Yet that sense of permanent, underlying order, with its preference for intellectual rather than surface beauty, is something which, once demonstrated as achievable in painting, would remain. It is a demonstration which separates the fifteenth century from the Gothic world, and indeed from antiquity. It becomes a principle

133

in Western painting, patent not only in Raphael but in Poussin and Cézanne, crystallizing in the group round Mondrian early in this century. The philosopher Schoenmaekers, who greatly influenced him, made a statement that would certainly have been understood by fifteenth-century Florentine artists and philosophers: 'We want to penetrate nature in such a way that the inner construction of reality is revealed to us.'

For this reason most painters there tended to ignore the appeal of natural atmosphere and surfaces, absorbed in building an 'inner construction of reality' which could be as mathematically planned as it is in a picture by Uccello *(Ill. 100)*, with its clear-cut defiance of the muddle of real warfare, and substitution of a decorative geometry drawn from helmets, lances, horses, even a dead body. To some extent, this abstracting principle is at work too in the much more animated – but no more realistic – pictures of Botticelli. He is indifferent to defining space in depth, but is uniquely sensitive to linear intervals. Out of these he built the intense, private reality of the *Birth of Venus (Ill. 101)*, in which it might be said that Gothic methods express a Renaissance concept. Perfect harmony reigns throughout the composition, symbolized in the weightless pose and poise of the goddess, effortlessly sure of sustaining her balance in the rhythm of propulsion. This is a morally serious picture, in which pagan mythology is treated with the earnestness previously reserved for Christian subjects. Wave-

100 UCCELLO *Rout of S. Romano*

101 BOTTICELLI *Birth of Venus*

borne Venus returns as if from exile, perhaps symbolizing love as the pivotal force of the universe but serene, spiritual love, almost closer to Dante than to any poet of classical antiquity. Nor are preoccupations with mathematical and ideal truths the prerogative of Florentine painters. With a subtle sense of interval rivalling Botticelli's, and with a much more subtle response than Uccello's to the poetry of geometry, Piero della Francesca created what are now among the most famous of fifteenth-century pictures, like the *Resurrection (Ill. 102)* in his small native town of San Sepolcro. The sepulchre here is a scarcely substantial rectangle, but its long horizontal divides the picture at exactly one-third of its height. Christ's absolutely logical 'rightness' is calculated by placing him vertically in the middle of the composition; he is its emotional and perhaps literal module, being half the height of the total picture.

Even the revolutionary naturalism of Masaccio is in the interests of an inner reality. Nature is penetrated rather than observed in the *Trinity (Ill. 103),* which is a more monumental

135

concentration of the interests shown by Ghiberti's Isaac panel. Masaccio's now much-praised bulky figures look back to Giotto, and though they lend themselves to being written about in sculptural terms they are not necessarily finer – or even more historically important – as a result. Indeed, Ghiberti's more fluid figures were probably much more influential. What is most significant in Masaccio's *Trinity* is the exploration in paint of space, and the painted architectural construction which is probably the nearest thing to a surviving painting by Brunelleschi.

Almost an exact contemporary of Ghiberti's, Brunelleschi was equally multi-talented. It is true that he lost the 1401 competition to Ghiberti, but he was to prove one of the most

103 MASACCIO
The Trinity
1425

potent demonstrations that not every important thing in Florence was by Ghiberti. Brunelleschi's concern with the question of mathematical perspective in painting perhaps literally lies behind the coffered barrel-vault in Masaccio's fresco – the indented lines being still visible – and is certainly inspired, if not positively executed, by Brunelleschi. Probably Ghiberti's own developing grasp of centralized perspective and response to architecture were also indebted to his rival – not only to the projects but to the actual buildings Brunelleschi constructed.

137

104 BRUNELLESCHI
Cupola of the
Duomo, Florence,
1432.
Unfinished at
Brunelleschi's
death in 1446

If Brunelleschi's greatest achievement was the vast dome of the cathedral *(Ill. 104)* where it was his turn to triumph over Ghiberti, it is in the small Pazzi chapel that he most clearly expressed the new architectural ideals of lucidity and order. The exterior is almost too neatly planned, with its geometrically precise use of classical motifs – entablature, rosettes, Corinthian columns – but used to create, as it were, a 'modern' classicism, not merely imitation. The façade uses the same vocabulary as the architecture in Masaccio's fresco, and inside the chapel *(Ill. 105)* the balanced, patterned symmetry is perhaps even more strikingly similar. There is the same passion for clarity, definition and what might be called a rich austerity. In the chapel, bands of grey *pietra serena* mark out and define the white walls – pattern-making rather than serving any real functional purpose, but giving an abstractly beautiful effect. Nothing is blurred or indefinite. The spectator is not challenged by doubts about reality; rather, the reality of space extending around him seems made palpable and controlled. Under the shallow cupola of the Pazzi chapel, man does not shrink but contentedly expands, harmonized into being part of this lucid scheme, able to relate himself to these proportions. If this is a simulacrum of the universe, man's place in it is central.

105 BRUNELLESCHI Pazzi chapel, Florence (interior). Work suspended
1443

The new architecture was not restricted to churches. More than one architect now thought again in civic terms, substituting ideal order for the incoherence which had grown up in medieval cities. At Florence there emerged the town palace to house those prosperous merchant citizens who were struggling for leadership – and who still struggled even after the Medici family had achieved domination. Something fortress-like and forbidding is still felt in the façade of Palazzo Rucellai *(Ill. 108)* designed by Alberti, the first palace to revive classical orders in the superimposed pilasters which help to articulate each storey and give visual coherence to the building. Leon Battista Alberti is also the first Renaissance theoretician, reviving antique forms in a more consciously classicizing way than Brunelleschi, more obviously learned and more eager to instruct others. He studied the writings of the imperial Roman architect Vitruvius (by whom no buildings are known) and himself wrote treatises on architecture, painting and sculpture. He represents a new figure, the artist-theoretician, and stands also for a new type of literate patron, anxious for learned, often highly personal, works of art. It is typical of Alberti that he should always use the word 'temples' to describe churches, and convenient that the most idiosyncratic of all churches – that of S. Francesco at Rimini *(Ill. 106)* – was designed by him. Its

106 ALBERTI S. Francesco, Rimini *c.* 1450

triumphal arch-like façade was never finished, but its Roman reminiscences are obvious enough, even without the Pantheon-inspired dome which was intended to crown the building.

Alberti described in writing the complete ideal city, with temples and public buildings, and regular palaces and houses graded for the grades of citizen. But the basically severe concept of a cube of palace, with windows and doorways equally severely treated, remained monotonously true of Florence. It is impossible to imagine there comparable effects to the *trompe l'œil* on Jacques Cœur's house *(Ill. 95),* so closely contemporary with Palazzo Rucellai. It was at Venice that a much richer style of palace architecture was to be encouraged, where Alberti's pilasters have become sturdy pillars grouped along a façade that is further animated by jutting balconies and clusters of high windows which at each storey curve up its full extent *(Ill. 107).* Instead of the 'blind' effect of Florentine palaces, with their suggestions of narrow, rather bare rooms behind the façade, there is an open spaciousness about these Venetian façades where the windows offer maximum illumination to the spacious interiors. The owners of such palaces were equally rich merchants, but more princely and frankly luxury-loving in their use of art.

107 LOMBARDO and CODUCCI
Palazzo Vendramin, Venice.
Begun *c.* 1481

108 ALBERTI
Palazzo Rucellai,
Florence 1445–57

Indeed, it was anywhere rather than at Florence that there developed the finest domestic interiors, where men could feel pleasurably at ease as well as uplifted. How much this was completely art's province is shown by the beautifully decorated rooms in the palace built at Urbino in the mid-fifteenth century for Federico da Montefeltro: a palace today stripped of much of its furnishings but giving no sense of emptiness or desolation. There a doorway *(Ill. 109)* becomes a work of art, delicately and crisply carved, while the door itself may be no less carefully designed to hold an inlaid pattern in the wood. Beauty rather than a grandiose effect is what matters. The palace itself is a marvel of harmony, a house rather than a fortress despite its

109 Doorway of the Sala dell'Iole, Palazzo Ducale, Urbino *c.* 1468

110 *Dame à la licorne* (tapestry). Early sixteenth century

huge scale, and a monument to a literate, artistic, humane ruler. In Northern Europe tapestries *(Ill. 110)* best exemplified art serving in a domestic setting, able to reflect countrified or courtly scenes in highly sophisticated decorative terms. In Italy, princes might have complete schemes of decoration, carved or painted, in the palaces they inhabited. At Mantua in 1474, Mantegna created for his patrons, the Gonzaga family, a unique painted room which is, as it were, a mirror of themselves *(Ill. 111)*. An almost Eyckian grasp on reality presents these people, and suggests their environment, without any flattery or idealization. Intimate rather than public events are commemorated, suitably personal for a private room. What had been a small-scale book of illuminations by the Limbourg brothers *(Ill. 77)* has here swelled into a large-scale fresco cycle.

The concern with man's setting, with relating him to the universe, argues fresh interest in man himself. The massive statuesque people of Giotto may be felt to be not sufficiently articulated; their bodies remain hewn, archaic blocks and their faces impassive in grief or joy. Man's physical appearance was equally to be re-scrutinized. Modelled by light and shade which gives relief, articulated, expressive, and naked, man and woman are driven from Paradise in Masaccio's Carmine fresco *(Ill. 112)* – the first of the new generation, banished from the Gothic Garden of Eden, to tread solidly on solid earth. But it was a sculptor, Donatello, who had made it possible for Masaccio to express this stark humanity in painting.

Donatello, older than Masaccio, younger than Brunelleschi and Ghiberti, outlived them all; he did not die until 1466, and he was working up to the end of his life. His art enshrines the full triumph of human beings – not only as bodies physically simulated in life-size free-standing figures of stone and bronze, but as containers of emotion, experiencing and conveying the subtlest states of mind. This intensely expressive character is what has stamped all Donatello's work, from the largest statue to the smallest relief. It is true that he was a revolutionary master of three-dimensional spatial effects (able to teach lessons to his teacher, Ghiberti), a revolutionary master of realistic monumental sculpture, able when necessary to convey classical gravity *(Ill. 113)*; but he was not a sculptor equivalent to Brunelleschi as architect or Masaccio as painter, despite their mutual friendship. By the end of his life, he had tacitly rejected their concerns. His pursuit of emotional expression had led to the bronze relief of the *Resurrection (Ill. 114)* which is barely bothered with space, and presents us with a wearily clambering, battered Christ – very different from Piero della Francesca's *(Ill. 102)* – grasping his banner like a battle-axe, emerging joylessly from the tomb as if from a nearly mortal struggle with death. Donatello's triumphant concentration on humanity is tinged with a considerable irony: when explored, the human condition is seen to be no perfect harmony of man and his

III MANTEGNA Fresco of the Gonzaga family (detail) 1474

environment; we are not monumental, archaic presences but vulnerable flesh.

Donatello aims at psychological truth. Ideas of victory, naturally associated with the saints and with the Resurrection, are implicit too in the story of David's conquest of Goliath. The keen, competent young shepherd, victorious and ready to take on another giant, is seen in Verrocchio's *David (Ill. 116)*, a famous and popular statue by a great Florentine sculptor of the next generation after Donatello. Not a tremor disturbs his proud features, softened – if at all – by the faintest complacency.

145

112 MASACCIO
*Expulsion from
Paradise*
1425/6–8

But Donatello's statue *(Ill. 115),* historically remarkable as the
first nude cast in bronze since antiquity, is aesthetically,
emotionally, remarkable too. It pays tribute, no doubt, to
Donatello's study of antique sculpture, but its ethos is far
removed from any classical god's. If we did not know the

113 DONATELLO
Equestrian statue of
Gattamelata 1447–53

114 DONATELLO *The
Resurrection c.* 1462–6.
Relief from the pulpit
of S. Lorenzo, Florence

story, nor had Goliath's head to form the statue's base, this *David* might almost seem to embody defeat. That is not subtle enough to do justice to Donatello's imaginative concept, whereby suggestions of lassitude in the midst of victory and sadness after exertion have slightly slackened the limbs. The long-bladed sword seems too heavy for the boy to hold any longer. Complete nudity, only enhanced by the shepherd's hat, conveys an idea of innocence. There is something shocking, even perhaps to the divinely-inspired perpetrator, in killing a man; David seems bemused by his feat, brushed by disturbing sensations as his leg is brushed by the feathered wing of his victim's helmet.

Perhaps it is not surprising that we know nothing of contemporary reactions to this, and to some other now familiar statues by Donatello. His very late works, the S. Lorenzo bronze pulpits (of which the *Resurrection* is part), were not set up in Florence until 1515 – at which time they made a con-

117 ANTONIO
POLLAIUOLO *Hercules
and Antaeus*

siderable impact, at least on painters. Indeed, Donatello's wide
influence was, even in his lifetime, perhaps most marked on
painters – from Masaccio to Mantegna. In any case it could not
be a single effect, for his own style shifted and evolved, and the
complexity of his achievements left hardly any category of art
untouched. Physical study of the body, so patent in his *David*,
was pursued in both painting and sculpture by the brothers
Antonio and Piero Pollaiuolo. Antonio produced what seem
to be the first 'modern' bronze statuettes, where the nude is
often thrown into violent action *(Ill. 117)*, studied here for its
own sake rather than for its classical subject-matter. Even in the
clothed figures of Luca Signorelli, in turn influenced by the
Pollaiuolo brothers, there is a harsh sense of strongly modelled
anatomy and a defiance of conventional beauty. Perhaps, like
Michelangelo, Donatello would have responded to the
violently expressive nudes who stir into life in his Last Judgment
frescoes at Orvieto *(Ill. 119)*. Although there are saved as well

149

15 DONATELLO *David* 1440–3
16 VERROCCHIO *David*. Before 1476

as damned in this apocalyptic vision, Signorelli's imagination fastens with grim vividness on mankind's awe. Heaven rains fire; angels sound their trumpets; and trembling naked men and women await their fate.

From Donatello came also technical innovations. He had set up the bronze equestrian memorial to Gattamelata and also evolved a new style of tomb, with equal emphasis on immortality, constructing round the image of the deceased ever-increasingly elaborate niches with heaven hovering close at hand in a group of Virgin and Child. Death is softened into a dreaming sleep, and indeed is defied by the immortality which art gives.

Out of the originally quite modest wall-monument emerged finally the richest of all fifteenth-century funerary chapels, that at Florence for the Cardinal of Portugal *(Ill. 118)*, created by the brothers Bernardo and Antonio Rossellino. In this there is a positively Baroque variety of gilding, coloured marble, *trompe l'œil* painting – so much busy decoration amid which the quite un-Baroque, calmly sleeping figure of the Cardinal lies at rest.

Donatello's withdrawal from spatial obsessions into an increasingly emotional sphere, peopled by beings conventionally ugly in their expressiveness but passionately human, is itself a significant result of newly scrutinizing nature and man. Escaped from Gothic uncertainty, man had reacted by building temples perhaps too rigorously lucid and ordered. Space may prove not susceptible of being organized into a neat three-dimensional cube. The penetration of nature, which might seem to promise a fundamental coherence, could reveal disconcerting facts. Even the desire for universal knowledge might lead to a knowingness which missed the essential mystery of things. In the sixteenth century, the English poet Spenser's friend, Gabriel Harvey, was to scold those who behave 'As if they had a key for all the locks in Heaven.' Some doors must remain closed even to the most potent conjunction of *ars* and *scientia* and it is this perhaps which ultimately Leonardo da Vinci understood. 'Nature is full of infinite causes that do not come within experience,' he wrote; and again and again over sheets of drawings: 'Tell me, if ever anything was finished.' Certainly the *Adoration of the Kings (Ill. 97)* was not, remaining a dream of grandeur, a confusedly rich palimpsest from which others could pluck a vocabulary, but which was never brought to full, final coherence.

In some ways, the empirical attitude of Jan van Eyck might prove a truer perspective in which to look at the universe. The warmly atmospheric, natural world of Giovanni Bellini, himself influenced when young by Donatello and sharing much of his poignant power, is quite unintellectual. He responds with all his senses to light and colour, almost palpably fused into an envelope to wrap round the Madonna quietly praying over her sleeping Child *(Ill. 121)*. Light is graduated in a subtle way that comes from no scientific study but plain observation. Even about the composition's coherence there is a natural air, so that we scarcely realize it *is* composed – accepting this woman and child seated in the stony fields with the herdsmen and their oxen, the castle on its hill, all held in a perfect, glowing prism of translucence.

118 ROSSELLINO BROTHERS Tomb of the Cardinal of Portugal *c.* 1461–6. S. Miniato al Monte, Florence

119 SIGNORELLI *Last Judgment frescoes* (detail) 1499–1503

As for the disturbing aspects of nature, sensed in Leonardo and Signorelli, and no less in Dürer, they are patent in the contemporary pictures of Hieronymus Bosch, as sensitive as Bellini to atmospheric effects but in a weird universe *(Ill. 120)*. The world is like a great apple cut open, and found to be full of maggots. Man is no monumental hero but a shrimp, created in a strange universe, alien to the humanity of della Quercia. The world is full of wonderfully delicate organisms that seem set in motion not by the great Architect but by some crazy clockmaker. It is a frightening cosmos that Bosch presents, but we may feel it is closer to the truth of things than the spacious halls of Ghiberti's palace *(Ill. 99)*. Combined with complete confidence in conveying the illusion of physical appearances, painting could now begin to serve hallucinatory purposes – suggesting visions and nightmares, with visionary or nightmare intensity.

152

120 BOSCH *Garden of Earthly Delights* (detail) c. 1500

121 BELLINI *Madonna of the Meadow*

Everywhere art was in command of its technical resources. It had mirrored the natural world and sketched a blueprint of an ideal world. It had discovered unified perspective. Although it had not discovered antiquity in a single dig, it had raised antiquity out of myth into historical fact and produced antique-inspired works – like Donatello's *Gattamelata* – which challenged antiquity.

Yet young artists all over Europe in the late fifteenth century, like young artists at most other periods, felt there was something new to be done. It was not, however, to be done so much out of the reaction to the immediate achievements of their elders as in consolidating and improving those. The ore had been extracted by diligent craftsmen; the next process must be refinement.

CHAPTER FIVE

Perfect Manners

The first twenty or so years of the sixteenth century saw art refined in a blaze of creativity which burnt throughout Europe, turning craftsmen into artists of princely stature who have never lost their prestige. Leonardo da Vinci, Michelangelo, Raphael, Dürer, Titian – these are only among the first names in an extraordinary concourse of talents working contemporaneously, and posthumously at work for centuries in the influence they exercised. As long as some sort of naturalistic canon governed painting and sculpture, the achievements of a Titian or a Michelangelo would retain their relevance – to the point of making later generations of artists almost despair. Impressionism and its aftermath could claim an ancestor in Titian's late work; and Renoir's enthusiasm for him is significant: 'Titian! He has everything in his favour.' Rodin is the last heir of Michelangelo – very different though the two sculptors' working methods were.

These are only the extreme limits of styles and influences that were formed in the sixteenth century but which constantly went on revitalizing and inspiring art in a way previously unparalleled. What is unparalleled is not the continuation of a style as such but its continual evolution under manipulation from fresh geniuses. If a style may be likened to a stream, then these are streams of molten metal – here made to follow a finely drawn channel in which it runs as a mere glittering thread, there pouring hotly into a scooped-out hole, now cooled into twisted artificial shapes and now again left in apparently rough state. Goldsmiths, alchemists, magicians, the great sixteenth-century artistic creators each seemed to strike the earth at a different point and cause to flow a spring which would prove the source for the great artists who followed them.

We can trace the phenomenon in all the three major arts (in the architectural style that begins with Palladio at least as much as in Michelangelo's sculpture) but in none is it more patent than in painting – the new predominance of which is itself

122 LEONARDO
Mona Lisa c. 1503

something created by the sixteenth century. What Raphael painted would be admired and influential in the eyes of Rubens, Rembrandt, Poussin and Bernini in the seventeenth century, still exercise great influence in the eighteenth century, be worshipped in the nineteenth century by Ingres – and praised too by Renoir. Nor is it just a matter of Raphael's own huge prestige. What emerged in the early sixteenth century were manners of painting flexible enough to serve Western art for several centuries. Even the 'revolutionary' attitudes of Caravaggio and Courbet are in fact contained within these well-established styles, and we may doubt if their revolutions would have seemed so shockingly novel to the contemporaries of Raphael and Titian. The periods art-historically labelled 'Baroque' and 'Rococo', and that always continuing current of 'realism' which accompanied them, are all in essence contained in early sixteenth-century achievements. The airborne visions of Tiepolo *(Ill. 221)*, the last great exponent of high Rococo manner, find their ultimate origin in Michelangelo's Sistine ceiling frescoes *(Ill. 127)*, completed in 1512.

156

123 RAPHAEL *Portrait of Baldassare Castiglione*

All the new refinement, its sophistication and also its effortless command of realism, is summed up in Raphael's portrait of
Baldassare Castiglione *(Ill. 123)*. The sitter alone is significant
enough, introducing us to a new concept of society, populated
not by monks or burgher-merchants but by gentlemen. He was
the author of a famous book *Il Cortegiano* (published in 1528,
although written several years earlier) which is concerned not
just with the courtier but with good behaviour and social
standards. In an age in which painters could be treated like
gentlemen, Castiglione suitably recommended that gentlemen
should acquire some knowledge of painting as part of their
education. And an important aspect of the new century was
the new respect which was paid to artists. Even if it is only
a legend that the Emperor Charles V stooped to pick up
Titian's brush, the existence of the story is significant. Other
factual testimonies confirm what that anecdote implies. When
Dürer reached Venice, he actually wrote: 'Here I am a gentleman [ein Herr].' Even as imperious a patron as Julius II recognized in Michelangelo a genius who must be honoured.
Castiglione was a close friend of Raphael's, and something of
the portrait's spell comes from a *rapport* sensed as existing
between painter and sitter.

Probably no comparably subtle and complex portrait of a
man had ever before been painted. It owes a good deal to its
spiritual mother, Leonardo's *Mona Lisa (Ill. 122)*, but what is
there veiled mystery has become confident clarity in Raphael's
handling. The result is certainly natural-seeming, but it goes
beyond nature. That particular step shows the direction of the
new sixteenth-century art, more varied, graceful and finished
than nature itself. No longer is it a sufficient achievement to capture the likeness of a person; Raphael, indifferent to Castiglione's
environment (reduced to a portion of wall and slightest
indications of a chair), seeks to capture Castiglione's personality.
The sitter relaxes in a pose devised by the painter, effortlessly
absorbed into becoming a work of art – a chromatic harmony
of silver-grey and black and white, a compositional one of
sinuous, interlocking curves – at once ideal and naturalistic.

At first glance the portrait is wonderfully convincing simply
as an eloquent likeness; it has all, and more, of the vitality so
much prized by fifteenth-century art. Yet, when examined
again, it is noticeably timeless, formal for all its vitality, a very
conscious arrangement – as in the dark silhouette of circular hat
against the luminous background – which bespeaks conscious

intention. The choice restriction of Castiglione's costume (embodying his own precepts against bright clothes) is merely the first of nonchalant-seeming but carefully devised effects. In place of fifteenth-century detail, so lovingly scrutinized and recorded, we have these plump, almost generalized forms, where form matters more than surface texture.

Within this beautifully constructed image there lie two distinct stylistic potentialities. Blended here, they could be drawn out separately, refined on and transmuted in their turn, so that in one way the *Castiglione* is an ancestor of the intimately naturalistic art of Rembrandt, while in another it lifts the sitter out of temporal associations, making a courtier-hero out of this man so perfectly composed – in both the temperamental and the artistic sense of the word. Verisimilitude as such is then less important than the ideal series of shapes, all curvilinear, yielding gracefully to the eye, which have been constructed by Raphael to convey a sense of artistic confidence and satisfaction that actually seems in disaccord with the sitter's somewhat anxious gaze. Even the duality of the portrait is part of art's new perfection. Soon there would be painted eye-deceiving effects, ambiguous visual tricks comparable to those mentioned in Shakespeare's *Richard II*: 'Like perspectives, which rightly gaz'd upon / Show nothing but confusion, – ey'd awry / Distinguish form . . .'.

These are more than clever virtuoso devices. They reveal art managing to mirror the ambiguities of human existence, sometimes presenting Christian and historical subjects with new psychological awareness, as in Pontormo's *Visitation (Ill. 159)*, or introducing a perspective reminder of death into the straightforward-seeming portrait of two friends – as Holbein does in his so-called *Ambassadors (Ill. 162)*.

What Raphael had blended in the Castiglione portrait would eventually harden into two opposing forces – fully hostile to each other by the nineteenth century, but both strangely irrelevant for modern art. The actual portrait may well have been known to Titian (who could have seen it at Mantua). In the seventeenth century it was certainly seen by both Rubens and Rembrandt – one executing a full-scale copy of it, the other hastily noting down its composition and utilizing it for self-portraits; and late in the nineteenth century it was to be copied by Matisse. What is crystallized by Raphael in this portrait is expressed on a variety of scale in the variety of his other work. Yet Castiglione remains the perfect figure for the period: the sophisticated connoisseur who may be imagined appreciating the new, heroic achievements of sculpture *(Ill. 125)*, or the richness of the new medium of engraving *(Ill. 149)*, the ideal inhabitant of some elegant villa with its superbly planned garden, equally a product of art's refinement and response to social needs. Finally, Castiglione's nationality is symbolically correct, because Italian art had taken the leading place in Europe, along with Italian manners. What is usually called the High Renaissance style was almost an entirely Italian creation; it remained Italianate even when disseminated through Europe, and was indeed often carried there by expatriate Italians. In itself this points to the prestige of Italian art; and among the first of such expatriates was one of the very greatest, Leonardo da Vinci, whose final years were spent in France.

124 LEONARDO *A Deluge*

Although Leonardo's life was peripatetic and some of his finest works left unfinished (or, like the *Last Supper*, ruined in his lifetime), he is in an extraordinary way the animating principle behind the new, perfect styles. In him is first apparent an effortless conquest of nature. He is also the first of the perfectly mannered artists, a legend in his lifetime for his graceful elegance, beautiful clothes, his mysteriously universal knowledge – all reflected in the suave people of his drawings and paintings, themselves so often hauntingly graceful, supernaturally beautiful in youth or supernaturally wise in old age.

In the *Adoration of the Kings (Ill. 97)* he already set a press of such people about the Virgin and Child, and made a fitting environment for them by turning the Bethlehem stable into a palatial ruin with a great double staircase, where noble horses pace with equal suavity. He took the factual fifteenth-century portrait and created the memorable image of *Mona Lisa (Ill. 122)*, where the mystery is not only in the woman but in that melting background, an unvisited country of sunken, ribbon-like rivers winding among inaccessible crystalline peaks – an eternity no less disturbing than is the sitter's expression. Leonardo's imaginings would cast their spell over many great sixteenth-century artists including Raphael, being felt by Giorgione and Correggio – both magician-like painters whose art would aim in turn at casting a spell over the spectator. And even where he did not positively execute but only brooded on possibilities, Leonardo seemed to exercise a fertilizing influence. He dreamed of a centrally planned domed church, occurring in various designs among his manuscripts, prophetic of Baroque achievements and providing more than a hint probably for Bramante's plan of the new St Peter's.

It scarcely matters that Leonardo seldom worked his concepts into actual execution. Probably he began to lose interest once the idea was formulated. Increasingly he seems to have thought of himself not as a painter. His interests were as much in science, anatomy, geology, and in 'machines' – from pageant mechanisms to projects for flying. But he had introduced a new concept of grace into art, in his uncanny, supra-real figures and in that twilit, smoky technique which hints at impermanence, flux, dissolution. Leonardo's contribution seems symbolized by one of those swirling deluges he liked to draw *(Ill. 124)*, graceful, energetic, and yet ultimately alien: a world from which man is swept away. Nature as we know it has certainly been vanquished, but this elemental vision is not altogether optimistic.

Art's ability to create a supernatural world – realistic-seeming but far beyond our ordinary experience – may frighten as well as delight us. What it will certainly do is affect us in an overwhelming way. Just as the *Mona Lisa* surpassed the plain humanity of fifteenth-century portraiture, so the closely contemporary *David* of Michelangelo *(Ill. 125)* has made a giant hero out of Donatello's shepherd boy *(Ill. 115)*. Not blood but some divine ichor flows in the veins of this vast figure, totally nude and aggressive in nudity, a positive Goliath beside Donatello's *David* – an impossibly heroic, magnificent statue which forbids any identification with mankind, despite all the suggestions of muscle and sinew carved in marble. Nor does this David require any miraculous help from God; it is he who is a god. After Leonardo, Michelangelo is the next overpoweringly revolutionary creator of a new style, himself trained within the fifteenth century but much younger than Leonardo and outliving him by almost half a century. Leonardo was on the committee at Florence in 1504 to decide the placing

127 MICHELANGELO *Creation of Man* Sistine Chapel, Rome 1508–12

of Michelangelo's *David*: the two men seem to have always felt an uneasy rivalry, and neither would have thought of himself as primarily a painter. It was left to Raphael to bring the two men together – artistically speaking – and become the first painter to fuse and apply their divergent manners.

Michelangelo replaces Leonardo's universal speculations with a single obsession, already declared in his *David*: the human body. It is symbolically apt that he should have frescoed the Sistine chapel ceiling with scenes from Genesis, and that the most memorable of those frescoes is the *Creation of Man (Ill. 127)*. In himself both Jehovah and Adam, Michelangelo crystallizes here the whole myth of artistic creation. Energy is embodied in the sweeping ovoid group from which Jehovah, borne along on the impetuous bodies of his own angelic creation, extends one finger to vitalize his last creation, man: a perfect, about to become living, statue. The principle of energy – that spark already jumping in the tiny gap between the finger-tips of Creator and created – has communicated itself to the

163

most extraordinary aspect of the ceiling: the twenty seated youths, more living painted sculpture, who serve to frame each scene from Genesis, and who are like a triumphal chorus to illustrate God's words: 'Be fruitful, and multiply, and replenish the earth. . . .'

Although we know how much Michelangelo hated the huge and terrible task of frescoing the Sistine ceiling, it remains his most perfectly accomplished work. It contains, as Vasari said with permissible exaggeration, every perfection, so that painters might well not bother to seek other inventions, attitudes, methods of expression, striking subjects; a whole vocabulary was there. Yet the medium remained uncongenial to Michelangelo. His concept of creativity was connected with real plasticity, weight and volume – not merely the feigned suggestion of these in paint. Thus, though never completed, the Medici chapel at Florence is closer to his ideals. It is rich for art's sake – with pilasters, mouldings, niches, and even door-ways that have no structural or utilitarian purpose. One is hardly conscious of the walls, since they are sculpted and delicately wrought into a series of projections and recessions, with little space left unadorned; they have become skeleton frames of shallow ledges and brackets, so much background to the dominant sculpture *(Ill. 128)* which would have filled more of them had it been executed as intended.

This is capricious, deliberately invented architecture, not based on study of ancient examples, nor mirroring a coherent cosmos with man centrally placed in it. The uneasy figures on the tombs, and the heroic, armoured effigies of the Medici princes who are commemorated – but not realistically por-trayed – increase the effect of having penetrated into a strange temple, marvellous, dignified, but scarcely reassuring. How calmly by comparison the Cardinal of Portugal could sleep in his tomb *(Ill. 118)*, but Michelangelo's own vision would deepen into a more tragic view of existence than had ever apparently been guessed at by the Rossellino brothers. Michel-angelo evolved from being the creator of the *David*, with its superb physique and physical pride, into the sculptor of the Rondanini *Pietà (Ill. 126)*, where Christ is a flayed and broken body, kept upright only by the rigid Virgin, herself angular and broken by grief. In 1564, in the last weeks of his life, Michel-angelo hacked away at this group until nothing was left but the marble bones we see. Yet the result could hardly be more expressive; its daring style is not by any means just an accident (for Michelangelo had long before cracked the mould of his early, polished style).

Perhaps it was the pursuit of energy which led Michelangelo to that final group – still a valid work of art, undestroyed for all the blows inflicted on it. What Leonardo had sought in natural phenomena, Michelangelo found in man. For the first arch-synthesizer of their styles, Raphael, Leonardo probably represented grace and Michelangelo force. Fused in the *School of Athens (Ill. 129)*, the two qualities make a perfect marriage.

128 MICHELANGELO Medici Chapel, S. Lorenzo, Florence (interior) 1524–34

129 RAPHAEL *School of Athens* 1509–11

This is no strange or disturbing scene, but a triumph of accomplished manner. Graceful, ideally noble forms – active too, as well as contemplative – move with assurance through an ideal, vaulted architectural setting on giant scale, spacious, open to the sky but somehow itself elemental, unchanging. All the variety and invention of pose shown by Michelangelo's nude Sistine figures is rivalled by Raphael's clothed ones. The graceful people Leonardo made to press about the Virgin in the *Adoration of the Kings* have swollen to a leisurely concourse, planned to cohere and flow from group to group, yet all depending from that central pair of Plato and Aristotle, framed by the curve of the furthest arch, themselves as it were married here to express full philosophical harmony. And, very different in this from Leonardo or Michelangelo, Raphael puts vivid portrait heads on to his ideal people.

Raphael was far the youngest of the creators of the High Renaissance, but he outlived Leonardo by only a year. The tragedy of his early death interrupted a career of almost too ideal success, an increasing accumulation of problems and tasks tackled with ease and untroubled assurance, an increasing train of pupils and assistants engaged under the master's direction, not only on paintings but complete decorative schemes, including sculpture, and some architectural projects. Both Leonardo and Michelangelo experienced difficulties and failures: tragedy for them lay in their flawed careers. Leonardo, obsessed with ideas of eternal incompleteness, perhaps hardly minded; but Michelangelo was plunged into pessimism by the protracted, hopeless history of the tomb he was commissioned to build for Pope Julius II, which he wished to build and on which he seemed continually frustrated. The Medici chapel too is quite unfinished, though he lived for thirty years after his last activity on it. Against such uncompleted works, Raphael may appear to offer the 'closed' perfection of the *School of Athens*, but that fresco marks merely one peak of his achievement – the culmination in him of fifteenth-century concern with figures in an ordered architectural framework.

A quite new language is spoken by the *Galatea (Ill. 130)*, so utterly simple in its setting but so rich in its composition, consisting of bodies alone, perfectly modelled, graceful, but in quite distinct action. Botticelli's *Birth of Venus (Ill. 101)* looks positively austere and pinched beside the carefree accomplishment of Raphael's picture, with its variety, invention and sense of ease. And Raphael was to push beyond this to a more elaborate style, more charged with emotion, more powerful and complex. His last painting, the *Transfiguration (Ill. 131)*, is a cosmic drama, where celestial vision and earthly reality are united by the spectator, witness of the ecstatic, uplifted Christ and of the troubled, epileptic boy. This world is more mighty, artificial and awe-inspiring than ours; the apostles are giant, gesticulating figures, each wrought to convey a different emotional state; the foreground kneeling woman alone is a triumph of eloquent art. With her elaborately braided hair, her gracefully disposed yet monumental draperies, her effective commanding pose, she embodies all that would be meant by 'the grand manner'. The whole picture is a carefully arranged stage for Baroque drama, and she is a heroine consciously moulded to perform in public. Nothing about her appearance or performance is to be judged natural – from the musculature of her impossibly powerful body to the bronze-like draperies that have been twisted round her, emphasizing the contorted pose.

The rich yet open language of the *Galatea* has become rhetoric, with its own laws and rules, a daring manner for other artists to imitate because its effects will seem stilted, tepid, even tasteless, unless they are achieved through energy. Even then, perhaps, they will always require the spectator to be educated in the laws of such artistic rhetoric. The danger in extreme manners is that those who do not respond to them will loathe them. And those educated to one style of rhetoric or realism will be disconcerted by others. The sixteenth century thus saw – along with highly personal styles – the phenomenon of certain styles being objected to by patrons and connoisseurs. In Venice one member of the Scuola di S. Rocco was to stipulate that he would contribute to its decoration only on condition Tintoretto was not employed. Philip II of Spain disliked El Greco's style. To Michelangelo the fault of Titian's work was its lack of art and design; their aid was needed to build out of his natural gifts – which Michelangelo thought great – a completely artful style. And though we may feel Michelangelo has missed the point of Titian's achievement, he aptly condemns in advance much Dutch seventeenth-century picture-making.

Raphael had woven something marvellous and personal out of hints which originated in Leonardo and Michelangelo. Only a genius could do that, and to many subsequent artists he would seem the most perfect of painters for this very power of synthesis. In the other arts the position was much more

130 RAPHAEL *Galatea c.* 1511

131 RAPHAEL *Transfiguration*

complicated, partly through the lack of a comparable figure.
Indeed, even here Raphael remained perhaps the most influential figure. Michelangelo's sculpture suggested an epic yet
private world in which lesser men might well hesitate to
intrude; but its achievement centred on the idea of the perfect
human body, inevitably nude and usually male. Concepts of
Mars had mingled with Apolline ones in his statues: a fierce
pride, which was his own, investing the figures sometimes with
a sense almost of outrage that they should be gazed on at all; and
even at their most frankly sensuous they retain a strange

132 SANSOVINO *Apollo c.* 1537–40   133 FLÖTNER *Apollo* 1532

virginity. Something more graceful and Praxitelean, softer and more yielding in manner, was to be evolved. Sansovino's *Apollo (Ill. 132)* at Venice is shown elegantly shrugging one shoulder, a slender, disdainful god. On his fountain at Nuremburg, Flötner's *Apollo (Ill. 133)* is almost exaggeratedly slender, effortlessly commanding a vast bow with arms scarcely thicker than the wood he bends. The most famous, though by no means the finest, of these unheroic heroes who have come from the dancing class rather than antiquity, is Cellini's *Perseus (Ill. 134)*. If Michelangelo instinctively thought on a colossal scale, the sculptors of these statues seem more interested in suggesting the proportions of the statuette; they concentrate on detail – as the

172

134 CELLINI *Perseus*. Commissioned 1545, set up in 1554
135 GIANBOLOGNA *Apollo*

intricate bases of Flötner's and Cellini's statues confirm – and
graceful refinement. It would be quite wrong to say that they
lack energy or inventiveness, but these qualities are channelled
into the direction of astonishing us by their sheer manner.

All is summed up by the small bronze *Apollo (Ill. 135),* of
exquisite ingenuity, by probably the greatest sculptor between
Michelangelo and Bernini, Jean Boulogne. He came from
Flanders, but settled in Florence. Gianbologna, as his name was
Italianized, was certainly able to work equally brilliantly on a
monumental scale with a sense of drama and movement, shifting
sculpture from Praxitelean terms into ones closer to the Pergamum altar. The *Apollo* is taut for all its apparent negligence,
with a complicated, sinuous silhouette, an echo of Raphael's
Galatea, developed in other work by Gianbologna into fully
three-dimensional terms, so that one feels stirred to walk round

one of his groups, discovering further aspects of its effectiveness. Throughout, there is a dynamism which Gianbologna has inherited artistically from Michelangelo – so that his figures are like graceful swimmers, enjoying the element around them and making the atmosphere vibrate – and which will return to sculpture in the ecstasy of Bernini's *St Theresa (Ill. 195)*.

Such art, whether Bernini's full Baroque or the sixteenth-century grand manner, needs an arena in which to perform – the larger the more effective in most cases. With that goes a need for the sort of sophisticated audience which was once likely to be found at a court. France under a king such as François I offered these possibilities in the first half of the sixteenth century, attracting first the aged Leonardo – an exhausted magician – and then a series of talented painters and sculptors, including Cellini. What was achieved at Fontainebleau *(Ill. 136)* is the quintessence of art freed from allegiance to religious or dynastic faith, performing with absolute assurance before an audience who completely believe in the prestige of art. Once again, it is a fusion of all the arts that is attempted, including pictures amid the stucco reliefs, giving an architectural importance to the tall, caryatid-like statues that animate the long walls – so much transference into fully plastic terms of what Michelangelo had frescoed on the Sistine ceiling, but capriciously varied for variety's sake, more playful than serious. Space too is played with, broken into juts and runs and scrolls of decorative motifs; and the figures grow elegantly tall, boneless, anatomically adaptable, to suit the decorative rhythm. The Galerie François I, designed by the Florentine Rosso – a painter of considerable emotional power in religious pictures – is a triumph of manner applied in a way unparalleled before in richness and artifice. What began as scarcely more than a corridor has become a grotto-like tunnel, overgrown with white unnatural stalactites, all paying tribute to the bizarre inventive powers of art to transform the ordinary into the unexpectedly extraordinary. Native French sculptors preferred a less extreme manner, perhaps even more accomplished but less ingeniously graceful. Even so, a problem is stated and solved by the narrow stone panels of the Fontaine des Innocents by Jean Goujon *(Ill. 137)*. Without apparent effort, the nymphs are disposed to fill the restricted area, their draperies as fluid as the water which pours from their water-pots, and the whole flat hard surface rippling all the way down from the crisp hair to the weightless, dancing feet.

136 ROSSO and PRIMATICCIO Galerie François I, Fontainebleau *c.*
1533–4

This almost lyrical effect animates the much wider-ranging
work of Germain Pilon, who was not just a decorator but a
sculptor of penetrating three-dimensional power. The head of
the bronze statue of Cardinal Birague *(Ill. 138)* shows a mastery
of realistic portraiture, rivalling anything fifteenth-century
Flemish in candid intensity, while the sweeping folds of the
Cardinal's robes flow and curl behind him in a musical arrangement that obeys the rules of art, not nature. Photographs which
show this wonderful monument without its literal coda cannot

175

137 GOUJON
*Fontaine des
Innocents* (detail)
1547–9

138 PILON ▶
*Cardinal
Birague.* After
1583

do justice to the Raphaelesque mingling there of natural and ideal, of pungent realism with suave artifice; Pilon's interest is in what art can make out of a cardinal's robes. How brilliantly he has applied his manner can be seen in strict art-historical terms by comparing *Cardinal Birague* with the usually cited precedent of the tomb of the Amboise cardinals in Rouen cathedral, where their robes lie behind them in flat, lifeless slabs. Not for a long time after Pilon would French sculpture achieve anything at once so truthful-seeming and so stylish as his work.

There is the same triumphant emergence in the sixteenth century of perfect manners in architecture as in sculpture and painting, and Italy remains the scene of such emergence. A new vocabulary was created out of those elements which had existed since Roman classical times and which are united in the Pantheon: the dome, the pediment and the pillar. Modern Papal Rome, even in the years before Raphael and Michelangelo settled there, already seemed to offer the ideal climate to foster the style which would become the Baroque. In the complex of St Peter's *(Ill. 140)* the general effect is homogeneous, despite the time gap between Michelangelo's dome and Bernini's colonnades – and even despite Maderno's long nave and façade which have spoilt the visual impact of the dome. This is architecture not only on a new giant scale, but with a dramatic richness which makes earlier achievements seem ineloquent. Brunelleschi's dome for Florence cathedral *(Ill. 104)* rises as quickly as possible from the structure below; Michelangelo's is built up on an elaborate drum, with projecting doubled columns, itself crowned with a wreath-hung ring which is also the base from which the dome finally rises.

A mass of material is boldly sculpted and thrust upwards, rising in triumph but not without effort, to provide the typical silhouette that has replaced Romanesque tower or Gothic spire in a form that swells as well as soars. The positively Corinthian richness and variety of imposing design are equally effectively seen in contrast to the Doric style and austerity of Bramante's Tempietto of S. Pietro in Montorio *(Ill. 139)*, executed in 1502.

139 BRAMANTE Tempietto S. Pietro in Montorio, Rome 1502

140 St Peter's and Piazza S. Pietro, Rome 1655–67

Yet Bramante's building, small in scale though it is, has a harmonious symmetry and a concentrated effect which makes it
something of a Janus temple. It is the culmination of fifteenth-
century aspirations for order and coherence, yet in its monumentality and its curving rhythm (extending to the curving
platform of steps on which it stands) looking forward to the
later achievements of the sixteenth and seventeenth centuries.
It is the actual expression of projects and designs for the ideal
circular church which had haunted Brunelleschi and interested
Leonardo, and which would not be without their relevance for
Bernini.

Bramante's Tempietto is calm rather than dramatic, austerely
free from decoration, and almost the architectural equivalent
of Raphael's *School of Athens*. Like that, it is classical in the sense
of balance and serenity, in its respect for antiquity, and even in
partly closing an epoch. Bramante was Raphael's uncle, and it
is his style of lucid architecture that frames the figures in
Raphael's fresco. Just as in painting Raphael disturbed the
equilibrium to achieve a richer, more dramatically 'engaged'
style, so he later came to consider Bramante's architecture in-
sufficiently rich. Antiquity could mean not merely Doric

179

severity but the almost florid effects of imperial Rome – and these were more relevant to modern Papal Rome, especially under Popes like Julius II.

Acting very much as a Roman emperor, Julius II required a new St Peter's to replace the old basilica which was inadequate to contain the tomb he intended Michelangelo to build him. Bramante was the first architect, and his plan of virtually a square church crowned by a huge dome replaced horizontal emphasis, and the long basilica nave, by a dominant verticality – an effect which was consolidated and made more dramatic by Michelangelo when he came to be the architect. Had Bramante completed it before his death, the church might well have seemed not rich enough. As it stands, its grandiose elaboration, its sensuous and dramatic use of colour and space, even the alterations and additions over several centuries, combine to make it an ideal both Renaissance and Baroque. Bramante's plan was significantly altered to provide a long nave for processional purposes. In the form of a dome rising behind a pedimented façade, with giant pillars, and an interior of long nave opening into a centralized space, a church was created that would

141 PERUZZI Palazzo Massimi, Rome. Begun 1535

142 SAN GALLO Palazzo Farnese, Rome 1534–45

serve as the standard. When, towards the end of the seventeenth century, Wren tried to return to Bramante-style complete centralization for St Paul's, he had to yield to tradition and provide once again a long nave.

Looked at by a sophisticated age, ancient Rome was not a city of stern Republican virtue so much as a great luxurious capital which had built on a vast scale often for pleasure. It was in Raphael's lifetime that there were discovered, appreciated and copied, the paintings and reliefs which survived from Nero's Golden House which had covered the Esquiline Hill. Even Julius II had not attempted to rival the statue of Nero which once stood there, described by Suetonius as being a hundred and twenty feet high. But new palaces and villas, and public buildings, could echo something of the sheer luxury, as well as grandeur, which had made Rome so famous. Palazzo Farnese *(Ill. 142)* develops positively antique Roman motifs, as well as consolidating with quite new and imposingly modelled style earlier Renaissance palace ideas. Palazzo Massimi *(Ill. 141)* is an entirely fresh solution. Palazzo Farnese was designed by the younger Antonio da San Gallo and became a standard for

143 LIGORIO Villa d'Este

145 PALLADIO S. Giorgio ▶
Maggiore, Venice
(interior). Begun 1570

144 SANSOVINO The
Library, Venice 1537–54

Roman palaces; Palazzo Massimi is by Baldassare Peruzzi. Both architects were involved in stages of the evolution of St Peter's, but San Gallo was really a believer in Bramantesque symmetry, in distinction to Peruzzi's orientation towards Raphael and the more daring, delicate effects seen in Palazzo Massimi – with its gently curving façade and unusual pillared entrance. It refuses to impose by strength, but its almost swaying ingenuity – extending to the oddly shaped 'picture-frame' upper windows – suggests a concept of grace which fits in well with sculpture like Cellini's *(Ill. 134)*.

These are town palaces, but it was equally in antique classical tradition to build country villas and to teach nature how it could be improved by art. Villa d'Este at Tivoli *(Ill. 143)* is only one example of sixteenth-century re-creation of that concept, but it is among the most superb. Stone, earth, trees and – above all – water, have been organized into a constant series of vistas, steps and fountains, meant to be encountered in ascending so that the villa itself and the extensive view over the Campagna are the final experience. A bare hillside has become this artful construction which forms a series of visual adventures – like progress down the Galerie François I at Fontainebleau or survey of the varying aspects of some statue by Gianbologna.

Although Rome, ancient and modern, provided the most stimulating climate for new architectural manners, architects themselves moved from Rome to disseminate their own highly individual idioms. At Venice, Sansovino – architect as well as sculptor of the *Apollo (Ill. 132)* – built opposite the Gothic Doge's Palace the Library *(Ill. 144)*; and the word's connotations do not prepare one for this pageant-style building, regular and yet highly picturesque, a vibrating screen of arches and pillars, topped by a statue-adorned balustrade. Its theatrical grandeur prepares the way for the most influential of all Italian architects, Palladio. He was not trained in Rome, but he was devoted to the Roman antique standards of Vitruvius and he visited Rome three times, benefiting from the example of Bramante perhaps as much as from antiquity.

The villas that he built influenced Northern Europe well into the eighteenth century and by that time were being copied also in America. Indeed, his classicism came to stand for classical antiquity – and in many ways he deserves that this should have happened. Despite his real learning, his buildings do not seem learned, still less pedantic. They have a delightful quality – communicating delight – which is far removed from anything by Alberti or by Michelangelo. His classicism, his purity of design, even his desire for lucidity, were all perfectly serious but governed by a basic picturesqueness which was the secret of his popularity. This made him no less great as an artist. His manner was completely his own – and his style must be one of the most immediately recognizable of all architectural styles, though it has not proved easy for historians to give it any of their usual labels. His church of S. Giorgio Maggiore at Venice *(Ill. 145)* might indeed exhaust the vocabulary of art-history. Its white, light-filled interior is austere and intensely exhilarating: space is contained and yet seems boundless without any suggestion of being beyond control. It is as if atmosphere had piled up within this bright, scrubbed, vast marine temple, ready to billow out to support the spectator, himself as if encapsulated, bounced effortlessly by gusts of energy down the gleaming floor. Roman Baroque churches, with their encrusted decoration and elaborate fresco schemes, are picturesque and theatrical in a way very different from Palladio's, stunning rather than cheering the spectator. But in seventeenth-century Venice, Longhena's *S. Maria della Salute (Ill. 182)* has much of the exciting quality of his architecture. And many eighteenth-century German churches share the same sense of control amid apparent excess, culminating in the superb interior of Vierzehnheiligen by the great architect Neumann *(Ill. 185)*.

In the sixteenth century, the new Italian style was disseminated through Europe particularly by books of architectural designs. One of the most influential was that by Sebastiano Serlio, a popularizing theorist who had worked with Peruzzi in Rome but later moved to Venice. Palladio may well have met him, and his own *Four Books of Architecture* provided patterns for arches, bridges, theatres and temples, as well as villas and palaces. Serlio was also summoned to France, though his design for the Louvre was not used. What was built instead by Pierre Lescot *(Ill. 146)* is perhaps more classically Roman than Italian, and considerably more graceful and less massive than the contemporary Palazzo Farnese *(Ill. 142)*. But it speaks a new 'renascent' language, most obviously in its central motifs, which via Serlio goes back to Vitruvius, and which all over Europe was replacing the Gothic style for architecture. It was probably due to Serlio's book that the huge town hall at Antwerp *(Ill. 147),* built by Cornelis Floris about 1560, had a triumphal arch-like central feature, with coupled pillars, statues and tall obelisks. In England, French and Flemish

185

influences mingled with Italian ones, and a rather startling new richness, more vigorous than refined, is displayed in the central pavilion of Burghley House *(Ill. 148)*, dated 1585; this has become its own peculiarly idiosyncratic style – barbaric and untidy when compared with Italian architecture – which yet pays almost touching tribute to the urge for highly-wrought novelty.

Italy probably represented individuality as well as just the classical tradition. Dürer in Venice – as has been mentioned – enjoyed his new status, without mentioning antiquities; and it is unlikely that he ever visited Rome. The self-portrait that he painted *(Ill. 152)* in 1498, after his first visit to Venice, crystallizes the sense of the artist-gentleman, fashionably dressed, at ease with no tools of his trade, and with a view of the distant Alps which suggests his travels: 'Heureux qui, comme Ulysse, a fait un beau voyage. . .' Nevertheless, it is not as a painter that Dürer was important. It might almost be said that his symbolic importance is altogether greater than his artistic one; he aimed at artistic and even social manners which did not always find much scope in his native Nuremberg. His intense curiosity, his observation of natural phenomena (not allied to

146 LESCOT Square court of the Louvre, Paris. Begun 1546

147 FLORIS Town Hall, Antwerp *c.* 1560

148 Central Pavilion, Burghley House, Northamptonshire 1585

intellectual speculation, however) and his instinctive literari-
ness are fascinating aspects of a mind that never quite emancipated itself. Leonardo – to whom he is so often compared – was
constantly being sought out by great patrons, remaining private
even when he had been purchased, idle, preoccupied, loitering
– almost – into fame.

Dürer's travels were at his own instigation; he often solicited
a patron, anxious to be public and published, working neurotic-
ally hard, and not so much alone as lonely. But he was acknow-
ledged as a unique artist in a new medium: 'the Apelles of black
lines', as a contemporary called him, recognizing that in his
engravings and woodcuts there was an artistic power as great
as that usually reserved for paintings. Unlike pictures, prints
could easily travel; and it was not merely Dürer's compositions
which were admired, and which were certainly influential, but
the richly wrought, detailed invention which is present through-

187

out an engraving like the *St Eustace (Ill. 149)*, executed in 1500, when Dürer was only twenty-six. This *tour de force* is almost painting with the graver, ranging from delicate hatching that conveys the muscles of the animals to the concentrated blackness of the tree-fringed lake where a tiny swan floats reflected on the dark water. Man, beast, landscape – all nature is here, but assembled through the artist's invention, more varied than anything we have seen before, more copious and more ingenious. Thus, by Vasari's standards for the new art of the sixteenth century, Dürer was already qualified to join the company of his great Italian contemporaries; and this particular engraving was singled out for praise by Vasari. And within Dürer's lifetime another Northern painter-engraver, Lucas van Leyden, was to produce even more subtle prints – enriching the Prodigal Son's return with every variety of costume, architecture, extensive landscape *(Ill. 150)*.

The highly individual, interacting and yet contrasting geniuses of Leonardo, Michelangelo and Raphael set the sixteenth century off to a complex start. Dürer's engravings introduced another element. In Venice even Bellini's work might seem stiff and ineloquent against the much more fluent, graceful, moody art which begins under the impetus of Giorgione – a revolutionary dead before Michelangelo had finished the Sistine ceiling or Raphael begun his *Galatea*. Giorgione's few

149 DÜRER
St Eustace 1500

150 LUCAS VAN LEYDEN *Return of the Prodigal Son* 1510

surviving paintings – of which the *Tempesta (Ill. 151)* is among the most haunting – are personal in a way hardly found again until Watteau. The *Tempesta* has a strangely surreal quality, so calmly conveyed that one scarcely ponders on why these figures should be in the countryside during a thunderstorm. Even if the subject is ever identified with certainty, still the picture will retain its un-public, almost improvised air – which is deliberate. The composition's elements are not far from those in Dürer's engravings, but the mood is lulling and more sensuous: the storm not dramatic but like summer lightning, and the woman absorbed into the wonderful natural setting as she suckles the child. A hint of this mood is sensed in Bellini's sacred picture, the *Madonna of the Meadow (Ill. 121)*, but Giorgione has broken the timeless spell, making light and landscape more capricious and dream-like. The paint is moody too, making patches of colour as if for colour's sake rather than dutifully recording three-dimensional shapes with clear outlines. Indeed, in this stylish use of paint in a way personal like handwriting, Giorgione goes further than any of his contemporaries – except Titian.

189

151 GIORGIONE *Tempesta*

152 DÜRER
Self-Portrait
1498

Titian's manner was not to be demonstrated by *recherché* subject-matter, nor even by a particularly novel approach, still less by intellectually pondered concepts of art. It was in his style of painting, of actually handling the medium – and in his last pictures he used his hands as well as brushes – that he virtually established the convention of oil painting in Europe up to Renoir. Though he was only a painter (in the same sense that Jane Austen was only a novelist) he already spoke the new heroic language, more Baroque than Renaissance, in the *Assunta* (*Ill. 153*) of 1518 – a huge picture which seems orientated away from Bellini, or even Giorgione, and full instead of the ethos being created by Michelangelo and Raphael. The Virgin sweeps

153 TITIAN *Assunta* 1518

up to heaven amid a hectic cloud of cherubs, ecstatically greet-
ing the hovering God the Father in a blaze of light, while
gesticulating figures of giant Apostles fill the foreground –
brothers to those in Raphael's *Transfiguration*. Titian tells the
story of the Assumption in physical terms, with swelling forms
of flesh and drapery which turn the subject from a mystery into
a palpable drama. The Virgin's very clothes are made eloquent

of assumption, gracefully swirling across her to emphasize the rushing motion of flight; and light aids the drama, as it blazes above, falls patchily on the clouds and scarcely illuminates the earthbound Apostles.

This almost scientific and psychological exactness – with which the painter seeks to communicate intense sensations to the spectator – is seen at its literally most stunning in the nearly contemporary *Resurrection (Ill. 154)* by Grünewald. The extraordinary elements of this are perhaps too often stressed – as if the German painter was Blake *avant la lettre*. Grünewald's style is undoubtedly different from Titian's, but both painters give visionary intensity to depicting a vision in dramatic terms, heightening naturalism. Titian idealizes his figures in a world of grand gestures and noble poses, but builds them with light and colour just as Grünewald does. Grünewald's psychological intensity is sharp, even shrill. Giorgione's summer thunder and Titian's sultry blaze seem tame beside the phosphorescence of Grünewald's risen Christ, burning orange and yellow in darkest night, blinding even while he calmly illuminates, a rocket whose upward force hurls men to the ground. To novelty of

154 GRÜNEWALD
Resurrection (detail)
1515–16

155 ALTDORFER *Battle of the Issus* 1529

concept is allied novel observation which gives scientific intensity to the vast gaseous halo into which Christ's face is actually absorbed; the Light of the World is interpreted as a real light, of decreasing strength as it moves outside Christ's orbit, melting into a cold ring of blueish flame. His grave-clothes are like charred paper twisting and writhing in a blaze.

Nor need such intense effects be restricted to religious subjects. Complete confidence of technique could lead the painter to such superb atmospheric effects – painted for their own sake –

as were caught in Altdorfer's *Battle of the Issus (Ill. 155).* The battling armies of Alexander and Darius are out-battled by the cosmic drama of the sky where the sun sinks hotly, reflected in great sheets of sea and glinting on the jagged, glassy ridges of distant mountains. This is not only an extraordinary aerial pageant – its atmospheric intensity to be equalled by Rubens and Turner alone – but the vast panorama emphasizes the clash of East and West, and dwarfs man and his doings to insignificance beside the eternal round of day and night.

Even Bruegel was not to achieve anything as revolutionary as Altdorfer's blazing sunset, but his seasonal pictures are peopled by ordinary figures, peasants or bourgeois, at their common tasks. It is not history but plain, daily fact that is illustrated, and yet the affecting thing is the atmospheric intensity. This art too impacts on the spectator in a new way: conveying almost physical sensations of a bitter winter day or hot June afternoon. Bruegel did not catch only extremes, but subtly, scientifically, painted those in-between hours which affect us most of all. In *November (Ill. 156),* the light is slowly

156 BRUEGEL THE ELDER *November (Return of the Herd)* 1565

fading as the cows are driven home; clouds are gathering, and soon this landscape will be deserted. It is on this realization that the whole mood tremblingly depends – as if the dying day was a foretaste of man's dying too.

Although the development of landscape painting may be largely a Northern phenomenon, the pursuit of atmospheric subtleties was a European one – a single aspect of the general urge towards more subtle art. Again and again that leads back to Leonardo, himself the writer who had linked subtlety of light to subtlety of manner. He had mentioned the charm arising through effects of muted light, and it is frank charm that breathes from Correggio's *Nativity (Ill. 157)*, where nothing is too startling or abrupt or sublime. It is not only the divine brightness of the Child shining out in the misty night that marks accomplishment here, but the luminous group of angels, almost Rococo figures in their aerial grace. And grace has been given to the scarcely rustic shepherd, doffing his cap with a suave courtesy worthy of a Magus, no less than to the pair of refined women whose hands assume artlessly graceful poses evocative rather of the boudoir than of Bethlehem.

Allowed to give his suavely alluring manner to a totally alluring subject, Correggio painted pictures ravishing in themselves which form not so much a cornerstone as a pillow for eighteenth-century painters like Boucher. More disturbing aspects of nature, seen psychologically heightened and therefore strange, also develop from Leonardo. In Pontormo, who was influenced by him, though also by Michelangelo and by Dürer's prints, tension has replaced Correggio's melting charm; yet there is grace in the crackling, swaying forms who express the *Visitation (Ill.159)*. This is no narrative picture but a moment of contact seized and frozen – barely localized, timeless, haunting in its intense spell. Just like Grünewald, Pontormo is trying to convey the significance of the subject in the most concentrated and psychologically exact terms. It was not a piece of charming daily life when the Virgin visited St Elizabeth, but the solemn meeting of God's mother and the mother of St John the Baptist: a mystery of the Child leaping in Mary's womb and Elizabeth 'filled with the Holy Ghost'. A comparable thinking into the significance of a scene, conveying the sensation of what it might be like if an angel erupted into a room, is apparent in the

157 *(far left)* CORREGGIO *Nativity* c. 1530

158 *(left)* LOTTO Annunciation 1526/8

159 *(right)* PONTORMO *Visitation* c. 1528

160 TITIAN *Pietà* 1573–6

Annunciation (Ill. 158) by Lorenzo Lotto, closely contemporary with Grünewald and Pontormo. Giotto's sense of cosmic order is rudely jolted here in the interests of dramatic accuracy; and the frightened cat is at once 'realistic' and yet a refinement no painter had dared introduce before.

Not every emphasis on art's ability to outdo nature produced results as apparently bizarre as those of Grünewald, Pontormo or Lotto; Titian's *Assunta* and Correggio's *Nativity* show that. Yet Titian too, in his search for emotional impact, moved away from the dignified surface of that confident picture, breaking up composition and surface to achieve finally the moving, mysterious *Pietà (Ill. 160),* unfinished at his death in 1576. More than similarity of subject links this to Michelangelo's Rondanini *Pietà (Ill. 126).* Nor is Titian's evolution connected just with subject-matter, for all his other work – whether his magical pagan pictures or superb portraits – shows him steadily evolving, displaying greater and greater confidence in the power of paint to obey his wishes. In the *Pietà* there is the same plangency as he gave contemporaneously to a picture of the *Flaying of Marsyas*. There is wildness in the *Pietà*, with the

198

distracted Magdalen rushing from the picture, as if calling on the spectator to share her grief. Even the grey architecture seems to obey emotional laws, ghostly rather than substantial in its form, a building conjured up from nowhere to shelter the Virgin; its statues grow strangely animated, disturbed partakers of the human suffering below them; and the paint throbs to the same grieving rhythm.

There had never been such a painter as Titian – nor has there been since. Effortlessly, and to vast applause, fame and wealth, he vanquished nature by producing art more natural than anything seen before. Between the *Assunta* and the *Pietà* – that is, over a period of about sixty years – he ceaselessly painted great pictures which were despatched across Europe and which everywhere affected painters. At the centre of his art lay a concern with mankind which was not elevated or theoretical but a rough physical familiarity, beyond cynicism and beyond being impressed. From his art certain strands could be separated: Van Dyck borrowed the glamorous appearance of his sitters; Velazquez was inspired by Titian's directness. But in Titian it had all been tightly bound into one whole. His portrait supposedly of the Lord of Atri *(Ill.161)* achieves a splendour that might well be called 'Renaissance', turning a man into Duke Theseus of *A Midsummer Night's Dream,* a hunter of women as much as animals, superbly incongruous in raspberry-red and gold pageant-style clothes in a chill grey landscape. With all the splendour goes a shrewd grasp on reality, on that common clay which lies under the glaze of finery, and this grasp gives the picture a sting of wit.

The very variety of sixteenth-century manners perhaps conceals some of the underlying similarities. If stylistically it seems a shock to turn from Titian's portrait to Holbein's *'Ambassadors' (Ill. 162),* it is not one emotionally, for the two pictures inhabit much the same climate – despite their different settings. Holbein is not just the craftsman–cum–photographer that the sheer accomplishment of his style sometimes suggests. His two 'ambassadors' look like very naturalistic portraits, but they are disposed with the formality of supporters in a coat of arms; a shield is formed by the what-not with its litter of skilfully drawn objects in foreshortening – many, if not all, having personal associations for the two sitters. That more than one plane of reality is intended is revealed by the skull painted in perspective across the foreground, existing in the space between pictured men and ourselves – a shadow of mortality which

162 HOLBEIN THE YOUNGER *The Ambassadors* 1533

literally puts the rest of the composition into a new perspective. All that such a portrait means is still not clear to us, but at least we can guess that surface naturalism is not sufficient for painter or painted; nor are the sitters seen, like the Arnolfini *(Ill. 92)*, in their ordinary environment, but in one specially devised and quite artificial (the patterned pavement, for instance, being derived from one in Westminster Abbey, which is clearly *not* the setting).

Holbein shows that the idea of improving and refining on nature – whether in portraiture or other pictures – was not restricted to Italy. In some ways, portraiture best reveals the transmutation of nature into art. How much science lies under the elegance and 'surprise' quality of such transmutations is shown in the self-portrait *(Ill. 164)* painted by Parmigianino, a tragically short-lived artist of graceful, handsome appearance

164 PARMIGIANINO *Self-portrait in a Convex Mirror* 1524

163 BRONZINO *Lodovico Capponi* c. 1550–5

as well as a supreme exponent of graceful style. The *Self-portrait* is unexpected because Parmigianino has not corrected the effect of its being painted from a convex mirror reflection; indeed, the curved shape combined with the illusionism of shining glass, the distorted hand, the reflected lights of a background window, all suggest that this object is no painting but itself a mirror. And perhaps the most complicated of all refining of flesh into art was achieved at Florence by Bronzino, polishing not only the surface of his pictures but the people in them *(Ill.163)* figures of marble or ice, with ivory hands and jewelled eyes, perfectly enamelled simulacra beside whom Raphael's *Castiglione* looks artless and prosaic.

Bronzino is indeed a last refinement of high artifice and manner, beyond which there could be only reaction or extinction. That is particularly true of Florence, whose greatest impetus in the arts was exhausted – and has never revived. One final petal of the gilded lily of art appeared in England, at Queen Elizabeth's Court, where the jewel-like miniatures of Nicholas Hilliard *(Ill.165)*, shadowless yet vivid likenesses, are

165 HILLIARD *Young Man amid Briar Roses c.* 1588

the perfect amorous tokens to be exchanged in the allusive, complicated, Illyrian world of *Twelfth Night*: '. . . wear this jewel for me', Olivia says lovingly to the apparent boy, Viola, ''tis my picture.' That the artist and his own personal style are still of paramount interest is testified to by Donne who wrote: 'a hand, or eye/By *Hilliard* drawne, is worth an history' by a lesser painter.

It was by a return, in effect, to the artistic sources of the early sixteenth century that there evolved the final triumph of sheer manner that is the Baroque. Where Bronzino almost disdained to affect the spectator, this style gathered up the resources of Raphael and Michelangelo, taking in Correggio's graceful illusionism and Titian's earthy vitality, and produced one great artist – Rubens – able to digest such potent influences and from them forge his own powerful, 'engaged', highly personal style. The edifice which he crowned was already being built by Tintoretto and Veronese, orientated respectively towards Michelangelo and Raphael but both indebted also to Titian. Between them – and they certainly affected each other's style – they virtually fused the elements of striking dynamism and physical splendour which would characterize Rubens' art. To typify them as spirit and flesh is too simple, for both were complex creators of increasing subtlety, whose late works are often surprisingly similar.

Yet it is inevitable to think of Tintoretto as the master of dramatic moments of divine intervention in human affairs – cosmic dramas where miracles replace Altdorfer's merely natural atmospheric effects. Bronzino, incidentally, had studied

166 TINTORETTO *Miracle of St Mark* 1548

Michelangelo's work to achieve his polished, remote marble pictures. Tintoretto's equally intense study of Michelangelo fastened on the energy contained under the surface, releasing it in great canvases that are stages lit by lightning-flash, catching us up in their drama so that we cease to be spectators and become participants. It is at our feet that the slave lies in the *Miracle of St Mark (Ill. 166)* and over our heads that the saint hurtles down, saving and illuminating – a firework tossed into the box-like, exploding construction. Tintoretto's manner was increasingly one of highly personal expression, using his brush and paint as if tracing with white fire, culminating in the *Last Supper (Ill. 167)* painted some forty years after he had burst on to the Venetian scene with the *Miracle of St Mark.* The long tunnel of this room is not disturbed but mystically illumined by the glowing Christ whose manifestation of his divinity has brought the transparent angels – painted with no more solidity than glass – to wheel in worship, unseen by men.

In some ways, Veronese is a more complicated phenomenon than Tintoretto. The balance and harmony which drew him to Raphael produced the good manners of the *Family of Darius (Ill. 170),* where East and West meet without shock, and where

167 TINTORETTO *Last Supper* 1592

168 VERONESE *Venus and Adonis c.* 1580

a conqueror displays magnanimity to the family of his foe with modern, Castiglione-style courtesy. This picture is Veronese's *School of Athens,* more worldly in its lesson, opulent, exotic but wonderfully well-bred. Like neither antiquity (despite its subject) nor sixteenth-century Venetian actuality (despite topical touches in heads and costumes) it creates an ideal middle state, a pageant world but not an impossible one, where Titian's *Lord of Atri (Ill.161)* might well feel at home. With all the resources of naturalism, Veronese conceived a climate as deeply imaginative as Tintoretto's but peopled by solid lovers rather than air-borne saints. His *Venus and Adonis (Ill. 168)* shows no struggling mortal trying to evade an ardent goddess, but a man contentedly collapsed on a woman's lap, being fanned against the heavy afternoon sultriness which bathes the whole picture in its sensuous spell: a tangerine-clad Antony and a blonde, bare-breasted Cleopatra, characters half-historical, half-mythological, who represent as much the heart's longing . for happy love as Tintoretto's the aspirations of the soul.

The fusion that Rubens would achieve totally was already aimed at, with very different results, by El Greco whose style

206

169 EL GRECO *Burial of Count Orgaz* 1586

was a positive anthology of most of the great artists discussed in this chapter. His now famous personal manner reduced itself to some extent to a refinement of Tintoretto's, a narrowing to candlelight power of what had been a blaze of energy, but flickeringly strange in its effect on the spectator. The whole of the large *Burial of Count Orgaz (Ill. 169)* is like a vision – earth being no less hallucinatory than heaven, both inhabited by insubstantial, spectral figures. There is no sense of space or weight; everything seems to burn upwards, in an agitated, crowded, windy world of smoke and flame. Its logic is artistic dream-logic, expressing what the artist feels rather than suggesting anything he has actually seen.

El Greco's is undoubtedly a flight from Renaissance daylight, and the painter is significantly recorded to have been found in his studio one spring day with the room deliberately darkened. Nor is it surprising if his style resists conventional classification. Coming from Crete, trained at Venice partly under the very old Titian, settling at Toledo at least by 1577, El Greco survived until 1614. By that time he had outlived Caravaggio and Annibale Carracci; the youthful Bernini was already astonishing Rome with his virtuoso sculpture; Rubens had been in Italy and was established as the leading painter in Antwerp. Such facts in themselves point to the development of that last of perfect manners – the Baroque – which was fostered especially in Rome: its roots lay in those great artists like Michelangelo and Raphael whom Greco had studied, and its final flower was Tiepolo, a Venetian who died in Spain – in one of the last countries where was acceptable the style which most of Europe had by then rejected as false.

170 VERONESE *Family of Darius before Alexander*

CHAPTER SIX

High Art and Low Nature

Few things better illustrate how easily one age misunderstands the artistic conventions of another than the for-long-held belief that the grand manner of the seventeenth century – the Baroque style – was false, morally depraved and meretricious. The reaction which brought into existence the Baroque style had actually originated in a desire to be more natural and less artificial, to overwhelm the spectator with emotional truths that had been absent too long from art: to be solid not fanciful, to impress and instruct rather than merely please. It was necessary to revitalize art; thus the seventeenth century saw a 'renaissance' which seemed to begin by going back to the early years of the previous century, putting blood into the frozen veins of Bronzino's people, warming into life the whitened, etiolated simulacra of Fontainebleau.

At its most vigorous, this new naturalism easily burst the frame of natural reference, as it does in Rubens and Bernini, the greatest Baroque masters, who are yet intensely natural, fully aware of humanity under all the trappings of grandeur. It is not surprising that these great exponents of the Baroque style were supreme in their grasp on vivid, candid nature. Whether giving tremendous conviction to imaginative ideas or catching nature with unrivalled directness, they were really using the same idiom. The public art that could apotheosize James I *(Ill. 172)* or set angels and clouds cascading around the Chair of St Peter *(Ill. 171)* was based on an awareness of humanity at least as intense and moving as Rembrandt's; and it could therefore produce with no sense of discrepancy such private work as Bernini's stunning bust of his mistress Constanza Bonarelli *(Ill. 174)* and Rubens' closely contemporary portrait of his second wife and young son *(Ill. 173)*.

In architecture too, the style of the seventeenth century was to begin by being dignified, solid and, at least externally, often quite plain. Bernini's church of S. Maria dell'Assunzione at Ariccia *(Ill. 175)* is a positively austere reduction of the Pantheon

171 BERNINI *Chair of Peter*, St Peter's, Rome. Begun 1624

172 RUBENS *Apotheosis of James I*. Ceiling, Whitehall Banqueting Hall, London 1635

174 BERNINI *Constanza Bonarelli c.* 1635

173 RUBENS *Helena Fourment
and her Son* 1636–7

to its basic terms of temple-style portico and dome: in its
austerity, what might be called a Doric version of that imperial
Roman building, with its rich porch of Corinthian columns
reduced by Bernini to three plain archways. Its concentrated,
almost Cubist form makes it a church that might have been
designed by Poussin rather than by someone traditionally
associated with extravagant effects. The interior is scarcely less
austere, beautifully lucid and decorated only by angels holding
up wreaths at each segment of the coffered dome. In England
Inigo Jones had spoken of the principle which he was to follow
in his buildings: 'Ye outward ornaments oft to be sollid, pro-
porsionable and according to the rulles, masculine and unaffected.' Nothing more perfectly expressive of these senti-
ments exists than his St Paul's, Covent Garden *(Ill. 176),* derived
from Palladio but with much sturdier effects, partly obtained
by a strict following of Vitruvius' rule for massive eaves.

175 BERNINI S. Maria dell'Assunzione, Ariccia 1662–4

176 INIGO JONES St Paul's, Covent Garden, London 1631

177 VIGNOLA Gesù, Rome.
Begun 1568

178 GAULLI *Adoration* ▶
of the Name Jesus.
Ceiling, Gesù, Rome
1676–9

The traditional, sixteenth-century base from which Inigo Jones has set out is reinforced by architecture other than Palladio's. The church of the Gesù *(Ill. 177)* at Rome, begun by Vignola in 1568 and executed by his pupil della Porta, is in fact plainer in its façade than Vignola's original statue-animated design. But in that design it lacked the great rolling scroll-like volutes which support and connect the upper pedimented portion to the lower. The whole church is on a huge scale, with giant pilasters and a dramatic central doorway, framed, pedimented, arched – as if to prepare the visitor for the large yet simple nave planned to be filled by a vast congregation and the reverberations of some dramatic sermon. More than a hundred years after the church had been begun, Gaulli frescoed the nave with the crushingly illusionistic *Adoration of the Name Jesus* *(Ill.178),* a final double triumph of the Baroque and the Jesuit Order for whom the church was built. This is the sort of high art associated with the Baroque, yet it has not only carefully planned, forceful illusionism but a carefully planned programme of meaning. Gaulli's allegorical figures are solid enough, falling out of the framework and apparently into the actual church. A concept of divine illumination and damnation on epic scale is given a plastic conviction and intensity as realistic-seeming as any scene of peasants or low life.

179 MANSART and LEMERCIER Val de Grâce,
Paris 1645–67

180 WREN St Paul's, London

As a type of modern church, the Gesù was disseminated almost as extensively as the Jesuits themselves. Its long nave and its scrolled and pedimented façade remained the pattern of the Baroque church, sometimes varied and made more dramatic by clustering pillars, or calmed into cooler dignity with more vertical effect – as in the church of Val de Grâce *(Ill. 179)* at Paris. The final echo of it is in Wren's St Paul's *(Ill. 180)*, blended from Italian and French examples; but Wren's own personal wish for St Paul's to be a centrally-planned church is itself an indication of the alternative interest of the period – a church like Bernini's at Ariccia. Taking the concept both of centralization and that of longitudinal emphasis, another great architect, Baldassare Longhena, produced the unique solution of S. Maria della Salute at Venice *(Ill. 182)*, an octagon crowned by a dome, with a subsidiary dome over the sanctuary beyond. Its smaller dome is usually forgotten or invisible, and the effect is of a huge, dramatic Palladian-style porch, approached from a great platform of steps, which leads into a somewhat challenging space – perhaps not accidentally recalling the effect of Justinian's S. Vitale at Ravenna *(Ill. 50)*.

Out of the two concepts present in the Salute evolved another interesting but popular mixture, the oval, which was perhaps the most significant of all Baroque designs (though to be found already in Serlio's book of 1547), playing with space in a new way, sending the eye on journeys that may prove exciting and precarious rather than harmonious in the Renaissance sense of certainty. Energy seems to have been pulling and pushing ordinary geometrical shapes into quite novel dynamic ones which need a new vocabulary to describe them in such a church as S. Carlo alle Quattro Fontane *(Ill. 181)*, by Bernini's great rival, Francesco Borromini. There is something sculptural in Borromini's attitude to architecture, ironically because he was – unlike Bernini – no sculptor, and indeed nothing but architect. His sculpture was the carved column, scooped-out niche and almost putty-like squeezes which are placed around his windows. Everywhere there is animation. The undulating interior of S. Carlo is prepared for by the undulating façade *(Ill. 181)* where the eye traces serpentine rhythms up and across the building. This is not rhetoric, still less a bizarre effect for its own bizarreness, but an exploration in terms of energy. Borromini's extremes are intellectual ones; though no universal man, he was a brilliant technician and mathematician. His buildings are very much of their century

217

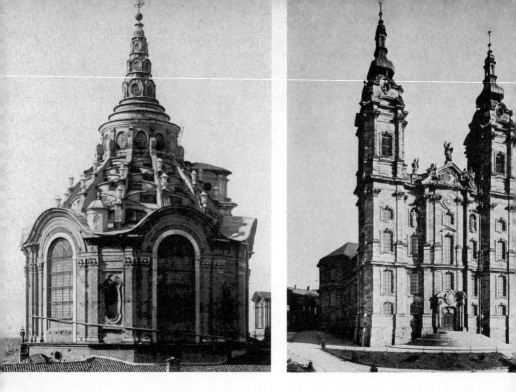

not in their presumed theatricality and 'caprice', but in their three-dimensional expression of the poetry of science and mathematics – and these things too are part of nature revealed.

Borromini's achievements were in Rome, but it is not without significance that he came from the extreme North of Italy, virtually Switzerland. His greatest heirs were not even active in Rome, and the harvest of his example is in the finest Rococo churches of Austria and Germany. Even more subtle effects, with positive dissonances and uneasy complexities, appear in the buildings of Guarino Guarini, priest, philosopher and mathematician, as well as architect, working chiefly at Turin, on palaces as well as churches. A view into the dome of the Cappella della SS. Sindone is almost like looking into the interior of a complicated piece of machinery. Perhaps the exterior of the chapel *(Ill. 183)* best reveals Guarini's extraordinary delight in extreme, spiralling effects, where solids are dissolved ultimately into hair-like plaiting in stone, topped by a final twirl which was even more extreme in the drawn design than as executed.

183 (*far left*) GUARINI Spire of the
Capella della SS. Sindone, Turin
1667–90

184, 185 NEUMANN Church of the
Vierzehnheiligen (*left*) exterior,
(*right*) interior 1744

Here the basic dignity of the Gesù, and the masculine weight
of Jones' St Paul's, have disappeared in a realm where imagination and mathematics continue to astonish the spectator. This
mixture – if indeed it *is* a mixture – lies at the heart of Rococo
architecture. It calls for a pursuit of intellectual extremes which
never appealed to French or English architects in general, and
which in Italy – as elsewhere – died away in the eighteenth
century under pressure of the apparent 'return to order' of
neo-classicism.

In Germany and Austria there was an instinctive response to
the ideas adumbrated by Borromini and Guarini: instinctive
to the point where several masterpieces were created by men
who were in status no more than humble masons. The most
distinguished, however, was trained engineer, artillery-officer
and theoretician, Balthasar Neumann. The interior of his church
of Vierzehnheiligen (*Ill. 185*) is the supreme triumph of the oval
in a series of great bursts of light and air which recall Palladio
but which are contained by a glowing yellow sandstone exterior
(*Ill. 184*), dignified and suitably vertical for its commanding

219

186 Palace at Versailles, the garden façade

position on a hill. The exterior alone is sufficient to show that such architecture is not wedding-cake confectionery or highly-coloured stage scenery but completely serious; and inside, the church has the hard delicacy of a huge shell, tinted in shell-pink and other pale tones, all clear-cut curves which sway and intersect not in dizzy extravagance but with a rightness gradually perceived as part of an organic, overall plan. Far from launching out into eternity, we are brought back finally to the oval central altar of the Fourteen Saints, itself like a gilded, curving shell: as it were, stating the architectural motif which recurs on a big scale in the surrounding fabric, and which is also the emotional focus and reason for the building.

Vierzehnheiligen is a culmination which is also the close of a style, as definitely a farewell masterpiece as in sculpture Pigalle's monument to Marshal Saxe *(Ill. 198)*, while in painting Tiepolo represents equal culmination and close. Such extremes are likely to encounter criticism in their own period, and already Borromini's architecture had been stigmatized by Bernini as 'chimerical' – based on fantasy rather than the fact of man and human stature. Pursuit of dignified splendour, and the constant presence of classicism as represented by Palladio, resulted notably outside Italy in architecture which was no less vigorous for being ostensibly more 'correct'. It would be convenient if this style had naturally been adopted by Protestant countries, while the more extreme Baroque style remained typically Roman Catholic. Indeed, this is often supposed to have been what happened, but art did not obey religion so neatly. France remained suspicious of excess – perhaps of all imaginative extremes – and though Versailles *(Ill. 186)* is vast, it is sober and

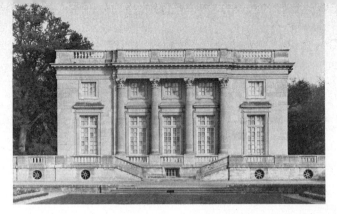

187 GABRIEL
Petit Trianon,
Versailles 1762–8

188 PERRAULT, LE VAU, LEBRUN
East Front of the Louvre,
Paris 1667–70

189 HÉRÉ The Hemicycle,
Nancy 1750–7

190 VANBRUGH Blenheim Palace, Oxfordshire 1705–20

regular to the point of monotony. Mansart's Val de Grâce *(Ill. 179)* had earlier hinted at a preference for calmness and balance, and there is a certain irony in the fact that Bernini's criticism of Borromini was spoken in France – a country which was to show increasing reserves about Bernini's own work.

Louis XIV abandoned Bernini's plan for the Louvre and what was built instead, probably as a result of collaboration by le Vau, Perrault and the painter Lebrun, was the colonnaded East Front *(Ill. 188).* This has no real precedent but begot many imitations and adaptations; it announces a particular type of French classicism which survived well into the nineteenth century. It was suited to solve some problems of town-planning, and a direct borrowing from the Louvre design lies behind the work of Jacques-Ange Gabriel, Louis XV's architect, in the Place de la Concorde at Paris. Much more spontaneous and varied is the town-planning achievement of Emmanuel Héré at Nancy *(Ill. 189)* begun only a few years before the Place de la Concorde – an enchanting Rococo liberation which was perhaps possible only in what was technically the small capital of another kingdom, being ruled by the titular King of Poland. Though the scale of Gabriel's Petit Trianon *(Ill. 187),* begun in 1762, offers a relief from the oppressive palace at Versailles, its style continues the classicism of the Louvre façade; it seems a building expressly designed to rebuke any latent tendency towards Rococo movement.

Like France in this, but unlike it in religion, England also returned to 'masculine and unaffected' Palladianism from which it had only rarely departed. Yet the departures – into the tremendous weight and vigour of Vanbrugh's Blenheim *(Ill. 190)* for example – show unmistakably that England was capable of producing its own version of Baroque. Were there any doubts about this, the attacks at the period of Wren's St Paul's and on a tendency of certain noblemen to build 'false and counterfeit Piece[s] of Magnificence' show that such a dangerous style was already thought to exist. It was often associated directly with the 'wildly extravagant' designs of Borromini, and contrasted with the purity of Palladio. In fact, there is something magnificent and original about the rhetorical pile of Blenheim; Vanbrugh, no less than Inigo Jones, wished his architecture to be masculine, as well as magnificent – suitably so for a great military commander. Blenheim is a deliberate national monument, erected to a hero in his lifetime and much more useful than a posthumous memorial.

Palladian classicism was suitable both for less grand houses, villas, planned often to follow Palladio's own villas very closely, and for extension on the urban scale that is found at Bath, associated with the two John Woods, father and son. It is hard to select among that embarrassment of architectural riches, but the younger Wood's Royal Crescent *(Ill. 191)*, of which the foundation-stone was laid in 1767, combines dramatic grandeur with regularity and remains unequalled even there. Royal Crescent forms a single palace block –

191 WOOD THE YOUNGER Royal Crescent, Bath. Begun 1767

192 LEDOUX
Barrière de
Courcelles, Paris
1785–91 (destroyed)

sweeping around a huge lawn which falls away from it; but it is also a solution to providing thirty houses, both varied and elaborate in décor, behind a giant, pillared, uniform façade. Something much more ambitious was almost contemporaneously being attempted in London by the Adam brothers – the Adelphi terrace destroyed in the 1930s. Robert Adam, the leader of the three brothers, used the word 'exploded' to explain his substitute of light decoration, grace and variety (mannered if not mannerist concepts) for the too severely regular Palladian style.

As far as can be seen from engravings and descriptions, the Adelphi combined plain massiveness on its lower-level arcades with an elegant, lightly pilastered and wreathed terrace above. This duality is typical of the complexity of the late eighteenth century. Classicism itself, when re-examined, took one back far beyond Palladio. It could lead to a sturdy simplicity of basic geometric forms, deriving from true Doric architecture such as that at Paestum *(Ill. 24)*, and resulting in the Barrière de Courcelles *(Ill. 192)* in Paris – classical beyond Gabriel's imagining – by the revolutionary architect Claude-Nicholas Ledoux. And classicism could also mean the more familiar decorative Adam style, sometimes exploding weight and severity in extreme filigree refinement in which Pompeiian seems virtually Rococo. Adam was a great architect, capable of a whole gamut of styles; and his antiquity could be as effectively grand, cool and unfevered as it is in the black and white hall at Syon House *(Ill. 193)*.

224

193 ADAM The Hall, Syon House, Middlesex 1762–9

194 DE MENA *Virgin of Sorrows*

In painting and sculpture the final Rococo fling can be paralleled best in the contemporary work of Fragonard and in the fragile yet earthy and intensely vivacious terracottas of Clodion *(Ill. 196)* – artists who lived through the French Revolution but who still dared to speak the language of Rubens and Bernini. They close what had begun in Rome in the early seventeenth century. Bernini's was a universal talent, harnessed under Pope Urban VIII to become a much happier seventeenth-century Michelangelo: 'born by Divine Disposition and for the glory of Rome to illuminate the century' the Pope wrote of Bernini, whom he encouraged as architect and even as painter.

Yet it was as a sculptor that Bernini had first astonished Rome, and it is his sculpture that remains the truest expression of his genius. The bust of his mistress *(Ill. 174)* and the Chair of St Peter *(Ill. 171)* loosely represent his response to nature and his dramatically decorative ability to express the visionary. It is faith that Bernini invokes – and is always invoking. There is nothing of Michelangelo's Olympian air, nor of his tortured sense of a body escaped from imprisonment in a marble block. One can scarcely think of a block at all before the fluttering fluid movement of a statue like the *St Theresa* whose draperies are animated into a storm of disturbance which seems to mirror her emotional state *(Ill. 195)*.

The core of Bernini is energy; obviously this is true of any creative artist, but in Bernini the energy seems to burn its way

to the surface with few or no obstacles. Nature, the rules, classical concepts of repose – all have to bend and melt before a fiery quality which can be expressed negatively by saying his work is never dull. And it is prodigious in scope. 'The glory of Rome' meant not only his religious sculpture but his portrait busts of the Popes, his fountains and his piazza before St Peter's *(Ill. 140)*. Yet it is ultimately on his creative power in realizing religious drama that one fastens. The complete expression of this – not on a huge scale, it should be noted, but with every device of art in setting and presentation – is the Cornaro chapel at S. Maria della Vittoria where the *Ecstasy of St Theresa (Ill. 195)* is the focus of a surrounding solidly three-dimensional theatre. The vision is physical in concept and realization: the Saint's dangling marble foot extraordinary in its flesh-like smoothness against the rough-textured, pumice-like cloud on which she swoons in palpitating abandon. The group is raised up, floating in a more effectively visionary way because of the firm framework of polychrome pillars, the carved spectators in theatre-boxes at either side. The intense natural observation, in which mystic experience is transmuted into physical terms, is worthy of St Theresa's own description of her experiences. Bernini's is a

196 CLODION
The Intoxication of Wine

197 COYSEVOX *Mercury*

deliberate conjuring with the strongest of illusionistic effects
so that one shares – not the Saint's ecstasy but something of her
faith. Its reality can be expressed only by the maximum reality
of artistic appearances.

The dangers of such means, when not fused by molten
energy like Bernini's, are patent. Like Borromini's architecture,
Bernini's work was often attacked and reacted against increasingly by the invoking of classical standards. He and Urban
VIII 'corrupted public taste' for over a century afterwards, the
sculptor Flaxman pronounced in 1805, with the strong moral
bias of his period. Leaving aside this confused charge, it
happens that Bernini's own tastes were extremely classic: he
admired Raphael, Annibale Carracci and – notably among his
contemporaries – Poussin. That admiration is further evidence
for a basic homogeneity in seventeenth-century art.

The powerful emotional reality seized by Bernini was being
aimed at by sculptors all over Europe, whether influenced or not
by him. In Spain there developed statues of startling reality,
usually of painted wood, often dressed in real fabrics, sometimes
tortured into masks with crystal tears and apparently liquid
blood – but sometimes more truly affecting in their sober
grief. The *Virgin of Sorrows (Ill. 194)* is tragically calm; plainly
clad with her heavy-lidded eyes and mouth turned down, she

229

is a straightforward, psychologically convincing image, almost classically restrained in sorrow. Elsewhere, even in France, a vigorous poetry now animated decorative sculpture; the equestrian *Mercury (Ill. 197)* by Antoine Coysevox is pitched between earth and heaven, a symbol of Baroque energy that is touched also by Rococo hints – as in the horse's curled-over, ornamental tail.

Coysevox, like Bernini, was also a great portrait-sculptor, and it was this category of sculpture that was to be demanded in steadily more truthful, and more prosaic, terms. The too-famous busts of Jean-Antoine Houdon represent an absolute return to the natural, but monuments still offered sculptors throughout the eighteenth century opportunities to combine the allegorical with the naturalistic, to make great drama out of those Rubens-like themes of immortality and honour. One last real-life hero, Marshal Saxe, was commemorated by the last of such monuments *(Ill.198),* by Jean-Baptiste Pigalle. Here a recognizably individualized, armoured figure of the great soldier-lover goes, like Don Giovanni, bravely down into the tomb that death has opened for him. Approached frontally, as it must be, the vast monument is one bold, challenging statement: a pageant of heroic departure set round with angry weeping allegories, a vainly interceding France and falling campaign banners, all of which make glorious the approach of death.

The trumpets and thunder of that farewell cannot, however, drown out the pan-pipes of Clodion, closer to earth, gallant rather than glorious, yet still instinct with energy. And just as the final triumph of Rococo architecture is in Germany and Austria, so it was there that one final sculptural style evolved which married almost rustic nature and high art: to produce elegant, vigorous, high-coloured statues whose very fingers are bent to hook the beholder's attention. The vision of the *Assumption (Ill. 199),* devised by Egid Quirin Asam is still visionary in Bernini's terms, but it has exploded his unified concept into highly-charged fragments even more astonishing, with the Apostles gaping in fluid amazement while the Virgin – herself an open-mouthed astonished *diva* – is rushed to heaven with reckless Rococo verve. The artifice of this vision is obvious enough: an almost Firbankian refinement upon the physical languor of the *St Theresa.* The classic beauty of Greek art, as it was to be inculcated by Winckelmann, has nothing to do with Asam's art; his statues act in every way as if they were not

230

statues, refusing to be calm and dignified, anxious rather to communicate and express emotion. In that they are – for all their gilt draperies and rouged cheeks – more true to nature than the chilly people of Canova's sculpture *(Ill. 200)*, where even in direct portraiture idealization has laid a cold, congealing hand upon the actual. Pauline Bonaparte would be a fit inhabitant of Adam's hall at Syon *(Ill. 193)*.

In all Bernini's sculpture there exist not merely pictorial but positively painterly qualities. He himself, as his admiration for certain painters reveals, had a particular interest in painting. He should certainly have recognized the quality also in Rubens, but his silence is explicable when one remembers that he was barely nine years old when Rubens left Rome, never returning to Italy. In painting Rubens is undoubtedly the century's dynamo – one which retained some current to animate even up to Van Gogh – and a symbol of the century's internationalism. He absorbed the Venetians and Raphael and Michelangelo, was influenced by both Caravaggio and Carracci, and built up an individual style which not only formed Van Dyck, touched Velazquez, once at least affected Rembrandt, but animated Watteau, even in ill-health, with the energy to create that culminates in the *Enseigne de Gersaint (Ill. 224)*. In England Gainsborough was markedly influenced by Rubens' landscapes, and Reynolds owned a fine landscape by him.

200 CANOVA *Pauline Bonaparte* 1808

202 RUBENS *An Allegory of Peace and War* 1629

Like Bernini, Rubens burnt with energy. He saw the natural world quite clearly in its surface appearances, but was able to re-make it, re-people it, charge it with an additional electricity which pulsates under all his greatest work and gives its meaningful vitality to enhance life itself. Warmed by his imagination, allegory and personification took on solid flesh. *An Allegory of Peace and War (Ill. 202)* is movingly full of artistic and personal conviction. There is even something splendid in the armoured Mars, reluctantly led by the wise Athena from the fecund scene where jewels, spurting milk, a cornucopia of glossy fruit, as well as eager children, all give reality to the concept of Europe enjoying peace, released from the threat of havoc. He could give restless, pageant-like splendour to such subjects as the *Mystic Marriage of St Catherine (Ill. 201)*, where the whole composition is excited and inspired, a tossing, curving wave which sets even the architecture in motion, rolling up to the Madonna, enthroned and, almost alone of the figures, calmly at rest. St Catherine's vision may be compared with St Theresa's,

235

but Rubens makes his interpretation more public than Bernini's group; it is not a privilege to attend the mystic marriage of St Catherine so much as something enforced on us by the gesticulating saints, conjuring us to an occasion as much festive as mystic.

Rubens was easily fired by ideas of triumph, whether of church or monarchy. He responded to a stable social framework where nature was beneficent in its manifestations. There was no irony in his vision of the blessings of James I's reign *(Ill. 172),* any more than there was scepticism in Bernini's sculptured glorification of the *Cathedra Petri.* It was within such concepts of a God-directed universe and beneficent nature that Rubens was able to produce such pictures as that of Helena Fourment with her young son *(Ill. 173),* the private blessings enjoyed by Rubens and celebrated by him in paint. This candid intimacy rivals Rembrandt's intimate portraits. And towards the end of his life, Rubens seemed to turn back in a new mood of intimacy to his native countryside, extending as it were to landscape the personal pride and tenderness which he had given to paintings of his family.

Yet Rubens' nature had needed Italian artistic stimulus before it could develop. The Rome not only of the past but of modern masters such as Caravaggio and Annibale Carracci had guided his energy into expression. Just as Baroque architecture goes back to the sobriety of the sixteenth-century Gesù church, so the equally seminal fresco scheme in the Galleria Farnese *(Ill. 203),* for which Annibale Carracci was summoned from Bologna to Rome in 1595, is sober, unillusionistic decoration in part – still closer in many ways to Raphael than to the dramatic extreme of Gaulli *(Ill. 178).* Cardinal Alessandro Farnese had built the Gesù for the Jesuits, and it was for his great-nephew that the Galleria in the family palace was frescoed. There are painted a series of classical love-stories composed as pictures on the ceiling: so many flat canvases, it might seem, on a framework most remarkable for the solidly-realized living nudes who inhabit this world above the cornice, and who contrast with the feigned architecture of herms, roundels and putti which they flank.

Elements of Veronese and Correggio mingle here with Raphael and Michelangelo, indicating that vein of colour (almost, colourfulness) and nature which was going to be brought into academic conflict with design, or draughtsmanship, and intellect – though, in fact, the conflict was really based

203 CARRACCI Galleria Farnese (detail). Palazzo Farnese, Rome
1597–1604

on false premises. In late seventeenth-century France, Rubens
and Poussin were to be made leaders of the two opposing
factions, in a way that did little justice to Poussin's response to
colour or Rubens' intellectual, antique interests. Like Raphael,
Annibale Carracci himself makes it clear that there need be no
such conflict. And like Raphael again, he offered work out of
which the twisted strands could be separated and drawn: highly
illusionistic, dramatic, light-filled ceilings could be developed
from the Galleria Farnese, or the more 'classic' picture on the
ceiling which was never more effectively achieved than in the
Aurora (Ill. 204) of 1613, by Guido Reni. A pastel-coloured,
cool vision of antiquity, it deserves its great fame for its perfect
solution to decorating a room, its mild but genuinely poetic
response to mythology and its glimpse of still-dark landscape
that Constable was to praise.

237

Annibale's own landscapes display an increasingly ordered vision, in which nature remains the inspiration but has been re-arranged in an ideal way. In the *Flight into Egypt (Ill. 205)* the Roman Campagna falls into a pattern more perfect than any in reality, somehow made to mirror the concept of departure and exile, with the Holy Family already cut off by the river from the rich pastoral countryside behind, and about to enter a dark, strange new land. The elements of Giorgione's *Tempesta (Ill. 151)* are here more intellectually restated. But the seventeenth century, even in Rome, the capital of classical idealizing tendencies, also required an almost scientific observation of nature and natural phenomena. It fostered the sensitive light effects of Adam Elsheimer's small landscapes *(Ill. 206)* where nature seems to rustle and stir under subtle, trembling atmospheric moods, and man is merged with nature – no longer its lord. Though he worked chiefly in Rome, Elsheimer was a German, and the tradition he continued was Altdorfer's.

Out of the intensely ordered arrangement of man and nature came the 'classical landscape', made by Nicolas Poussin to hold the deepest possible philosophical implications, as Bernini recognized. It was in front of one of these classical landscapes that Bernini, putting a finger to his forehead, remarked: 'Signor Poussin is a painter who works up here.' Atmospheric nature, closer to Elseimer's than to Annibale Carracci's, floods the pictures of the third great foreigner working in Rome, Claude Lorrain *(Ill. 207)* Here the re-ordering of nature has been conducted as stringently as by Poussin, but by the laws of a dream world rather than of logic or intellect. Although figures always animate these scenes, the permanent hero of

204 RENI *Aurora* 1613

205 CARRACCI *Flight into Egypt*

them all is light: caught at the subtlest moments of vapour-veiled brightness. Poussin's world is all solids, cubes and cones of landscape and cloud, where even water becomes a heavy, metallic liquid; everything remains graspable by man. But Claude's is a world where earth is only a slim crust between shimmering sky and sea: often reduced to no more than two stage-scenery wings which provide the bare framework within which insubstantial atmosphere hovers.

Claude's landscapes represent an extreme, yet it is notable that he never painted pure landscapes without some human presence and association. Nature inevitably retained its Renaissance significance of humanity, and it was as an emotional, sheerly affecting drama that Domenichino's *Last Communion of St Jerome (Ill. 209)* was for long appreciated. This large and famous picture is as much a key to the period as Bernini's group of *St Theresa in Ecstasy*, and its influence lasted longer. It tells of no miracle but instead of the tenacious faith of the dying Saint, emaciated and feeble, who has insisted on being borne to a chapel from the desert to receive Communion for the last time. Awe, devotion and pity are expressed by the Saint's attendants and by the ideal trio of ministrants: priest, deacon and subdeacon, in their very gradations of age making up a symbol of human life. Domenichino tells the story in recognizable realistic terms, but with emphasis not on any dramatic action but on decorum and dignity. It is almost a stoic picture, for the old man's resolution may be admired without sharing his faith; and it is probably the ancestor of all affecting deathbed pictures. In many ways, Domenichino's severe ideals – in composition as much as in concept – anticipated and influenced Poussin. Pictures like Poussin's *Death of Germanicus (Ill. 208)* create a new climate of attitude to antiquity, tacitly challenging Christianity by their emotional seriousness and their celebration of natural virtue; the poisoned Germanicus is mourned for his learning and benevolence, as well as his military qualities. A hero even to Suetonius, he is one of the first of Poussin's pagan martyrs. An antique Roman scene is painted in modern Rome, and destined for the Barberini family whose head would become Pope Urban VIII.

Rome was also the scene of the supposedly 'realistic' art of Caravaggio, sometimes strangely treated as a pioneer of

206 ELSHEIMER *Flight into Egypt*

207 CLAUDE *Embarkation of the Queen of Sheba* 1648

modern art. If Annibale Carracci is less ideal and contrived than he at first appears, Caravaggio is less naturalistic and revolutionary than he would have liked to appear. Like Annibale he came from Northern Italy; like him he was influenced by sixteenth-century Venetian painters, with more response perhaps to the emotional assaults planned by Lotto *(Ill. 158)* than to the imperturbable good manners of Veronese. And in subject-matter he remains remarkably conventional, preferring religious themes. His effects of theatrical realism may well be called 'Baroque'. The *Spiritual Exercises* of St Ignatius Loyola, the founder of the Jesuits, had encouraged palpable, physical sensations akin to the drama of Caravaggio's *Calling of St Matthew (Ill. 210),* but Caravaggio seems to linger more on the group round the Saint than on Christ – a figure in timeless draperies whose pose is oddly stilted. It is rather as if Caravaggio

241

needed to invoke Raphael's late rhetoric for his religious figures but in his own idiom could respond to the genre scene of the group around the table. The elements of theatre uneasily linked with 'realism' – perhaps unfairly suggesting Italian touring company *verismo* – are emphasized by the shallow space of the picture area and the harsh contrasts of light and darkness: a darkness that is black and flat rather than atmospheric. To some extent, Caravaggio was perhaps the victim of an artistic delusion, for the closer he came to imitating realistic surfaces in paint the more inner significance is lacking. There is some hollowness behind his apparently hardest modelling, and an absence of conviction under the waxwork appearances. The effects may be eye-deceiving, but they do not deceive the mind.

Caravaggio caused a great stir, and for a while exercised great influence chiefly outside Italy. He did perhaps mean to bring nature back into too ingenious-seeming and sterile art; and the plebeian quality of his models, his touches of carefully

209 DOMENICHINO *Last Communion of St Jerome* 1614 ▶

208 POUSSIN *Death of Germanicus* 1627–31

210 CARAVAGGIO *Calling of St Matthew*

painted naturalistic detail, and his determinedly dramatic effects might suggest exciting possibilities to greater painters. But the century that was to produce the electric realism of Rubens, the dignified truth of Velazquez and the poignant naturalism of Rembrandt, can scarcely claim in Caravaggio more than a pioneer – pioneer, rather than peer of those great painters. Nor was his revolution one that would lead to anything we can legitimately call modern art; its aftermath was the exhibition picture of the nineteenth century, where glossy paint and shocking subject-matter would briefly create journalistic sensations around painters now totally forgotten.

Truth in art is an elusive substance. Yet within the conventions of naturalism in Western painting, it was clear to the seventeenth century that Titian was the artist who had come

211 VAN DYCK *Charles I*

212 VELAZQUEZ
Francisco Lezcano

213 REMBRANDT
Margareta Trip
c. 1661

closest to it. Rubens studied and copied his work; so did Rubens' most gifted pupil Anthony van Dyck, whose *Charles I (Ill. 211)* captures an outdoor naturalism, amid refinement, which eluded the brash pursuit of Caravaggio. Van Dyck can even suggest the passage of time: the King negligently strolling, barely pausing for his portrait before drifting out of the picture. Between ruler and gentleman, formality and informality, the picture is delicately balanced; though art has refined and sieved nature here into an elusive, fluid substance, the nervous vitality of nature is still present. In Italy portraiture languished. After Van Dyck, it was Velazquez in Spain who best knew how to pick up Titian's brush. If it is the illusion of being confronted by real people that is required, Velazquez can produce the astonishing *Las Meninas (Ill. 218)* which is a positive life-size box of trick effects – but much more than that.

Where Rubens elevated James I to a heaven of flashing allegory, Velazquez places royalty on earth: in a framework of common nature, the plainest and yet the most vivid of environments. Van Dyck subordinated all to the King – even bending the horse to his design. Velazquez' art has gone into making the whole scene appear quite natural, even artless; his portrait is not of any single person but of a Court which includes himself. In one way, this is a self-portrait with other figures: the artist in his studio, much as Vermeer in Holland was to depict him *(Ill. 216)* not many years later. Yet Velazquez is stubbornly unideal. As much emotional weight is attached to the dwarfs and attendant women as to himself or the youthful Infanta: they have their lives too, and in single portraits of the Court dwarfs *(Ill. 212)* Velazquez indeed painted – with overwhelming dignity – the 'natural', in the sense of the mental defective. How ideal the humanity of the fifteenth century seems in the presence of this penetrating vision, and how foppish and fancy-dress Caravaggio's characters. But Rembrandt's *Margareta Trip (Ill. 213)* has something of the same essential, stubborn humanity; she is physically weak where the dwarfs were mentally so, and Rembrandt gains part of his effect from the associations of tremulous old age; sunken face against starched ruff, withered hand clasping the intensely clean white handkerchief.

Nature is not only humanity but our environment; Jan van Eyck had already stated so much in the Arnolfini group *(Ill. 92)*, and a good deal of seventeenth-century genre painting, especially in Holland, records appearances of ordinary life without his intellectual power and penetration. The topical,

247

214 ZURBARÁN *Still-life*

215 RUISDAEL *The Mill at Wijk c.* 1670

216 VERMEER *The Artist's Studio c.* 1666

gossipy aspects of this art may well give it the appeal of diaries and newspapers; and it is easy to say, as is usually said, that such art developed in opposition to the Baroque visionary art of Rubens or Bernini. Yet it needed just as much visionary power to seize on the natural, subordinate its distracting elements, and produce such almost mystically ideal realism as Vermeer's interior with an artist *(Ill. 216)* or the grave intensity of Zurbarán's *Still-life (Ill. 214)*. It is hardly too paradoxical to claim that these painters have, in their own fashion, practised St Ignatius' *Spiritual Exercises*: meditating on their subject, they have conjured it up with the conviction of inner reality. They make it mean more to the spectator than could an ordinary light-filled room or a pile of fruit. And they also point to the complete emancipation of the painter from the tyranny of subject-matter.

217 REMBRANDT *Christ preaching* 1652

A painter like Jacob Ruisdael has turned landscape into being a moody reflection of his own states of mind *(Ill. 215)*. What interests him, and us, is not the topographical accuracy of the scene but the play of light and shadow in an entirely natural universe. There are no cataclysmic events; to some extent the earth is of no more importance than it is in Claude. It is the always changing atmosphere that is Ruisdael's subject. He seems absorbed by mutability, and though he painted no 'Allegory of Time' his landscapes are full of feelings of transience. In Rembrandt's portraits time is always passing, through suggestions of changing mood, transient light and something momentarily seized – it seems – in the actual sitters. The nature that he sees is as direct as Velazquez'; its central concern is humanity, neither elevated nor scorned, placed in the framework of its daily environment – as we see it in the *Syndics (Ill. 219)*. This was painted only a very few years after *Las Meninas,* and the two pictures provide fascinating, eternal food for comparison. When Rembrandt took up conventional religious subject-matter it was touched with a sense of humanity deeper than anything Caravaggio had known. In his etchings – and perhaps Rembrandt was at his most personal in this medium – he would depict a Christ *(Ill. 217)* whose divinity does not separate him from the people to whom he preaches. He is one with them – and they are ordinary humanity indeed, not dressed-up actors but plain, puzzled beings, utterly convincing as the species to which we ourselves belong.

Such 'nature' would be instinctively responded to by Goya, who named as his teachers Rembrandt and Velazquez, along with Nature herself. The coming of the eighteenth century did not shift the emphasis from nature; and it is a gross error, as well as an irony, to confuse Watteau's personal revolution with an increase in artificiality. Like Goya, he invoked nature – and could have named Rubens and Veronese as his teachers from the past. The eighteenth century had inherited the tail-end of the tradition of perfect manner; it increasingly stigmatized that inheritance as false and outworn, and invoked nature to lead it back towards the unvarnished truth. Goya, perhaps more profoundly than any other painter, understood that there is something confused and irrational at the heart of nature. But what he feared was positively enjoyed by an artist like Blake, whose highly visionary subjects were expressed in a technique deliberately 'primitive', disdaining the illusionism of oil paint *(Ill. 226)*.

218 VELAZQUEZ *Las Meninas* 1656

219 REMBRANDT *The Syndics* 1662

The paintings of Tiepolo *(Ill. 221)*, themselves consciously echoing Veronese, are intended to exceed and improve on nature. That they are 'false' is part of the artist's intention; and it is clear that as a document of dark age history, this *Marriage of Frederick Barbarossa* is quite worthless. No more do the petit-point pastorals of Boucher *(Ill. 220)* provide instruction about what the actual countryside is like. These are works of art that justify themselves by power of the imagination: they mean to take us into a world which does not exist and never has existed outside art. It is really no different an aim from Blake's – different as the results are – but it has no particular moral conviction. Both Tiepolo and Boucher showed themselves aware of, and able to delineate, ordinary nature (Tiepolo in his caricatures, for example, and Boucher in his genre scenes). Their lifetimes were those also of Canaletto, recording often with poetic response even the gritty workaday reality of Venice *(Ill. 223)*, and of

253

220 BOUCHER *Shepherd piping to a Shepherdess*

221 TIEPOLO *Marriage of Frederick Barbarossa* 1752

222 CHARDIN *Morning Toilet* 1741

223 CANALETTO *The Stonemason's Yard c.* 1730

224 WATTEAU *Enseigne de Gersaint* 1720

Chardin, whose interior scenes have an unreal perfection *(Ill. 222)* recalling Vermeer's, yet with an intensely human concern, warmer than Vermeer but not sentimental. And Gainsborough was their contemporary too, in himself uniting natural observation of people with silken graceful artificiality, as in *The Morning Walk (Ill. 225).*

In all this art, even Chardin's, the deepest truths of human nature might seem to be lacking – for one reason or another. Certainly they are not lacking in Watteau's work, whether in the dialogue of passion that makes tense the surface of his scenes of lovers and dancers or in the naturalism of the *Enseigne de Gersaint (Ill. 224),* where a genre scene is shot through with electric, erotic energy to make this interior the shop of the human heart. But Watteau is concerned, seriously concerned, with love; and the eighteenth century was spoiling for a fight. Like Madame de Merteuil in its own great novel, *Les Liaisons Dangereuses,* it replied to hedonistic appeals, relaxation, amorous unity, with the words: 'La guerre.' Hogarth tried to disturb his period by satiric, modern moral subjects which are perhaps too entertaining *(Ill. 228)* for their purpose. Several painters sought increasingly in history – even in contemporary

225 GAINSBOROUGH *The Morning Walk* 1785

226 BLAKE *The Spiritual Form of Pitt* 1808

227 COPLEY *Death of Chatham* 1779–80

228 HOGARTH *After the Marriage (Marriage à la Mode) c.* 1744

history – for stirring, true events. Death remained the most popular basic concern. The American-born Copley was something of a pioneer in this field of the modern history picture, stirringly but inaccurately showing, for example, the *Death of Chatham (Ill. 227)*. A much greater fright was needed; it was given to all Europe by the French Revolution. When the tremors caused by that event died away, the mould of perfect manner and high art was seen to be one of the casualties. In art, as in politics, new realities had to be faced.

Two artists, Goya and David, born within two years of each other, invoked nature in a revolutionary way and were caught up in the events of the stormy years around 1800. What they witnessed was shockingly natural, or romantically exciting.

259

229 DAVID *Death of Marat* 1793

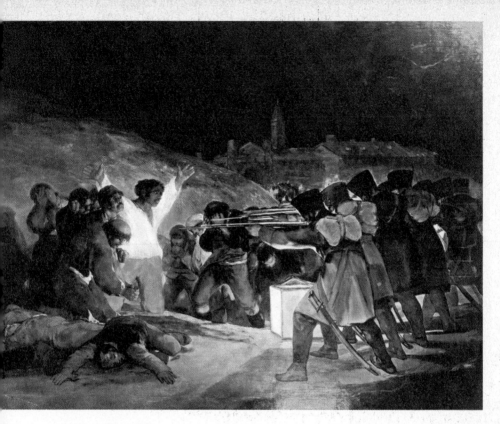

230 GOYA *3 May 1808*

The art they made from these events assaults the spectator with
full Baroque force, so that we too become witnesses; and in
several ways the *Death of Marat (Ill. 229)* and the *3 May 1808
(Ill. 230)* are the last great religious pictures. They mark too the
end of all Renaissance ideals; the blood that had been vigorously
restored to humanity after etiolation by artists like Bronzino is
here shed. And before they had painted these pictures, both
David and Goya had, as it were, crystallized their beliefs concerning art and nature. Desire for the truth had led, via such
pictures as Poussin's *Death of Germanicus (Ill. 208),* to David's
famous *Oath of the Horatii (Ill. 231),* a severe, exhortatory view
of antique history which delighted most of late eighteenth-
century Europe; regenerating art, much as Ledoux's archi-

tecture or Canova's sculpture might be supposed to do, substituting classical truth and moral fervour for Rococo falsity and light-heartedness. That is high art indeed.

Goya was less confident but more profound; he exposed the irrational weakness in our natures, and originally intended that the frontispiece of his book of etchings, the *Caprichos,* should show *The Sleep of Reason produces Monsters (Ill. 232).* After the self-portraits of Velazquez and Rembrandt comes this one, which shows Goya dreaming, his reason lulled to sleep, and the air thick with monsters. When he prepared this etching, Goya had not yet seen the results of reason's breakdown which the *3 May 1808* so vividly depicts; but he drafted a caption that serves as epitaph on the old half-Renaissance world into which he was born and as foretaste of the modern one into which he lived: 'Imagination, deserted by reason, begets impossible monsters. United with reason, she is the mother of all the arts, and the source of their wonders.'

231 DAVID *Oath of the Horatii* 1785

232 GOYA *The Sleep of Reason produces Monsters* 1799

233 TURNER *Ulysses deriding Polyphemus* 1829

234 CONSTABLE *The Haywain* 1821

CHAPTER SEVEN

Facing up to Reality

Eight years after Goya's death, John Constable delivered the first of his series of lectures on landscape painting at the Royal Institution in London. His opening phrases stated his own beliefs about painting: 'that it is *scientific* as well as *poetic*', and 'that imagination alone never did, and never can, produce works that are to stand by a comparison with *realities*' (the italics are his own). And Constable's own paintings *(Ill. 234)* reveal what he meant by 'realities', as well as showing the scientific truths which he sought to convey.

Not for the last time, an artist claimed that art was concerned with depicting what concretely *is*: 'la représentation des choses réelles' was to be Courbet's definition. No doubt by accident, Constable seemed to offer a standard by which we can judge art according to its verisimilitude to the exterior world. Such was probably the standard adopted by most people in the nineteenth century. There did not seem much place for exercise of the imagination, and though Turner's pictures *(Ill. 233)* may most immediately and obviously refute this, one must remember that all Ruskin's enormous, eloquent defence of Turner before his contemporaries rests on Turner's truth to nature. Indeed, Ruskin virtually provided as well a defence of the Impressionists (not so unexpectedly, because he shared their abhorrence of average French academic art), in his emphasis on the great 'modern' subject of landscape, in his quasi-scientific observations on colour and variation of light, and above all his stress on truth to appearances. No one before Ruskin had ever denigrated the old masters so violently – he proposed, among other things, the burning of the majority of Dutch landscape pictures – with a view to praising so violently a living painter. In other circumstances he might have championed not Turner but Monet.

It was a brave attempt, and it was also central to the problems which all the arts faced with the arrival of the nineteenth century. Ruskin himself increasingly could not see a solution.

No accident turned him from concern with art to concern with the society amid and for which art is produced; and it is no accident either that he, who had compared himself with Swift, should ultimately be drawn into despair and insanity. 'One day mimicking, the next destroying . . .', was how he saw his age's alternating attitude to the work of those who had made possible its intellectual and artistic life. This was the essence of the dilemma, and it is remarkable how much art produced by the nineteenth century can be divided into tame imitation of the past (buildings in Greek, Gothic or Renaissance style) and unprecedentedly violent rupture from it (Cézanne, Gauguin, Van Gogh).

Ruskin, like Tolstoy, proposed a middle way: truth to natural appearances should be wedded to moral truth. Unfortunately, the results meant – especially in the eyes of both these critics – a triumph of moral subject-matter; what was depicted came to matter more than how it was depicted. Tolstoy inevitably praised peasant pictures that unite everyone in the same feelings, indifferent to whether they were by Millet or Bastien-Lepage. And the champion of Turner finished by praising a dance 'of two girlies outside of a mushroom' by Kate Greenaway.

Constable's unfortunate, but typical, distrust of the imagination chimed only too well with the fears and aspirations of a world trying to settle down and forget the shock of the French Revolution. Increased literacy also proved deeply inhibiting to the visual arts, so often collapsing into sheer illustration during the nineteenth century. Never before had there been such a gap between contemporary estimates and those of posterity; Ruskin's *Modern Painters* is partly an attempt to make conservative opinion *avant-garde*. Art was, in many senses, up against reality: the reality of social conditions where it was not always apparent that anyone needed art, the reality of existence which was not heroic but prosperous or desperate, industrial and prosaic. Thackeray was merely one more person who welcomed artists cultivating 'the pathetic and the familiar' in place of the grandiloquent. He was glad to see the disappearance of such allegorical pictures as, in his own words: *'Britannia, Guarded by Religion and Neptune, Welcoming General Tomkins in the Temple of Glory'*. Yet, it ought to be only modified joy which saw that replaced by the intensely realized, realistic but no less absurd *Light of the World (Ill. 235)* by Holman Hunt, truest of the Pre-Raphaelite Brotherhood. The moral purpose here may be admirable; the artistic discipline –

235 HOLMAN HUNT
*The Light of the
World* 1853

working through cold nights in a real orchard – certainly was. But for all the surface reality of eye-deceiving weeds, wooden door and tin lantern, inner significance is absent; indeed, these very properties, like the tasteless crown of thorns and jewels, betray the basic banality. And Carlyle cruelly revealed this when he said in front of the picture, and the painter, that it was 'empty make-believe'.

In no medium was the dilemma posed by reality made more apparent than in sculpture, an art less utilitarian than architecture and more public than painting. And it is probably true to say that no medium sank to a lower level, where technical competence merely underlined artistic poverty. The squares of every large European city are, like graveyards, full of nineteenth-century marble and bronze statues where reality is enshrined in top-hatted figures, sculpted down to the last crease of trouser and welt of boot. Not that such factual detail is in itself the flaw; it proved no solution to dress up Queen Victoria and Prince Albert in Anglo-Saxon costume, as did William Theed, a pupil of the much more famous John Gibson. Gibson's life-size 'Tinted Venus' represents the logical end of realism: a statue apparently as successful and popular in mid-nineteenth-century Rome as had been David's Oath of the Horatii sixty-five years earlier. Gibson's is the last echo of neo-classicism, less severe than that of Canova – under whom he had studied – and here passing into a rigid yet waxen insipidity (Ill. 236).

Historically, his statue closes a tradition which goes back to Praxiteles (Ill. 32). Its conscious stillness almost demands to be disturbed; the best the nineteenth century could do was to put animation back into sculpture, first with the Rococo feverishness of Carpeaux whose work (Ill. 237) is almost pictorially fluid. Form seems eaten away from within by energy, while light falls over such surfaces as survive with flickering effect. There is a romantic elegance also in Carpeaux's best sculpture which made him a suitable choice to create a monument to Watteau. His fluidity of form – one escape out of straightforward realism – is carried even further by the sole nineteenth-century Italian sculptor of any importance, Medardo Rosso. His is a positive impressionism, remarkable daring and revolutionary for its period, in which the forms flow and coagulate without too much regard for what is realistic. His Conversation in a Garden (Ill. 238), of 1893, is scarcely representational at all; but the three beaky shapes are dynamic eruptions of bronze that seem still molten, its surface exciting in its alternations of

236 GIBSON 'Tinted Venus'
1850

237 CARPEAUX la Danse 1869

238 ROSSO Conversation in a Garden 1893

smooth and rough texture. The emphasis is on material, on movement and freedom – the artist's freedom to re-shape reality into forms more vital than could be found by modelling three little lifelike dolls conversing in a recognizable, miniature garden.

The problem of lifelikeness is acutely enshrined in the work of Rodin, the greatest sculptor of the nineteenth century but one who ends a tradition rather than opens up profoundly new possibilities. 'Three centuries of mannerism, academicism and decadence', according to Herbert Read, separate him from Michelangelo. Unfortunately, even were this true, strains of mannerism, academicism and decadence are all apparent in Rodin himself: sometimes so academically realistic that he could be accused of casting a statue from a live model, and certainly mannered, if not decadent, in the *Balzac (Ill. 239)*. There is, of course, no reason why a great work of art should not be mannered; the *Balzac* is highly personal, deliberately subjective, conveying an 'idea' of Balzac rather than providing the nineteenth century with its average concept of a portrait statue. Yet there is a surface of realism even here, a tendency to describe, so that what at first glance must have once seemed shockingly unnatural is quickly perceived nowadays to be the effect of a coat wrapped round the figure in a theatrical gesture. The result is a sort of realistic rhetoric, removed from the ordinary without being fused into something beyond the commonplace. Rodin has some affinity with G. F. Watts in England, and more than a touch of Victor Hugo. An 'hélas' must qualify our recognition of Rodin as the greatest of nineteenth-century sculptors.

Although architecture had the advantage of being free from the weight of traditional realism, it was deeply bound to tradition as such. Indeed, it was plagued by a historicism which consistently quoted from the styles of the past, making Renaissance clubs and banks, Gothic town halls and churches – not to speak of its more bizarre excursions into hybrid styles supposed suitable for museums and university buildings. But though it is usual to judge the whole architecture of the nineteenth century by some of these famous aberrations, that is no more just than judging its painting solely by the Royal Academy and French Salon artists. In many ways, it was actually in architecture that the century made its finest contribution to art – regardless, incidentally, of whether that contribution has proved influential. Bridges, stations, office and emporium buildings – and

239 RODIN *Balzac* 1897

exhibition ones like Paxton's Crystal Palace *(Ill. 240)* – show that the century was capable of original feats, particularly where it could feel confident that art and mechanical progress had come together.

In the early years of the century, the idea of the planned city, inspired by the modern example of Napoleon's Paris and the antique one of imperial Rome, produced some of the finest solutions to a practical yet agreeable urban environment. Natural scenery, whether wild or tamed into park and garden, also found its place in these schemes – most obviously in the splendid London designed and partly achieved under the Prince Regent and Nash. The neo-classicism which served Schinkel in Berlin for temple-style museums *(Ill. 241)* is more florid and yet more frankly scenographic in Nash's Regent's Park terraces *(Ill. 242)*: but there is a sense of order and elegance in this palatial way of creating private houses which contrasts with the huddled terraces and uncouth Baroque of mid-Victorian architecture. For some reason Nash has remained a despised figure in English architectural history; his very grandness and cool symmetry have been stigmatized, probably through a Puritan confusion about the aims of art, in comparison with the 'bold independence' of Philip Webb and Norman Shaw. The visual effect of Shaw's own house *(Ill. 243)*, built in 1875, as well as being prophetic of miles of later nineteenth- and twentieth-century suburban semi-detached villas, is so aggressively awful as to suggest that it was designed not by Norman, but by George Bernard, Shaw. In Nash's architecture, Vitruvian principles still retain their classic validity; and man can better measure himself against the unit of the pillar than amid the gables, leaded panes and fretwork balconies that Shaw presumably thought 'truer' than stucco capitals.

Yet architecture, no more than the other arts, need necessarily obey a single law of truth – whether truth to function or to materials. Schinkel, who was in London at the time Nash was replanning it, was capable of Gothic-style buildings and monuments – in which cast iron was used. Nash executed a Gothic country-house for himself as opposed to his opulent classical town-house in Regent Street, where the Quadrant columns were also of disguised cast iron. While Paxton's Crystal Palace may seem a triumph of 'modern' style, prophetic of later architectural developments in iron and glass, muddled historicism could create masterpieces really in no style at all: faintly monstrous and overblown public buildings like the British Houses

273

240 PAXTON Crystal Palace, London 1850–1
241 SCHINKEL Altes Museum, Berlin 1824–8
242 NASH Cumberland Terrace, London. Begun 1826–7

243 SHAW Architect's own house, London 1875

244 BARRY and PUGIN Houses of Parliament, London 1840–60

of Parliament *(Ill. 244)*, the unique child of Barry's Italianate classicism and Pugin's Gothic passion. Pugin, inevitably, loathed the Crystal Palace; he called it the 'Crystal Humbug', hinting thus at its falseness – unfortunately, since it is fitter for its function than his own building and quite free from superfluous ornament. Yet Pugin's romantic Gothic pile, partly dependent for its picturesque effect on the river and convenient mist, remains an achievement as well as a warning. The same is true of Charles Garnier's Opéra *(Ill. 245)* in Paris: a monument of highly personal Baroque, equally effective on its site, but almost grossly evocative of pleasure, as abandoned as the late pictures of Ingres. No performance inside the Opéra could equal its pleasure-dome exterior, and no parliamentary debate could approach the unworldly, religious air of Pugin's seat of government.

Of the two buildings, Garnier's was closer to contemporary needs; indeed, it led to a whole style of theatre architecture. It had been evolved for public social use. Although the odd great

245 CHARLES GARNIER Opéra, Paris 1861–74 ▶

building might emerge from brooding on the past, some solution beyond imitation was needed. 'Stations are the cathedrals of our century', wrote an English critic in 1875. Destruction was necessary – as Ruskin perhaps saw, certainly feared. It was not destruction of old buildings, however, but of preconceptions – extending beyond the forms used to a realization that whole new types of buildings would indeed prove as relevant to the nineteenth century as cathedrals to medieval man.

With new types of building went new materials, first iron and later steel. The first results were technically triumphs of engineering rather than architecture: bridges spanned in an unprecedented way and the huge yet skeletal Eiffel Tower (of 1889) which is the Gothic dream of a weightless, open-work spire (as at Freiburg, *Ill. 62*) come true on a vast scale in the modern world. Emphasis on engineering – on craft or science, rather than on the 'fine art' of architecture – meant a concentration on essentials, turning away from decoration and ornament, to produce such a stark result as the Monadnock Block in Chicago *(Ill. 249)*. After the richly Baroque Opéra of Garnier, the theatre designed by another architect of by chance the same surname, Tony Garnier, is effectively compact and plain *(Ill. 246)*. It illustrates his belief that in architecture 'Truth alone is beautiful.' His theatre is true to its materials of reinforced concrete and glass. Facing up to the reality of modern needs and modern materials is not something to be dodged but enjoyed;

246 TONY GARNIER Theatre, Industrial City 1901–4

and Garnier's design – dating from 1901–4 – retains an extraordinary validity. Only one year younger than Garnier, Adolf Loos produced a few years later in the Steiner House *(Ill. 247)*, at Vienna, the quintessential statement about the beauty of truth – truth seen here in a ruled-out, uncompromising simplicity, its structure unhindered by useless ornament. This is crisply reasonable and elegant domestic architecture, beside which Norman Shaw's picturesque house is illogical and sentimental, and not particularly 'true'.

Not every modern nineteenth-century architect was prepared totally to banish ornament. It is very much present in the work of the American Louis Sullivan, whose Wainwright Building *(Ill. 248)*, in St Louis, looks almost Expressionist and highly decorated in comparison with the exactly contemporary Monadnock Block in Chicago. It is not just Sullivan's building that faces two ways, but his own ideas; he condemned ornament as a luxury, and the Wainwright Building is basically a well-planned grid of regular piers and windows. Yet the top storey writhes in a very different rhythm, with round windows piercing lushly carved foliage. Sullivan restricts ornament,

276

247 LOOS Steiner House, Vienna 1910

without dispensing with it, but in the buildings of Antoni Gaudí the ornament virtually is the architecture. It is really a latent Gothicism which produced his extraordinary fluid effects, where stone seems to have melted and been moulded as if it were wax – and into this wax miscellaneous objects appear inserted. Alberti could have comprehended the principles of Loos' Steiner House, but Gaudí's utter novelty and almost shocking powers of fantasy are unparalleled in earlier architecture. His Sagrada Familia *(Ill. 250)* at Barcelona is not at all what Ruskin had in mind in saying that 'Ornamentation is the principal part of architecture'; yet it might be justified by that sentence. And, after too much purity and truth to material and function, Gaudi's architecture – which was after all actually built – may seem to have achieved something by its relentless breaking of every rule. For Constable's 'realities', it has substituted imagination of the wildest kind.

In painting itself, conflict revolved round the artist's liberty and the public's reserves over that liberty. At bottom, what was increasingly in doubt was whether society needed art. For this reason, men like William Morris denounced the whole social structure which appeared 'incurably vicious'. His solution was destruction of evil machinery and a return to an impossible

248 SULLIVAN
Wainwright Building,
St Louis 1890–1

249 BURNHAM and
ROOT Monadnock
Block, Chicago 1891

250 GAUDÍ Church of Sagrada Familia, Barcelona. Begun 1884

Middle Ages of primitive handicrafts. Wilde was much closer
to a solution when he said – already in 1882 – 'All machinery
may be beautiful. . . .' In 1901 Sullivan's pupil, Frank Lloyd
Wright, one of the creators of modern architecture, read a
panegyric on our 'age of steel and steam': exciting, prophetic
of twentieth-century developments, but finding little room for
the painter in 'the Machine Age'.

The Industrial Revolution and the French Revolution had catapulted the painter into a very difficult world, one experienced by and responded to, in different ways, by such artists as David and Goya. To some extent, their attitudes are inherited by Constable and Turner – both invoking truth to sensations yet with contrasting results. The proclamation of 'le Réalisme' made by Courbet in 1855, and presented pictorially in *'Bonjour, Monsieur Courbet' (Ill. 251)* of the previous year, remains the central concern for all painters. Increasingly it was realised, as Courbet's champion, Champfleury, said: 'there are no bad images for interested eyes'; but few artists painted themselves hailed as genius-Saviour on the road not to Emmaus but to Montpellier. Constable's *Haywain (Ill. 234)* is real enough, solid, even stolid, deliberately commonplace in subject-matter, and yet perhaps rather romantic in its associations of rural peace and lingering belief in the moral value of 'nature'. Turner's nature, as seen in *Ulysses deriding Polyphemus (Ill. 233)*, is romantically exciting, rather in the stirring, slightly vulgar manner of Wagner's early operas. Instead of Constable's pastoral scenery and summer sky, we encounter a whole range of exotic effects with blazing sky and glassy-cool sea, an elemental pageant amid which the sunset-dyed ship is itself a half-ridiculous and half-effective symbol. Turner was also the creator of pictures like the *Evening Star (Ill. 253)*, quietly revolutionary in dispensing with subject-matter, a tone poem rather than an opera. This absolute stillness of sea and sky, broken only by the minute crystal point of a single star, is truth to nature so intensely realized that beside it even the best contemporary landscapes of Caspar David Friedrich *(Ill. 252)* look contrived, 'Gothick' in their spookiness, and faintly dead in actual handling of paint.

In different ways, both Constable and Turner retreat before the urban social conditions of their century – indeed, before the whole spectacle of humanity. Their concept of nature is of a world not made by man and scarcely intruded on by him; like Friedrich's group, mankind's role is that of spectator. This does not make such painters' work any less great as art, but it divorces it from concern with the reality of life around them. The landscapes of Corot *(Ill. 254)* have a timeless innocence and a sort of Arcadian tranquillity which reflect the artist's own tranquil innocence. This 'nature' promises to turn into Impressionism, and Corot began with a tonal accuracy which unfortunately he could not retain.

251 COURBET *'Bonjour, Monsieur Courbet'* 1854

Dramatic human reality, in shocking, topical terms, had already been thrust before the public in Géricault's *Raft of the 'Medusa' (Ill. 255),* resuming as it were where David's *Death of Marat (Ill. 229)* had stopped. And there unheroic humanity is shown suffering in a way that can leave no spectator uninvolved – overwhelmed, more likely, by the size and emotional power of a painting which perhaps proves too extravagantly sensational. Ordinary life does not offer many opportunities for depicting such accumulated horror. Increasingly, and with less artistic energy, painters were to provoke such *frissons* by turning to famous incidents from past history: there queens were executed, cardinals expired, and the little Princes waited ominously in the Tower *(Ill. 257)*. With Delaroche, the story alone provides the emotional impact; he simply illustrates an historical anecdote in a way typical of the many mid-nineteenth-century Salon and Royal Academy painters. Indeed, Millais was later to paint the same subject, with even more flagrant *tableau vivant* air. This is exactly the sort of art against which Courbet rebelled – even more by his subject-matter, however, than by his technique. *'Bonjour, Monsieur Courbet' (Ill. 251)* is an almost crude breath of air, rough, tough, and arrogantly honest after the polished waxwork insipidity of Delaroche. Daumier's works *(Ill. 260)* more subtly confirm a determination to reveal what life was really like – interpreting with indignation or compassion, not merely recording it; in his work the humblest reality is faced up to and transfigured into art.

Daumier was one of a disparate trio indicated by Baudelaire when in reviewing the Salon exhibition of 1845 he said: '. . . let us love them all three'. The other two were Delacroix and

253 TURNER *The Evening Star* Before 1840 ▶

254 COROT *Pont de Narni* 1826/7

252 FRIEDRICH *Man and Woman gazing at the Moon* 1819

Ingres. Delacroix's subject-matter often scarcely differs from that of Delaroche, yet Baudelaire could praise him for colour that was 'scientific'. Delacroix himself retouched portions of the *Massacre de Scio (Ill. 256)* after seeing some of Constable's pictures in Paris, notably *The Haywain (Ill. 234)*. Although the *Massacre* was an appalling contemporary event, and Delacroix sympathized with the massacred Greeks, the picture is more stirring and colourful than shocking. It does not impact on the spectator with the force of Géricault, but it has its own energy and excitement – its brushwork vibrant in comparison with Delaroche's glossy surface. Strictly speaking, Delacroix's colour was not scientific, but in its very vitality there was a freshness and truth which would prove an inspiration to the Impressionists. It is this colour that gives conviction to scenes which otherwise strike rather a contrived note. Delacroix seems to urge on a basically sluggish temperament, one really quite at home in his own century, to conceive massacres and atrocities, wild horses and bleeding bodies; they are tribute of a not always happy kind to Delacroix's belief in human existence as the central concern of art.

255 GÉRICAULT *Raft of the 'Medusa'* 1819

256 DELACROIX *Massacre de Scio* 1824

257 DELAROCHE
*Little Princes in the
Tower* 1831

What Delacroix makes natural-seeming, Ingres refines into
the ideal. It used to be commonplace to see Ingres as an isolated
figure – a hot-house camellia blooming eccentrically amid
rising, *plein-air* naturalism – but his obsessive concern with
certain motifs links him to Cézanne, and his superb linear gifts
not merely inspired Degas but are part of an undying tradition.
Like Klee, Ingres can often be found taking a line for a walk,
and he already obeyed Klee's self-administered dictum: 'the
essence of the subject must always become visible, even if this
is impossible in nature'. Manipulating the surface properties of
reality, Ingres keeps producing effects that are virtually surreal
in their obsessive detail. His wonderful portraits *(Ill. 258)* are
remarkable for everything except, ironically, naturalism. To
some extent Ingres solved better than anyone else the dilemma
of the mid-nineteenth century. He was, in many ways, the
'painter of modern life' demanded by Baudelaire. Allowed to
exercise his imagination on the past, he became ludicrous and
pedestrian. Confronted by the prosaic reality of Madame
Moitessier, opulent, over-upholstered, a modern example of
conspicuous waste – a subject Delacroix would have turned
from and Daumier caricatured – Ingres became inspired. He
stalked her, plotted her, over the years, and finally evolved the
double-headed image where art has fused a masterpiece out of
heaviness and banality.

286

258 INGRES *Madame Moitessier* 1844/56

259 MADOX BROWN *Work* 1852–65

260 DAUMIER *Third Class Carriage* 1863/5

261 MANET *Déjeuner sur l'Herbe* 1863

There is something primitively tenacious and tenaciously primitive in Ingres' technique. Like the Pre-Raphaelite Brotherhood in England, but nearly half a century earlier, Ingres had perceived that art needed purification. Reality must be looked at clearly – with something of that clarity of outline (and clarity of purpose) which might be found in early, pre-Raphael paintings. A group of German artists in Rome – the so-called Nazarenes – had at the beginning of the nineteenth century produced a surreal type of picture, mingling literary subject-matter with a technique whose very precision contradicts optical truth: showing us what is known to be there, rather than what is immediately seen, and paying much more attention to line than to true colour relationships. The Pre-Raphaelite Brotherhood was more amateurish and muddled in its aims, while proclaiming with Ruskin the necessity of going 'to nature in all singleness of heart, selecting nothing, rejecting nothing'. Their nature remained quite unnatural, even though it had usually been the result of prolonged study.

289

Holman Hunt's *Light of the World (Ill. 235)* marks the failure of creativity when this principle was applied to an imaginative religious idea. The failure of *Work (Ill. 259)* by Ford Madox Brown – a picture that should have combined Courbet's 'réalisme' with Daumier's social concern – is ultimately a failure of fusion. This is not so surprising when Brown's own working methods are considered: 'Worked well at the shawl in the open air', he recorded of a small portion of this crowded picture. 'Now that the pattern is all drawn and covered with a tint, I put-in the outdoor effect.'

Other outdoor effects *(Ill. 261, 265)*, achieved not long afterwards in France, would prove artistically more valid. Like Ingres, like Delacroix, like Courbet, like the Pre-Raphaelites, the Impressionists were first to be attacked and then assimilated. The 'truth' they shared was on first sight too naked – literally so in Manet's *Déjeuner sur l'Herbe (Ill.261)*, though this is not truly an Impressionist picture. Yet, in the end, their essentially bourgeois, optimistic art – obsessed with appearances – became the standard by which thousands of people have gone on judging painting, to be disconcerted by styles and subject-matter which are superficially less related to the ordinary world we see. No artistic revolution, perhaps, is easier to understand. The Impressionists turned away from literary or historical subject-matter, remaining altogether somewhat uninterested in *la condition humaine*; they painted the ordinary world as a spectacle in which they were scarcely engaged except visually. Renoir's wet day in Paris *(Ill. 262)* is as enchanted as some picture of nymphs by Boucher, and this is one of his most ordered and coherent paintings, touched with lessons learned from Ingres and Cézanne. The hedonism released by Impressionist art rushes on every visual experience with a greediness that may eventually exhaust the spectator – and the artist too. Yet the whole movement was quintessentially formed by its period: an age without faith in imaginative myth or religion, challenged by, but equally proud of, its scientific discoveries, its industrial and urban development. And by inventing the camera, the nineteenth century had challenged in particular painting of all the arts.

It brought to a head the whole crisis of reality. Impressionism, the movement most closely linked to photography, did not at first seem to feel the challenge. In the paintings of Monet, the truest and most typical of Impressionists, there seemed to be a camera-like objectivity: the seizing in paint on

262 RENOIR *les Parapluies c.* 1884

263 DEGAS *Pouting* 1873–5

265 MONET *la Seine à Argenteuil* 1874

the actual spot of what is visible to the eye, catching momentary effects, fracturing solid reality into the dancing visual impression of fragments of light and colour *(Ill. 265)*. This may be how we see; it is less informative about what we see and experience. Just as so much great nineteenth-century painting dodged out of the city into the countryside, so Impressionism dodged the question of the real in concentrating on the visible. A very strong sense of the importance of physical facts, almost a moral sense of truth-telling, had lain behind Constable's pictures; in Turner, whose work Monet saw in England in 1870 (before the first Impressionist exhibition), nature is invoked in some eternal cosmic drama, symbol of the artist's own interior turmoil. Both English painters are involved with what they depict, and depict more than they see. It is legitimate to ask, what had Monet to say *about* the Seine at Argenteuil? And it is hard to find in his picture anything that could not be seen by the average spectator, with or without a camera.

Yet Impressionism, in this sense, was much shorter-lived than any of the painters associated with it. It had developed

293

haphazardly and gradually; and gradually it ceased to be practised. In Monet's very late pictures, objects have dissolved into pools of colour, and the relation to exterior reality is tenuous to the point of non-existence. The whole Impressionist movement was the last attempt of Western painting to deal scientifically with Constable's 'realities'. Instead of the outer eye, it would be the inner one that henceforward accounted for more. In Monet's art a positive brainlessness can be detected, but with some other painters associated, more or less willingly, with Impressionism the position is rather different. Renoir was much more directly stirred by life in the sense of people – ravishing, pretty people of such dangerously feathery prettiness that he himself came to correct his style; and the left-hand portion of *les Parapluies* shows a new, non-impressionistic sense of form. Degas had never painted in the open air; he was interested in catching the 'essential gestures' of life, making reality significant by his intense acid concentration and brilliantly unexpected compositional angles – stimulated by newly-imported Japanese prints and by photography, but not

266 SEURAT *la Grande Jatte* 1884–6

267 HOMER *Gloucester Farm* 1874

269 SARGENT *Graham Robertson* 1895

8 WHISTLER *Carlyle* 1873

emulating either. Even when he utilized photographs, he produced something vividly personal *(Ill. 263).*

In Manet there existed almost surreal ambiguities; they are present in the *Déjeuner sur l'Herbe*, which still possesses a challenging air, and they give their force to the silvery-sombre *Meal in the Studio (Ill. 264)*, a 'still life' indeed. These are modern 'history pictures', without overt incident and yet strangely removed from anything resembling a 'slice of life'. They are partly traditional pictures painted with no greater novelty of style than could be paralleled in the work of Velazquez or Goya. Reserved, dignified, undramatic, Manet's art is perhaps the most baffling of all the art produced by the nineteenth century. It is certainly full of the recognizable world and closes a tradition. Even there an ambiguity lurks, for Manet died prematurely of gangrene, whereas Degas, Monet and

271 REDON *Seahorse in an Undersea Landscape.* Before 1909

Renoir were all exceptionally long-lived – into the active lifetime of Matisse and Picasso. It is, historically at least, a sobering thought that they could all have seen Duchamp's 'signed' *Fountain (Ill. 1).*

Other painters came pointedly to challenge Impressionism. However different from each other, Cézanne, Van Gogh and Gauguin were in search of a reality deeper than that of visual impressions. They were much more aggressive, artistically speaking, in their attitude to their material, and more pro-

297

272 TOULOUSE-LAUTREC
Jardin de Paris: Jane Avril
1893

foundly imaginative. These three alone may be said to have released painting from its naturalistic obsessions. They were more violently divorced from public success than the Impressionists. Manet – who thought himself badly treated – may seem a popular success in comparison with the period's total neglect of Van Gogh. The importance of this trio must lie in their art, but their historical importance for the twentieth century is so colossal that it almost conceals their own personal achievements. Cubism, Fauvism, Expressionism – merely to begin a list of movements and styles that find their source in these painters – can too easily colour their art as we look back. From the point of view of modern pioneering, they lead in association with the magic, glowing unreality of Odilon Redon, whose dream-pictures *(Ill. 271)* are the vision of the inner eye; and the work of Redon's friend 'le Douanier' Rousseau, whose natural world *(Ill. 270)* is scarcely less visionary and magical; and the monumental, intellectual, achievement of Seurat *(Ill. 266)*, the painter whose attitude most closely approaches that of Cézanne.

273 BEARDSLEY *Ascension of St Rose of Lima* 1896

274 CÉZANNE *Mont Sainte-Victoire* 1885–7

It is necessary to see each achievement of the nineteenth century in its own right, before turning every great artist into being also a prophet. And amid the giant figures, those of such individual but not towering talents as Whistler and Sargent can easily be overlooked. Their American origin is a hint towards the slow but distinct emergence of an American School of painting. Where Whistler and Sargent sought Europe and the experience of European old masters like Velazquez, Winslow Homer remained – despite one European stay – much more nationally-rooted in his subject-matter (*Ill. 267*) and his attitudes. Homer's vision is very consciously of what he has seen; it is typical of its century in its realism and also in its tendency to lapse into illustration. Free from this danger, Whistler's art wavers uncertainly in a way surprising for such a would-be trenchant personality. Some lack of invention or, perhaps more truly, some failure of artistic energy, prevents his work from making any consistent impact. He

275 VAN GOGH *The Sower* 1888

remains the painter of one or two familiar masterpieces – like the *Carlyle (Ill. 268)* – which manage to be boldly austere and tonally effective, true to the artist's vision of life re-arranged, but also true to life.

While Whistler has always been treated respectfully, if not necessarily with enthusiasm, Sargent has been absurdly denigrated. His fashionable success as a portrait painter served him ill with posterity, but even his brashest, slickest pictures leave a distinct image – where Whistler grows vague and indeterminate. When he was quite free to choose his sitter, Sargent could paint with great sensitivity combined with a genuine romanticism. Clothes provide a permanent drama in his pictures, and the subtle portrait of Graham Robertson *(Ill. 269)* originated in Sargent's being attracted by the long overcoat Robertson wore.

There are, equally, certain isolated great artists who conform to no pattern of the period. There is considerable technical

301

importance in the work of Toulouse-Lautrec, whose posters and lithographs are 'modern' art: art in their achievement, and modern in their use of new processes of reproduction. Painting as a fine art is jolted into a more up-to-date world; the aura of the 'original' naturally diminishes when it is designed to be mechanically reproduced. Lautrec's brilliant draughtsmanship *(Ill. 272)* still triumphs in reproduction; and he is engaged, wittily as well as poignantly, with his subject-matter in ways closer to Daumier than to Degas. His gas-lit inferno is cheerfully humane compared with the satanic perversions of another great artist – if a painter, one only in black and white. Beardsley had been influenced by Lautrec's posters and he wrote his own remarkably accurate prophecy of the future: 'London will soon be resplendent with advertisements, and against a leaden sky skysigns will trace their formal arabesque.' All Beardsley's work was intended for reproduction, though it is in book-illustration rather than in posters that his exotic, erotic style best flowered. For his own erotic book, *Under the Hill,* he produced the *Ascension of St Rose of Lima (Ill. 273),* a much more successful religious picture than the *Light of the World,* in so far as its theme excites and creatively engages the artist. It also perfectly expresses the fact that art is not a reproduction of what already exists but a making visible of other things.

That paraphrase of Klee's dictum about art certainly illuminates the solution practised in different ways by Cézanne, Van Gogh and Gauguin. Yet while it is true that they sought for a reality beyond the transitory – Cézanne seeking it through an intellectual geometry, a structure of order, which recalls Constable, and Van Gogh by a passionate expressionism akin to Turner's – they all sought it in nature. Nature still meant the open-air countryside, and the peasants or workers most closely connected with the country. Less strangely than it might appear, the spirit of the Preface to *Lyrical Ballads* still haunts their art; rustic life – in Gauguin's case primitive Tahitian life – seeming the condition where 'the essential passions of the heart find a better soil . . .'. Thus, in subject-matter these great pioneers of modern painting are largely true to the tradition of their own century. In the landscape around Aix *(Ill. 274),* or in a still-life, Cézanne found significance enough. Given these objects, familiar and knowable (in a way no person can possibly be), he proceeded to reduce them to their essential forms: that is, nature slowly revealed itself to him, in colour as much as form. It is not too much to see a romantic concept even of the 'history

276 VAN GOGH
White Roses 1890

picture' lying behind his dreams of fusing the human body and natural environment, trying to make in *les Grandes Baigneuses* *(Ill. 277)* a final statement on a theme which had entered Western art with Giorgione *(Ill. 151)*. Renoir too was to come, late in life and in his own terms, to make his contribution to this general theme, re-doing Rubens as it were, in the richly fleshy *Judgment of Paris (Ill. 278)*.

Van Gogh's was altogether a much more urgent vision; it could not fail to upset – and indeed it is recorded as having upset Cézanne, to whom his pictures seemed a madman's work. And this is tragically apt, because Van Gogh's pictures are the work of someone fighting to preserve his sanity: 'trying to remain true', he wrote of his art, 'is perhaps a remedy in fighting the disease . . .'. To some extent, Van Gogh's pitiful life, harried by the threat of madness, tends to obscure the resolute quality of

277 CÉZANNE *les Grandes Baigneuses* 1898–1905

279 GAUGUIN *Whispered Words* 1892

his imagination; his pictures are as lucid as his letters, with a blazing intensity of colour that he himself compared to 'effects like stained glass'. The sheer boldness of pictures like *The Sower (Ill. 275),* where the influence of Japanese prints blends with Provençal countryside, results in a vision which is at once more coherent and more exciting than, for example, Monet's Impressionism. The purple plain and the vast yellow sun are not what had been seen before, but they are immediately convincing as an artistic metaphor. They have become real – more vividly real than nature itself.

The same is true of Van Gogh's still-lives, living but seldom still, which do not penetrate to an underlying essence analytically, as Cézanne's do, but pluck out instinctively the hot, essential heart of things. His sunflowers spin like fireworks of bright colour but he can also achieve the cool sea-green vividness of *White Roses (Ill. 276)* painted within three months of his death. No less than the more familiar sunflowers, this

305

picture is a symbol: it is intensely eloquent of that calm and harmony, only briefly recovered by the painter and for which he had always been searching. This is a green and white paradise for Van Gogh, as much his haven as the South Sea Island scene *(Ill. 279)* proved for Gauguin.

The incompatible characters of the two men are hinted at in these two pictures. In the yellow house at Arles they had tried unsuccessfully to live and paint together, but Gauguin's urge towards the primitive unsettled him even before he quarrelled with Van Gogh. Instead of merely using the exotic effects of oriental prints, Gauguin was directly to experience – and come to full artistic life in – an exotic world. An artistic tendency to retreat before urban industrial reality becomes geographical escape. His flight from Europe was itself prophetic of the discovery of non-Western art which would soon have significant effect on European painting (e.g. Picasso's *Demoiselles d'Avignon Ill. 292)*. In Tahiti, his wonderful colour bloomed to express an ideal mythical world, peopled by physically splendid beings who really seem to achieve a harmony with the brilliant flora amid which they live *(Ill. 279)*. Man and open-air nature are brought together, just as they are in the late work of Renoir and Cézanne. The sun still shines on warm flesh; nature is beneficent and somehow *au fond* ordered, truthful and peaceful.

Yet these were visions achieved in what Frank Lloyd Wright was by 1901 calling our 'age of steel and steam . . . the Machine Age'. Is nature really so ordered and peaceful? And what is truth? Do human beings not have some psychological perceptions and pressures more disturbing than calming? A person on a frighteningly steep bridge in an alarmingly wavering landscape suddenly puts hands up to face and screams *(Ill. 280)*. Munch's picture is of 1893, but in Bacon's work its echoes are still with us *(Ill. 312)*.

280 MUNCH *The Scream* 1893

281 MODIGLIANI
Italian Woman

282 PICASSO
Woman in a Blue Dress 1941

CHAPTER EIGHT

'We must go on searching'

At any period an artist might make such a statement, but in fact these words come from Paul Klee's aphoristic essay 'On Modern Art'. They may well seem to have a special application to twentieth-century art, so consciously and so continually searching that it has taken on some of the dangerous ephemerality of fashion. Media as well as styles have changed more and more rapidly as the search has continued. The very categories of what constitutes pictures and sculpture have themselves changed and expanded, and sometimes merged. Most people are less dogmatic than they would have been fifty years ago about defining what is – or is not – a work of art. Duchamp's 'ready-mades' have proved extraordinarily prophetic; but it has become increasingly difficult to shock and astound the public. Only too conscious now of the giant errors made by critics and public in the nineteenth century, our century has largely tried to protect itself by calmly accepting everything – but probably *au fond* caring for nothing much which has been produced. The sixteenth-century Venetian who disliked Tintoretto's work, or those many Victorians who were moved by Holman Hunt's *Light of the World*, at least expressed a judgment of taste. Posterity – if there is a posterity – may well wonder whether art any longer mattered to us, so little does it really affect anybody's life or interests outside very narrow circles.

This is the first difficulty underlying any survey of art in our own century. Historically, we can hardly be expected yet to comprehend its significance. Aesthetically, there has been little attempt to challenge or revalue the lazy estimates which have grown like weeds on the one-time battlefields of taste: Picasso is more famous than Matisse, and hence can be presumed to be a greater artist. Mediterranean culture and tradition exercise a glamour over the Anglo-Saxon world which guarantees a preference for art engendered within that magic territory; it is bad luck to be born a Northern artist and preserve a 'Northern' concern with emotion, expression or fantasy. Indeed, the sole prejudice that is developed and popular among art critics is against German twentieth-century art; Dessau has no emotive power compared with Aix-en-Provence.

There is another difficulty, connected with appreciation, which histories of art particularly like to emphasize: the break with previous visual traditions which can certainly be made to look abrupt if a Kandinsky is placed next to a Courbet. But this sort of comparison does less than justice to an artist like Modigliani – sculptor, it should be remembered, as well as painter – who managed to be 'modern' partly through response to art of the past; and his incisive images *(Ill. 281)*, graceful yet keen, deserve re-appreciation now that figurative art is again respectable. Of course it is true that the early twentieth century deliberately achieved several artistic revolutions which violently overthrew what was then currently passing as traditional – most patently in the sort of illusionistic realism practised by painting. But the presumed difficulty is only a Western one, and then came into existence only at the Renaissance. The contemporaries of Duccio would probably have experienced little difficulty in appreciating Kandinsky; certainly they could have responded to Klee. Byzantine mosaics, the Lindisfarne Gospels, Gothic stained glass are merely some of the examples of pre-Renaissance art which were able to invent images without copying exterior reality. We do not hear that the public experienced any bafflement in understanding such art; and one should reflect before saying that this was only because the public had faith in the concepts expressed by the art, since a modern public should also be presumed to have faith – in the concept of artistic inspiration. If one generation can believe in angels, another should believe in genius. And how the Gothic artist boldly trusted to art is shown by the eagle vase *(Ill. 66)* of Abbot Suger; without too much incongruity this could be associated with Picasso's sculpture created out of found objects. In both we enjoy, and are meant to enjoy, pleasure of recognition combined with pleasure of surprise: the vase become an eagle's body, bicycle handlebars become a bull's horns *(Ill. 283)*. And in neither case are we troubled that the result is not like a real bull's head or a real eagle. What the results do resemble, however, are ideas that existed in their creators' minds.

They too – the ideas – have their reality. Indeed, their absence from the work of, for example, Monet is what makes it so dangerously thin and dependent on what is seen. Munch's

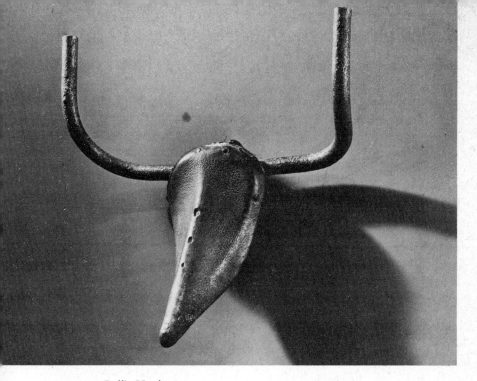

283 PICASSO *Bull's Head* 1943

Scream (Ill. 280) is a refusal to surrender to that outside envelope of reality which had clung like a shirt of Nessus to most nineteenth-century painters. He deliberately shakes that concept of harmony and gentle, intimist optimism that is exuded from the pictures of the 'Nabis'. Bonnard and Vuillard were close contemporaries of Munch. Bonnard's diluted Impressionism marks the end of a tradition, dying agreeably in patches of sunlight, domestic interiors and faceless, not very vigorous nudes. Vuillard is a much more sharply decorative painter *(Ill. 284)*, less in thrall to what is seen and more capable therefore of giving artistic independence to shapes and – especially – colour. What is certainly hinted at in Vuillard becomes triumphant fact in the work of Matisse. Explaining what characterized the movement he led, to be dubbed Fauvism, Matisse stated: 'we completely abandoned imitative colour'. He himself early painted a blue male nude, disconcerting even his friends – just as Picasso's friends were to be disconcerted when they first saw *les Demoiselles d'Avignon (Ill. 292)*.

Where Munch sought an intensity of feeling expressed partly through subject-matter, Matisse made colour in itself serve as expression. It is the coloured surface which is important in the red version of the *Dinner Table (Ill. 285)*: the table is as flat as the wallpaper, and the epergnes with fruit no more solid than the flower motifs which cover table-cloth and wall. The subordination of ordinary reality is much stricter than a 'Nabi' painting, and though one can easily recognize that the scene shows a maid at a table near a window, the picture is not 'about' this but about blue and red combined together near an expanse of green. The effect of these is controlled by pattern-making, in which sharp black lines not only delineate shapes but serve – as in stained glass – to intensify the patches of colour they surround. It is not therefore a paradox but part of Matisse's control of his effects, however brilliant in colour, that he should also have been a brilliant draughtsman. There is economy even amid his most apparent luxury, and the economy of effect in his drawings manages to be at the same time sensuous and colourful, despite the restriction.

284 VUILLARD
Interior 1893

285 MATISSE
The Dinner Table 1908

286 MATISSE *Negro Boxer* 1947

313

All Matisse's interests over a long life seem concentrated in the paper cut-outs which are typical of his late years: patterns made up of directly juxtaposed flat shapes of colour. The indifference to three-dimensional illusionism in the *Dinner Table*, of 1908, has become complete emancipation from any transcript of reality in the *Negro Boxer (Ill. 286)*, a paper cut-out of 1947. Colour is now patently the subject, with black a lively, pugilistic motif against rectangles of complementary red and green. In the black shape Matisse expresses his symbol of the boxer but beyond that no deduction is possible: 'When I paint a green, this does not necessarily mean grass.'

The emancipation which Matisse early achieved in his own personal way was prophetic not only of the twentieth century's ability to dispose as it liked of visual reality but had a direct influence on other painters – perhaps more significantly outside France. His recognition of the autonomy of colour has been developed as a principle in modern art and the almost magic sense of colour released, flooding pictures with its own vitality, is found as a force behind many quite diverse painters, including Nolde, Klee and Kandinsky. Something of this dominance is suggested, not altogether accidentally, by the very name of the *Blaue Reiter* group: preparing the spectator for a world where it is perfectly acceptable – indeed, artistically true – that a horseman should be blue. He becomes the champion of anti-naturalism but also the symbol of deeper reality.

In this determination to express something more 'real' than the Impressionists had seen, Van Gogh, Gauguin and Munch had already led the way. These three artists in particular inspired the short-lived German group *die Brücke* (founded in 1905), whose most distinguished member was Kirchner. No more than Matisse did Kirchner intend the recognizable references to reality in his work to be the real subject. His imagination played around street scenes in Berlin *(Ill. 287)*, for example, heightening reality with brilliantly jagged, often sinister shapes and lurid colour – expressing his view of a city, very different from the gentle atmospheric Paris of Impressionism. Kirchner bites more deeply and satirically into the spectacle of urban life than any French artist except Toulouse-Lautrec; and his lynx-faced ladies and shrill colour make him much more truly *fauve* than any of the historically Fauve group. Briefly a member of *die Brücke* but basically committed to nothing but his own intense vision, Nolde – two years older than Matisse – early subordinated exterior reality, transfiguring it into some of the most sensuously rich twentieth-century paintings. Colour seems to well out from centres within the composition – perhaps most superbly in his water-colours *(Ill. 288)* which blossom like the flowers he was fond of painting, blossoming with a vividness that has passed beyond anything lifelike. The flowers are flakes of burning fire or molten metal, hallucinatory in their effect: they are part of Nolde's sense of a mystic universe, with, in the words of the seventeenth-century mystic poet Vaughan, 'Bright shoots of everlastingness.'

287
KIRCHNER
*Potsdamer
Platz*
1913–14

315

288 NOLDE *Red and Yellow Poppies*

289 KANDINSKY *Composition IV* 19

290 KLEE *Flagged Town* 1927

Nature, in equally mystic sense, was vital to the slightly later *Blaue Reiter* group. The simplicity – not naïvety – which these artists admired was expressed better in le Douanier Rousseau (cf *Ill. 270*) than in the more strident, matter-of-fact world of Gauguin. Ideas of magic and primitivism take the *Blaue Reiter* painters' art back to the cave. They are one aspect of a twentieth-century dissatisfaction with Western civilization and culture, and a consequent interest in so-called 'primitive' art. Some *Blaue Reiter* artists may seem merely charming and decorative. Kandinsky and Klee, also both members of the group, cannot be dismissed in this way. Historically, Kandinsky's importance is considerable: finally, perhaps, for his treatise 'Concerning the Spiritual in Art' (1912) rather than for his actual pictorial work. The twentieth-century earliest determination – present before being articulated – to banish the object altogether from the picture was probably first expressed by Kandinsky, already in 1910. Despite their energy, their musical lyricism, their lively yet not quite witty inventiveness, Kandinsky's pictures *(Ill. 289)* remain faintly contrived; there is an element of exercise about many of them which contrasts with even the slightest, yet always authentic pictures and drawings of Klee. Kandinsky's spiritual intentions were perhaps too solemnly conscious; and sometimes Klee's wit may well seem directed at exploding such solemnity, letting the unconscious thumb its nose at everything that had been called art.

While some German twentieth-century painters have been underestimated through being supposed gloomy, clumsy and 'expressionist', Klee has probably been underestimated because of his light-heartedness, delicacy and charm. There was, however, nothing superficial in Klee's own continual search for ways towards great art. Picasso may have arrogantly declared, 'I do not search; I find.' Klee was humble, not out of any lack of pride in trying to be a good artist but because he realized that it is not 'I' but something working through the artist which produces art. And sometimes what Picasso found has speedily lost its lustre. Through doodling, through the example of child art, through a sort of lulling of the conscious, Klee was able finally to create something that seems slight but which remains tenaciously vivid. Unlike Kandinsky, he often retained images which are quite recognizable; unlike Kandinsky, he could control – and that most beautifully – his design. The sheer inventiveness of the images and colour produced pictures *(Ill. 290)* which are intensely poetic and timeless in a good sense.

They neither reproduce nor totally reject the exterior world we see; it is imagination which has coloured all Klee's images, products of an inner eye which sees much deeper than the ordinary one. This perhaps is Klee's final lesson, in a life of giving many lessons: that the imagination must be trusted.

Klee's finest work was done after the First World War when he joined the Bauhaus under Gropius, but the *Blaue Reiter* group had been formed before 1914. In the first fourteen years of the twentieth century, the diversity of its searching was already apparent; indeed, in those years were established many of the dominant styles and movements which still echo on, more than half a century later. Yet underlying the diversity is the common belief that 'all forms of imitation should be held in contempt'. These words are from the Futurist manifesto of 1910, which expresses in particular the views of a group of Italian artists (a poet and a composer, along with painters, formed the group). Eager for the truth of modern sensations, emphasizing the vortex of life, and trying to capture its speed and motion in their pictures, they produced paintings which are no longer effective in those devices that the cinema has made seem absurd but which in their very apparent absurdity anticipate Dadaism and Surrealism. Perhaps the most successful picture of this kind is the work of someone who was not an Italian Futurist, Duchamp's *Nude descending a staircase (Ill. 291)*, painted in 1912. This is a picture which still conveys a sense of hurtling energy, an almost noisy clatter of wooden planes against wooden steps, a deliberately aggressive, energetic dismissal of anything resembling a 'real' nude.

It was a different way of rejecting naturalism that led to the severely geometrical abstractionism practised in Russia by Malevich. In 1913 he painted his manifesto of the movement he called 'Suprematism': a picture of a black square on a white ground. Kandinsky, Russian by birth, may seem an obvious link, and yet Malevich probably did not know him and certainly had more purist, perhaps more truly painterly ideas. Very firm shapes and very deliberately restricted contrasts of colour make Malevich's pictures have much more in common with Mondrian than with Kandinsky. An entirely painted architecture is built up, a scaffolding which is intended to be a structure of the ideal world – harmonious as our world is not but ought to be. Reason, logic, seriousness mark all these efforts to dig down to the truth that underlies natural appearances. Already, in dealing with fifteenth-century Florence, the words of the philosopher Schoenmaekers, a great influence on Mondrian, have proved relevant: 'we want to penetrate nature in such a way that the inner construction of reality is revealed to us'. And these words supply a prologue to the most serious and sustained movement of the early twentieth century: Cubism.

Les Demoiselles d'Avignon (Ill. 292) is a shocking, seminal picture – an ugly, unfinished picture losing significance when it loses its power to shock – which marks the beginning of Cubism without being itself Cubist. The question of totally non-naturalistic art is not a very difficult one; indeed, it may well be that illusionistic work like Caravaggio's ultimately raises

292 PICASSO *les Demoiselles d'Avignon* 1907

291 DUCHAMP *Nude descending a staircase* 1912

more questions. What happens in *les Demoiselles d'Avignon* is the shocking juxtaposition of two quite grotesque heads to some figures who derive from Cézanne's *Baigneuses (Ill. 277)*. These two heads are in a completely new idiom, suggested by Negro sculpture but wrenching reality in a much more disturbed and disturbing way. It is an aggressive break with the Renaissance-established canons of illusionism, all the more aggressive since it is carried out not in landscape or still-life but in the most sacred of Renaissance subjects – mankind. Not only are the two heads not like anything we see in ordinary life, but the upper woman's left breast is a deliberate, shaded square: however tentatively, Cubism has already begun its radical work.

Picasso and Braque must be spoken of together as the founders of Cubism; and in the constant search for geometrical design and structure, Braque remained a Cubist. What they invented was an artistic language which emphasized its independence from reality by at first virtually banishing colour along with recognizable contours and shapes. Although it is sometimes described as vaguely scientific, it was perhaps basically more truly romantic and poetic. Picasso's portrait of Vollard *(Ill. 294)* and Braque's *Young Girl with Guitar (Ill. 293)* – different as they already are from each other in details of style – both exult in the freedom of having found a way to express their perceptions of the subject, regardless of what is actually visible. It is less science than magic which creates these fractured, multiple images which are like shifting kaleidoscopes. Braque's picture has an almost musical rightness in its placing of the lines (it is indeed more linear than Picasso's *Vollard*), and Braque was to develop this gift in a series of still-lives – his preferred theme – which might be called decoratively cubist in their effect and palpitatingly sensuous in their colour and surface when compared with the still-life in the foreground of *les Demoiselles*. Braque's intensely personal art produced some of the finest paintings of the first half of the twentieth century, but his apartness leads to his being somewhat overshadowed by conventional art history once the early years of Cubism are over.

The influences and effects of Cubism were speedily felt, and also its limitations. Braque and Picasso were the first to realize that there was something too hermetic, too dull perhaps, in the style; they provided a dose of fresh reality in the most real of ways, by applying to the picture surface actual pieces of cut-out paper and cards, and varying the paint texture by roughening it with sand. Something more colourful and playful was the result: a sense of *trompe l'œil* which can take on at times a surrealistic conviction. There is also a kinetic aspect of Cubism, whereby the images seem to move, revealing each facet – each cube – while the spectator remains still. To be developed by Futurism, it was achieved by Duchamp not by the suggestion of coloured lights playing over surfaces but by the series of hard, sharp planes presenting multiple images in the *Nude descending a staircase*.

Even there, in a style which Duchamp was to abandon, can be detected a deliberate overtone of anti-art: there is a greater discrepancy perhaps between the title and what we see than between title and picture in the case of Braque's *Young Girl with Guitar*. And perhaps the theme of the staircase itself provides another hint of the direction to be taken by Duchamp, for it is a common dream symbol (Freud's *The Interpretation of Dreams* had first been published in 1900). Duchamp's anti-art ideas were to become one of the stronger planks in the rather uneven platform of Dada – a movement which began in Switzerland, was suitably international in its membership and its influence, and which seemed to signal complete liberation from the past. At the same time, Duchamp was also to be praised by André Breton, leader of the movement which emerged as quite different from Dada, however mingled the two had at first seemed: Surrealism. In Duchamp's *The Bride stripped bare by her Bachelors even* – an early example of the new art object which refuses to be categorized – Breton rightly found intimations of eroticism, lyricism, science and humour; and though *The Bride* figures in histories of Dada, it is as far from being non-art as it is from being a 'ready-made'. The same is particularly true of the work produced by Dada artists like Arp and Schwitters. Although Schwitters made a point of assembling his compositions out of rubbish, the results *(Ill. 295)* are not only works of art, apparently casual yet carefully planned down to the application of the smallest fragment of torn paper, but they themselves have now taken on an aura of the past; they are the slightly dusty incunabula of modern art, and it no more matters that they are made out of wire, feathers and tram tickets than that early Italian pictures are painted with earth colours, gold-leaf and lapis lazuli.

If the original intention of Dada was to be against everything – especially the everything represented by Zürich, the city where it began – Surrealism represents liberation rather than mere revolution. Both movements began in literature; and

293 BRAQUE *Young Girl with Guitar*

294 PICASSO *Vollard* 1909–10

literary associations colour much surrealist painting. Reason is excluded so as to allow the unconscious mind to release images which are usually vivid and precise – like dream images – needing to be painted with extreme, almost 'primitive' detail. This role of making visible what is within him is Max Ernst's definition of the painter's task, when describing his discovery of the images and shapes provoked by the grainy floorboards of a seaside hotel. In his work *(Ill. 296)* imagination really seems to find free play. Certain images, like doves and forests, return

295 SCHWITTERS *Opened by Customs c.* 1937–9

296 ERNST *Grey Forest* 1927

again and again with haunting effect – an effect Ernst himself captures evocatively in two sentences about his original vision: 'In a country the colour of *"a pigeon's breast"*, I hailed the flight of *100,000* doves. I saw them invade the black forests of *desire* and endless *walls* and *seas*.' Against Ernst's authentic magic, the surrealism of Dali may seem too glossy and contrived; the chic surrealism of a shop-window rather than anything sprung from the unconscious. It is easy, however, to be unfair to Dali since his later work has become glossy academicism and because there is little point in praising someone so adept at praising himself. Perhaps it is not altogether an accident, however, that the more literal, figurative surrealists have had some difficulty in preserving the poetic, inspirational element in their work.

The searching which Klee spoke of had led, in painting alone, to such diversity of results by the 1920s. In 1926 Gropius built the Bauhaus *(Ill. 297)* at Dessau, typifying the new modern attitude to architecture and also the new modern concept of an artistic centre which should serve as a power-house of all the arts. In this too there is something of a return to pre-Renaissance standards: a cathedral rather than a palace seems the relevant comparison, and concern with the community rather than the individual. In architecture there might seem to be a less radical break with nineteenth-century standards, because the more advanced of those had already laid definite foundations for modern developments. In America Sullivan's architecture remained, still remains, acceptably 'modern'. The elements of steel and glass which make up the Bauhaus had been used in Paxton's Crystal Palace, romantic as that building may seem when compared with the logically coherent, skeletal design by Gropius, occupying space yet scarcely realized as mass.

One reason for a sense of continuity is that the nineteenth century had already initiated novel types of buildings – stations, museums, office blocks – which were to offer architects in the twentieth century some of their best opportunities. The tall office block created by Sullivan culminates in the weightless but triumphantly high Seagram Building *(Ill. 301),* seeming to rise unsupported, beginning as it were in the air. This is perhaps the last echo of Gothic chapels of glass, and certainly the last echo of Bauhaus ideals. The glass-roofed halls of nineteenth-century stations culminate in the undulating, spacious rather than massive, Stazione Termini at Rome. The problems of the museum building have demanded more radical solutions than the nineteenth century quite dared to propose; its impersonal cavernous halls for housing art have given way to something more flexible, dynamically exciting and dramatic in the winding layers of Wright's Guggenheim Museum, perhaps almost too personal a setting for works of art.

The problem of the urban centre – which had once occupied Julius Caesar at Rome – seemed solved by the early nineteenth century but had become acute again before the century ended. Agglomeration of houses in industrial cities (the very creators of the materials that ought to have meant better housing) had produced slums. And whereas people may question the relevance for them of 'art' in the sense of paintings or sculpture, architecture remains the art which directly concerns everybody; unfortunately, this has sometimes had the effect of preventing buildings from being architecture – rather as most newspapers fail to be literature. Le Corbusier, whose treatise on urbanism 'la Ville Radieuse' was published over thirty years ago, was one of the architects most obsessed with the problem of modern man's domestic existence. His Unité d'Habitation at Marseilles *(Ill. 298)* is a return to the horizontal grid of Gropius, opened up here to provide the maximum light through glass, making cells for existence which may encourage intimations of bee-like activity or tend too much to suggest prison uniformity.

The possibilities of the individual house in or near an urban environment naturally interested English planners; the garden city and garden suburb remain very much an English conception, exercising some fitful influence in Northern Europe, but a luxury of space – and an ideal – that most countries neither had nor desired. When it came to building blocks of flats for ordinary workers on a municipal scale, England lagged behind Continental and American example. Box-like, cell-like constructions in which to live were opposed by Frank Lloyd Wright, whose private houses are planned in relation to their natural setting, most patently in the Kaufmann House *(Ill. 299)*. Here nature has dictated if not the forms at least something of the effect. Long horizontals are complemented by trees; real rock is echoed by slabs of concrete built out over a mountain stream. Such a solution to the 'house' is as princely and personal as Villa d'Este. It aims at being a work of art, not imposing on but blending with its environment, where man and nature have created together in harmony. Such a view of their activity was to be expressed also by certain modern sculptors.

And in disassociating himself from cold functionalism, Wright has proved particularly significant. Glass and steel cubism has more recently been replaced by more expressive, personal qualities which may best be conveyed in stone and concrete materials. Having searched for and found ways to dissolve walls, architecture is now more likely to find ways to put massiveness back into walls – above all, perhaps, to find ways in which the individual architect may express his individuality. This is probably the only way in which a building can become a work of art. It is as an example of the new style, expressed in a personal idiom, that one can see Denys Lasdun's Royal College of Physicians *(Ill. 300)*: built in Nash's Regent's Park complex, a challenging environment which is partly garden as well as architectural into which it was planned to fit.

329

297 GROPIUS Bauhaus, Dessau 1925–6

298 LE CORBUSIER L'Unité d'Habitation, Marseilles 1946–52

299 WRIGHT Kaufmann House,
Bear Run, Pennsylvania 1936

300 LASDUN Royal College
of Physicians, London 1964

301 VAN DER ROHE and
JOHNSON Seagram Building,
New York 1958

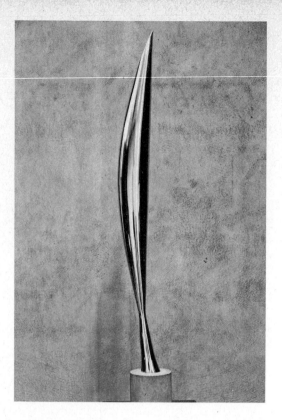

302 BRANCUSI
Bird in Space
1919

Since sculpture was probably the weakest art form in the nineteenth century, it was the one whose tradition was most obviously to be rejected by modern sculptors. In fact, freed from tradition, sculpture has proved the most fluid and flexible of modern media. Rodin was no Cézanne or Van Gogh. This was recognized by the most significant sculptor at the beginning of the twentieth century, Brancusi, even though he could praise Rodin. It was equally recognized by Matisse, by no means the first great painter to show interest in, and to practise, sculpture. Degas and Renoir indeed had produced perhaps the only truly 'modern' sculpture in France during the nineteenth century. Brancusi refused to become an assistant of Rodin's. He saw his task as one of purifying art, dispensing with surface realism and penetrating to that essence of things which was equally occupying painters in the early years of this century.

The shapes which Brancusi created *(Ill. 302)* achieve a purity and satisfying non-realism, while emphasizing bulk and weight

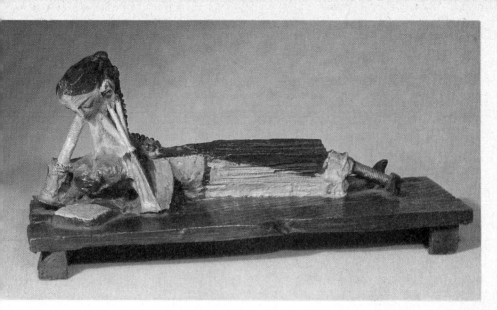

303 PICASSO *Woman Reading* 1952–3

304 MOORE *Reclining Figure* 1929

in a tactile way; but in aiming to penetrate to the essence of things, he perhaps did not go deep enough. At least in hindsight, there remains something rather obvious about his smooth egg-shapes and polished streamlined surfaces. Perhaps he was not very inventive; and by a strange irony he could even seem to be himself the victim of a sort of rhetoric – a fate liable to happen to any artist whose style does not evolve. Many of the problems of appreciating Brancusi are avoided by the sculpture of Arp, a founder of Dada, and creator of lively painted and sculpted reliefs. Arp's sculpture in the round was a later development; there his shapes are intended to be organic, to relate in some way to nature, and yet they are not so obviously abstracted from recognizable prototypes in nature as are Brancusi's.

Possibly there is a romantic fallacy in that tendency of some modern sculptors (and some of their admirers) to see their work constantly in relation to nature – presumably under the dangerous tutelage of Wordsworth. The language of eternal forms is often diffuse and misty rather than profoundly mystic. There

305 BOCCIONI *Development of a Bottle in Space* 1912

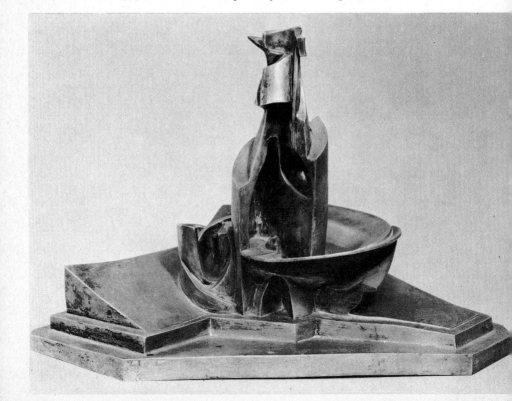

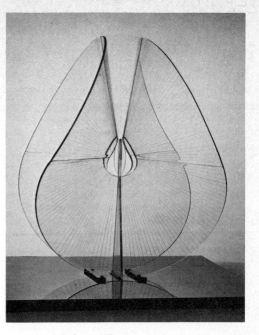

306 GIACOMETTI *Man Pointing* 1947   307 GABO *Spheric Theme* 1951

can be, it is true, the satisfyingly boulder-like maternity of, for example, Arnolfo di Cambio's *Madonna and Child (Ill. 89)*; but sculpture equally includes the high Rococo artificiality of Asam's *Assumption (Ill. 199)*. To some extent it may be that the work of Hepworth and Henry Moore marks the end of a phase of modern sculpture that began with Brancusi's definite and necessary revolution. Even the once much-praised concept of 'truth to material' – contradicted by Asam with beautifully flagrant effect – is being contradicted by young sculptors again today. And it can never be said to have had much effect on Picasso – fortunately. Although Moore probably still holds virtually official position as the most famous sculptor of our period, Picasso's sculpture (only recently shown in public *en masse*), in its sheer variety, its beauty as well as its wit, and constant energy, can challenge that position. Against Moore's typical reclining figure *(Ill. 304)*, monumental and timeless, Picasso's tiny *Woman Reading (Ill. 303)* may seem a mere impudent *jeu d'esprit*; yet it is a sparkling sample of that inventiveness (including finding use for nails, screws and bits of wood) which animates Picasso's other sculpture, whether the incisively

335

310 SMITH *Cubi XVIII* 1964

delicate cut-outs in metal or the Cubist constructions, executed some fifty years earlier.

No other sculptor has ranged as far and as successfully as Picasso who typifies the revolutionary diversity of twentieth-century sculpture. Yet amid the diversity there are apparent two main streams: one preserving some sort of link with the image made, however remotely, to resemble man; the other seeming to challenge nature by creating completely new forms, often preferring novel, unexpected materials, sometimes changing conventional ideas of sculpture by using only wire or glass. Braque and Picasso had pointed this way, in their use of real objects when breaking out of hermetic, analytic Cubism. In comparison with their experiments, Moore has remained traditional; in his work the basic human element is either expressed or strongly felt permeating the shape. And perhaps the last great sculptor to at least suggest the theme of man was Giacometti. His elongated figures *(Ill. 306)* have a hallucinatory quality, coming partly from their dream-like proportions and partly from molten, wax-like effect even though they are usually of bronze. They recall Giacometti's origin as a Surrealist sculptor. They are people like candles, burnt down to a thread of vitality which seems always on the point of being extinguished. In them perhaps does really die the Western tradition of figurative sculpture.

The new and more challenging sculpture, represented by Picasso's Cubist construction, quickly found its own champions. In Russia, the rival of Malevich and also originally a painter, Tatlin, had produced by 1914 under Picasso's influence constructions which have no basis in representation. He was to be influenced also by the Futurists, of whom the painter-cum-sculptor Boccioni was for this phase the most interesting. Boccioni seems to have done no sculpture when he issued his manifesto on Futurist Sculpture in 1912, but he briefly followed out what he preached. *The Development of a Bottle in Space (Ill. 305),* executed that year, is revolutionary in its opening up of forms, suggesting that space has pulled out and pressed around these shapes so that the bronze seems to have been wrought in a slip-stream of energy. Significantly, Boccioni had praise for Medardo Rosso's sculpture *(Ill. 238)*; and he called also for work with startlingly different materials from those tradition-ally in use: '. . . glass, wood, cardboard . . . cloth, mirrors, electric light'. He would probably have seen in kinetic sculpture the ultimate solution to that dynamism which art had to capture and enshrine. Another way, stimulated no doubt by Tatlin's ideas, was expressed by another Russian, who took the name Naum Gabo. Gabo's most typical plastic constructions (*Ill. 307*) are completely abstract, beautifully clean and balanced, glass-like architectural sculpture which occupies space without asserting mass – and thus belongs in the idiom of the Seagram Building (*Ill. 301*).

As architecture has turned back to an emphasis on mass and on materials, so more recent sculpture has preferred the apparently least tractable of all materials, iron. Some sculptors have shown an interest in surface effects, sometimes by use of mechanical debris assembled in the body of the sculpture, or combined with solid, geometric shapes. Machinery, geometry, use of discarded ironware: all these were elements in the work of the leading American sculptor David Smith (died 1965) who more than once worked as a welder in a factory. Indeed, he wanted his studio to become like a factory; he chose to work in iron or steel exactly because they had no 'art' associations apart from purely twentieth-century ones. Yet even the geometric, severely abstract shapes of his late sculpture, in an outdoor setting which Smith preferred for his work (*Ill. 310*), may seem romantic – with echoes of Frank Lloyd Wright – when compared with the concentrated, clear-cut single statement of Anthony Caro's work in England (*Ill. 309*). Brightly painted in one colour, boldly extended, this nakedly exists as a steel statement which refuses to be covered by explanations, whether artistic or art-historical.

In painting, too, it is easy to show comparable recent developments. Frank Stella's *Bampur* (*Ill. 308*) might reasonably be juxtaposed to Caro's sculpture – not to make the two artists say exactly the same thing, but to show that a certain cool impassivity and concern with construction represent one aspect of art in the 1960s. That diversity which makes it difficult enough yet to survey the arts at the opening of the twentieth century only increases as one approaches our own decade. Even more uncertain in some ways are the years that lie between – no longer the present and not yet become totally the past. It is all the more extraordinary to reflect that throughout the whole century so far Picasso has been at work; and his life and his work are easily confounded in one image of intense vitality. However posterity ultimately estimates him, he is evidence that art still mattered to the twentieth century. His vast international fame symbolizes the internationalness of modern art. And ultimately

339

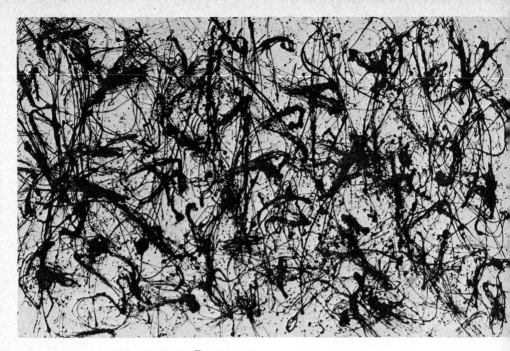

311 POLLOCK *Europe* 1950

it will probably be with him that posterity comes to associate that break with the imitative which was essential to all modern art. His own constant revolutions of style not merely mirror the restless quality of this century but help us as spectators to respond to the variety of styles which art has offered us: from the abstract expressionism of Jackson Pollock *(Ill. 311),* itself already a part of history, to the highly charged, personal expressionism of Francis Bacon *(Ill. 312).* The so-called 'Pop' painters put back into art a topicality which perhaps proved too attractive to the public who enjoyed recognizing commonplace images and things, and scarcely noticed the art. Already 'Pop' seems a movement that has ended, or is ending. Klee's exhortation to go on searching is still being followed. This book closes therefore with the sentence that opened it: 'Art is not something that has ceased to be created.'

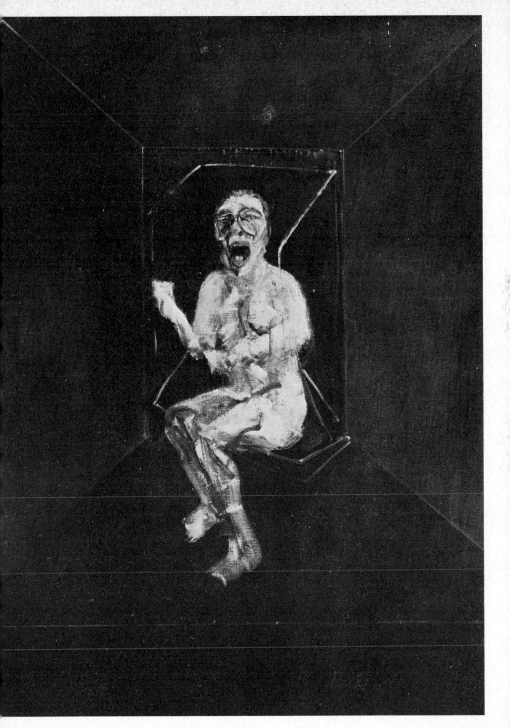

312 BACON *Study of the nurse from the film 'Battleship Potemkin'* 1957

List of Illustrations

Measurements are given in inches and centimetres, height preceding width

101 SANDRO BOTTICELLI *c.* 1445–1510
Birth of Venus
Oil on canvas $68\frac{7}{8} \times 85\frac{1}{2}$ (175 × 278)
Florence, Uffizi

102 PIERO DELLA FRANCESCA 1410/20–92
The Resurrection
Fresco
Borgo S. Sepolcro, Palazzo Communale
Photo Anderson

103 MASACCIO 1401–?28
The Trinity 1425
Fresco
Florence, S. Maria Novella
Photo Mansell-Anderson

104 FILIPPO BRUNELLESCHI 1377–1446
Cupola of the Duomo, Florence *c.* 1432
Photo Alinari

105 BRUNELLESCHI
Pazzi chapel, Florence (interior). Work suspended 1443
Photo Scala

106 LEON BATTISTA ALBERTI 1404–72
S. Francesco, Rimini *c.* 1450
Photo Mansell-Alinari

107 PIETRO LOMBARDO 1435–1515 and
MAURO CODUCCI d. 1504
Palazzo Vendramin Calergi, Venice. Begun
c. 1481
Photo Georgina Masson

108 LEONE BATTISTA ALBERTI 1404–72
Palazzo Rucellai, Florence 1445–57
Photo Mansell-Alinari

109 Doorway of the Sala dell'Iole, Palazzo Ducale, Urbino *c.* 1468
Photo Mansell-Anderson

110 Tapestry: *Dame à la licorne*. Early sixteenth
century
144 × 126 (366 × 320)
Paris, Cluny Museum

111 ANDREA MANTEGNA *c.* 1431–1506
The Gonzaga family (detail) 1474
Fresco
Mantua, Palazzo Ducale, Camera degli Sposi
Photo Scala, by courtesy of Sadea-Sansoni

112 MASACCIO 1401–28
Expulsion from Paradise 1425/6–8
Fresco
S. Maria del Carmine, Brancacci Chapel,
Florence
Photo Mansell-Alinari

113 DONATELLO *c.* 1386–1466
Equestrian statue of Gattamelata 1447–53
Bronze

Padua, Piazza del Santo
Photo Mansell-Anderson

114 DONATELLO
The Resurrection c. 1462–6
Bronze relief on pulpit of S. Lorenzo,
Florence
Photo Brogi

115 DONATELLO
David 1440–3
Bronze
Florence, Museo Nazionale
Photo Mansell-Anderson

116 ANDREA DEL VERROCCHIO *c.* 1435–88
David. Before 1476
Bronze
Florence, Museo Nazionale
Photo Mansell Collection

117 ANTONIO POLLAIUOLO *c.* 1432–98
Hercules and Antaeus 1475–80
Bronze h. $17\frac{3}{4}$ (45)
Florence, Museo Nazionale
Photo Mansell-Alinari

118 BERNARDO ROSSELLINO 1409–64 and
ANTONIO ROSSELLINO 1427–79
Tomb of the Cardinal of Portugal *c.* 1461–6
S. Miniato al Monte, Florence
Photo Mansell-Alinari

119 LUCA SIGNORELLI *c.* 1441/50–1523
Last Judgment (detail) 1499–1503
Fresco
Orvieto Cathedral

120 HIERONYMUS BOSCH *c.* 1450–1516
Garden of Earthly Delights (detail) *c.* 1500
Oil and tempera on panel, side panel $86\frac{5}{8} \times 38\frac{1}{8}$
(220 × 97)
Madrid, Prado

121 GIOVANNI BELLINI *c.* 1430–1516
Madonna of the Meadow
Originally on panel $26\frac{1}{2} \times 34$ (67 × 86)
London, by courtesy of the Trustees of the
National Gallery
Photo National Gallery

122 LEONARDO DA VINCI 1452–1519
Mona Lisa c. 1503
Oil on canvas $38\frac{1}{4} \times 20\frac{1}{4}$ (97 × 51·5)
Paris, Louvre
Photo Giraudon

123 RAPHAEL 1483–1520
Portrait of Baldassare Castiglione 1519
Oil on canvas $32\frac{1}{4} \times 26\frac{1}{2}$ (82 × 67)
Paris, Louvre
Photo Archives Photographiques

347

124 LEONARDO DA VINCI 1452–1519
A Deluge
Black chalk 6½ × 8¼ (16·3 × 21)
Windsor Castle, Royal Library
Reproduced by gracious permission of Her
Majesty Queen Elizabeth II

125 MICHELANGELO BUONAROTTI 1475–
1564
David 1503–4
Marble h. 198⅞ (505)
Florence, Accademia
Photo Alinari

126 MICHELANGELO
Rondanini Pietà 1555–64
Marble h. 98 (249)
Milan, Castello Sforzesco

127 MICHELANGELO
Creation of Man 1508–12
Fresco
Rome, Sistine Chapel
Photo Mansell-Alinari

128 MICHELANGELO
Medici Chapel, S. Lorenzo, Florence (interior)
1524–34
Photo Mansell-Alinari

129 RAPHAEL 1483–1520
School of Athens 1509–11
Fresco
Rome, Vatican Stanze
Photo Vatican Museums

130 RAPHAEL
Galatea c. 1511
Fresco 116⅛ × 88⅝ (295 × 225)
Rome, Villa Farnesina

131 RAPHAEL
Transfiguration
Oil on panel 159½ × 109½ (405 × 278)
Rome, Vatican Gallery
Photo Vatican Museums

132 JACOPO SANSOVINO 1486–1570
Apollo c. 1537–40
Bronze h. 58 (147)
Venice, Loggetta of the Campanile, Piazza
San Marco
Photo Mansell-Alinari

133 PETER FLÖTNER *c.* 1485–1546
Apollo 1532
Bronze
Nuremberg, Town Hall
Photo Helga Schmidt-Glassner

134 BENVENUTO CELLINI 1500–71
Perseus. Commissioned 1545, set up in 1554
Bronze h. 126 (320)
Florence, Loggia dei Lanzi
Photo Mansell-Alinari

135 GIANBOLOGNA 1529–1608
Apollo
Florence, Palazzo Vecchio
Photo Mansell-Alinari

136 ROSSO FIORENTINO 1494–1540 and
FRANCESCO PRIMATICCIO 1504–70
Galerie François I, Fontainebleau *c.* 1533–4
Stucco by Rosso, painting by Primaticcio
Photo Scala

137 JEAN GOUJON fl. 1540–62
Fontaine des Innocents (detail) 1547–9
Marble
Paris, Louvre
Photo Giraudon

138 GERMAIN PILON *c.* 1530–90
Cardinal Birague. After 1583
Bronze
Paris, Louvre
Photo Giraudon

139 BRAMANTE 1444–1514
Tempietto 1502
Rome, S. Pietro in Montorio
Photo Linda Murray

140 St. Peter's and Piazza S. Pietro, Rome 1655–67
Photo Mansell-Anderson

141 BALDASSARE PERUZZI *c.* 1481–1536
Palazzo Massimi, Rome. Begun 1535
Photo Linda Murray

142 ANTONIO DA SAN GALLO 1485–1559
Palazzo Farnese, Rome 1534–45
Photo Anderson

143 PIRRO LIGORIO *c.* 1520–80
Villa d'Este, Tivoli 1550–60
Photo Georgina Masson

144 JACOPO SANSOVINO *c.* 1460–1529
Library, Venice 1537–54
Photo Mansell-Anderson

145 ANDREA PALLADIO 1508–80
S. Giorgio Maggiore, Venice (interior). Begun
c. 1570
Photo Linda Murray

146 PIERRE LESCOT *c.* 1515–78
Square court of the Louvre, Paris. Begun 1546
Photo Jean Roubier

147 CORNELIS FLORIS 1514–75
Town Hall, Antwerp *c.* 1560
Photo A.C.L.

148 Central Pavilion, Burghley House,
Northamptonshire 1585
*Photo National Monuments Record, Royal
Commission on Historical Monuments*

149 ALBRECHT DÜRER 1471–1528
St Eustace 1500
Engraving 14 × 10¼ (35·5 × 26)

150 LUCAS VAN LEYDEN 1494?–1533
Return of the Prodigal Son 1510
Engraving 7⅛ × 9⅝ (18 × 24·5)

151 GIORGIONE *c.* 1476/8–1510
Tempesta
Oil on canvas 30¾ × 28½ (78 × 72)
Venice, Accademia

152 ALBRECHT DÜRER 1471–1528
Self-portrait 1498
Oil on panel 20½ × 16⅛ (52 × 41)
Madrid, Prado

153 TITIAN (Tiziano Vecelli) *c.* 1487/90–1576
Assunta 1518
Wood 270 × 141 (690 × 360)
Venice, Frari Church
Photo Mansell-Anderson

154 GRÜNEWALD *c.* 1470/80–1528
Resurrection (detail) 1515–16
Isenheim Altar
Oil on panel 105⅞ × 56¼ (269 × 144)
Colmar, Unterlinden Museum
Photo Bildarchiv Marburg

155 ALBRECHT ALTDORFER *c.* 1480–1538
Battle of the Issus 1529
Wood 63¼ × 48 (158 × 120)
Munich, Alte Pinakothek
Photo Bayerische Staatsgemäldesammlungen

156 PIETER BRUEGEL the Elder *c.* 1525/30–69
November (Return of the Herd) 1565
Wood 46⅛ × 62⅝ (117 × 159)
Vienna, Kunsthistorisches Museum
Photo Kunsthistorisches Museum

157 ANTONIO ALLEGRI DA CORREGGIO
1487/8–1534
Nativity c. 1530
Wood 100¾ × 74 (256 × 188)
Dresden, Gemäldegalerie
Photo Staatliche Kunstsammlungen, Dresden

158 LORENZO LOTTO *c.* 1480–1556
Annunciation 1526/8
Oil on canvas 166 × 114 (421·5 × 290)
Recanati, S. Maria sopra Mercanti
Photo Mansell-Alinari

159 JACOPO PONTORMO 1494–1566/7
Visitation c. 1528
Wood 79½ × 61⅜ (202 × 156)
Carmignano, Parish Church
Photo Mansell-Alinari

160 TITIAN (Tiziano Vecelli) *c.* 1487/90–1576
Pietà 1573–6
Oil on canvas 137¼ × 153½ (350 × 395)
Venice, Accademia
Photo Mansell-Alinari

161 TITIAN
Giovanni d'Acquaviva, Lord of Atri(?) c. 1550
Oil on canvas 88 × 59¾ (224 × 152)
Cassel, Gemäldegalerie
Photo Staatliche Kunstsammlungen, Cassel

162 HANS HOLBEIN the Younger 1497/8–1543
The Ambassadors (Jean de Dinteville and
Georges de Selve) 1533
Panel 81¼ × 82½ (207 × 209·5)
London, by courtesy of the Trustees of the
National Gallery
Photo National Gallery

163 AGNOLO BRONZINO 1503–72
Lodovico Capponi c. 1550–5
Oil on canvas 45⅞ × 33¾ (116·5 × 86)
New York, copyright The Frick Collection

164 FRANCESCO PARMIGIANINO 1503–40
Self-portrait in a Convex Mirror 1524
Panel 9½ (24)
Vienna, Kunsthistorisches Museum

165 NICHOLAS HILLIARD 1547–1619
Young Man amid Briar Roses c. 1588
Watercolour 5⅜ × 2⅜ (13·5 × 7)
London, Victoria and Albert Museum

166 JACOPO TINTORETTO 1518–94
Miracle of St Mark
Oil on canvas 161⅜ × 213¾ (415 × 543·5)
Venice, Accademia
Photo Mansell-Anderson

167 TINTORETTO
Last Supper 1592
Oil on canvas 144 × 224 (366 × 569)
Venice, S. Giorgio Maggiore
Photo Mansell-Anderson

168 PAOLO VERONESE 1528–88
Venus and Adonis c. 1580
Oil on canvas 83½ × 75¼ (212 × 191)
Madrid, Prado
Photo Mas

169 EL GRECO (Domenikos Theotocopoulos)
1541–1614
Burial of Count Orgaz 1586
Oil on canvas 191⅞ × 141¾ (487·5 × 360)
Toledo, S. Tomé

170 PAOLO VERONESE 1528–88
Family of Darius before Alexander
Canvas 92½ × 186½ (234 × 473)
London, by courtesy of the Trustees of the
National Gallery

349

171 GIANLORENZO BERNINI 1598–1680
Chair of Peter. Begun 1624
Bronze, partly gilt
Rome, St Peter's

172 SIR PETER PAUL RUBENS 1577–1640
Apotheosis of James I 1635
Oil on canvas
Ceiling, Banqueting Hall, Whitehall, London

173 RUBENS
Helena Fourment and her Son 1636–7
Panel 44½ × 32¼ (113 × 82)
Paris, Louvre
Photo Giraudon

174 GIANLORENZO BERNINI 1598–1680
Constanza Bonarelli c. 1635
Marble, life-size
Florence, Museo Nazionale
Photo Mansell-Anderson

175 BERNINI
S. Maria dell'Assunzione, Ariccia 1662–4
Photo G.F.N.

176 INIGO JONES 1573–1652
St Paul's, Covent Garden, London 1631
Photo National Buildings Record

177 GIACOMO BAROZZI DA VIGNOLA
1507–73
Gesù, Rome. Begun 1568
Photo Mansell-Anderson

178 GIOVANNI BATTISTA GAULLI 1639–
1709
Adoration of the Name Jesus 1676–9
Fresco, central part of ceiling
Gesù, Rome
Photo Scala

179 FRANÇOIS MANSART 1598–1666 and
JACQUES LEMERCIER 1585–1654
Val-de-Grâce, Paris 1645–67
Photo Giraudon

180 SIR CHRISTOPHER WREN 1632–1723
St Paul's, London 1675–1712
Photo Royal Commission on Historical Monuments

181 FRANCESCO BORROMINI 1599–1667
S. Carlo alle Quattro Fontane, Rome 1655–67
Photo Mansell-Alinari

182 BALDASSARE LONGHENA 1598–1682
S. Maria della Salute, Venice 1631–85
Photo Mansell-Anderson

183 GUARINO GUARINI 1624–83
Cappella della SS. Sindone, Turin
1667–90
Photo Mansell-Alinari

184, BALTHASAR NEUMANN 1687–1753
185 Church of Vierzehnheiligen, near Banz 1744
Photos Bildarchiv Marburg (exterior), A.F. Kersting (interior)

186 LOUIS LE VAU 1612–70 and JULES
HARDOUIN MANSART 1646–1708
Palace at Versailles, the garden façade 1669–85
Photo Giraudon

187 JACQUES ANGE GABRIEL *c.* 1710–82
Petit Trianon, Versailles 1762–8
Photo Giraudon

188 CLAUDE PERRAULT 1613–88, LOUIS
LE VAU 1612–70 and CHARLES LEBRUN
1619–90
East front of the Louvre, Paris 1667–70
Photo Giraudon

189 EMMANUEL HÉRÉ DE CORNY 1705–63
The Hemicycle, Nancy 1750–7
Photo Giraudon

190 SIR JOHN VANBRUGH 1666–1726
Blenheim Palace, Oxfordshire 1705–20
Photo A. F. Kersting

191 JOHN WOOD THE YOUNGER 1728–81
Royal Crescent, Bath. Begun 1767
Photo Edwin Smith

192 CLAUDE NICOLAS LEDOUX 1736–1806
Barrière de Courcelles, Paris 1785–91
(destroyed)

193 ROBERT ADAM 1728–92
The Hall, Syon House, Middlesex 1762–9
Photo A.F. Kersting

194 PEDRO DE MENA 1628–88
The Virgin of Sorrows
Painted wood, h. 16¾ (42·5)
London, Victoria and Albert Museum

195 GIANLORENZO BERNINI 1598–1680
Ecstasy of St Theresa 1645–52
Marble, life-size
Rome, S. Maria della Vittoria, Cornaro
Chapel
Photo Anderson

196 CLAUDE MICHEL called CLODION
1738–1814
The Intoxication of Wine
Terracotta h. 23¼ (60)
New York, The Metropolitan Museum of
Art, Bequest of Benjamin Altman, 1913
Photo The Metropolitan Museum of Art, New York

219 REMBRANDT VAN RIJN 1606–69
The Syndics 1662
Oil on canvas 75¼ × 109⅞ (191 × 279)
Amsterdam, Rijksmuseum

220 FRANÇOIS BOUCHER 1703–70
Shepherd piping to a Shepherdess
Oil on canvas 36¾ × 55¾ (93 × 142)
London, reproduced by permission of the
Trustees of the Wallace Collection
Photo Wallace Collection, Crown copyright

221 GIOVANNI BATTISTA TIEPOLO 1696–
1770
Marriage of Frederick Barbarossa 1752
Fresco
Würzburg, Residenz
Photo Hirmer Verlag

222 JEAN-BAPTISTE-SIMÉON   CHARDIN
1699–1779
Morning Toilet 1741
Oil on canvas 19¼ × 15¾ (49 × 40)
Stockholm, National Museum
Photo National Museum, Stockholm

223 CANALETTO 1697–1768
The Stonemason's Yard
Oil on canvas 48¾ × 64⅛ (123 × 163)
London, by courtesy of the Trustees of the
National Gallery
Photo National Gallery, London

224 JEAN-ANTOINE WATTEAU 1684–1721
Enseigne de Gersaint 1720
Oil on canvas 54½ × 121¼ (138 × 308)
Berlin, Charlottenburg Palace
Photo Staatliche Museen, Berlin

225 THOMAS GAINSBOROUGH 1727–88
The Morning Walk 1785
Oil on canvas 93 × 70½ (236 × 179)
London, by courtesy of the Trustees of the
National Gallery

226 WILLIAM BLAKE 1757–1827
The Spiritual Form of Pitt 1808
Tempera on canvas 29½ × 24½ (74 × 62)
London, The Tate Gallery
Photo Tate Gallery

227 JOHN SINGLETON COPLEY 1738–1815
Death of Chatham 1779–80
Oil on canvas 90 × 121 (228·5 × 307)
London, The Tate Gallery
Photo Tate Gallery

228 WILLIAM HOGARTH 1697–1764
After the Marriage (Marriage à la Mode) c. 1744
Oil on canvas 27 × 35 (69 × 89)
London, by courtesy of the Trustees of the
National Gallery
Photo National Gallery, London

229 JACQUES-LOUIS DAVID 1748–1825
Death of Marat 1793
Oil on canvas 65 × 50½ (165 × 128)
Brussels, Musées Royaux des Beaux-Arts

230 FRANCISCO JOSÉ DE GOYA Y
LUCIENTES 1746–1828
3 May 1808
Oil on canvas 104½ × 135⅝ (265 × 344)
Madrid, Prado

231 JACQUES-LOUIS DAVID 1748–1825
Oath of the Horatii 1785
Oil on canvas 129⅞ × 168½ (330 × 427)
Paris, Louvre
Photo Bulloz

232 FRANCISCO JOSÉ DE GOYA Y
LUCIENTES 1746–1828
The Sleep of Reason produces Monsters 1799
Etching 7⅛ × 4¾ (18 × 12)

233 JOSEPH MALLORD WILLIAM TURNER
1775–1851
Ulysses deriding Polyphemus 1829
Oil on canvas 52¼ × 80½ (132·5 × 203·5)
London, by courtesy of the Trustees of the
National Gallery
Photo John Webb, Brompton Studio

234 JOHN CONSTABLE 1776–1837
The Haywain 1821
Oil on canvas 51¼ × 73 (130 × 185)
London, by courtesy of the Trustees of the
National Gallery

235 WILLIAM HOLMAN HUNT 1827–1910
The Light of the World 1853
Oil on canvas 18½ × 9¼ (47 × 23·5)
Manchester, City Art Gallery
Photo City Art Gallery, Manchester

236 JOHN GIBSON 1790–1866
'Tinted Venus' c. 1850
Marble with slight pigmentation h. 68 (173)
London, Collection P. J. Dearden
Photo Victoria and Albert Museum

237 JEAN-BAPTISTE CARPEAUX 1827–75
La Danse 1869
Stone
Paris, Louvre
Photo Archives Photographiques

238 MEDARDO ROSSO 1858–1928
Conversation in a Garden 1893
Bronze 13 × 26⅜ × 15⅞ (33 × 67 × 40·5)
Rome, Galleria Nazionale d'Arte Moderna
*Photo Soprintendenza alla Galleria Roma II,
Galleria Nazionale d'Arte Moderna*

239 AUGUSTE RODIN 1840–1917
Balzac 1897
Stucco h. 113¾ (289)
Paris, Musée Rodin
Photo Martin Hürlimann

240 SIR JOSEPH PAXTON 1801–65, SIR
CHARLES FOX 1810–74 and HENDER-
SON
Crystal Palace 1850–1. Moved to Sydenham
1852–4, destroyed 1936
*'Architectural Review' photograph by Dell and
Wainwright*

241 KARL FRIEDRICH SCHINKEL 1781–1841
Altes Museum, Berlin 1824–8 (destroyed)
Photo Staatliche Museen, Berlin

242 JOHN NASH 1752–1835
Cumberland Terrace, London. Begun 1826–7
Photo Julian Wontner

243 RICHARD NORMAN SHAW 1831–1912
Architect's own house, London 1875
*Photo National Monuments Record, Royal
Commission on Historical Monuments*

244 SIR CHARLES BARRY 1795–1860 and
AUGUSTUS WELBY NORTHMORE
PUGIN 1812–52
Houses of Parliament, London 1840–60
*Photo National Buildings Record, Royal Com-
mission on Historical Monuments*

245 JEAN-LOUIS-CHARLES GARNIER 1825–
98
Opéra, Paris 1861–74
Photo Julian Wontner

246 TONY GARNIER 1869–1948
Theatre, Industrial City 1901–4
Drawing

247 ADOLF LOOS 1870–1933
Steiner House, Vienna 1910

248 LOUIS H. SULLIVAN 1856–1924
Wainwright Building, St Louis 1890–1
Photo Hedrich-Blessing

249 DANIEL HUDSON BURNHAM 1846–
1912 and JOHN WELLBOM ROOT
1850–91
Monadnock Block, Chicago 1891
Photo Dr F. Stoedtner

250 ANTONI GAUDÍ 1852–1926
Church of Sagrada Familia, Barcelona. Begun
1884
Photo Mas

251 GUSTAVE COURBET 1819–77
'Bonjour, Monsieur Courbet' 1854
Oil on canvas 50¾ × 58⅝ (129 × 149)
Montpellier, Musée Fabre
Photo Giraudon

252 CASPAR DAVID FRIEDRICH 1774–1840
Man and Woman gazing at the Moon 1819
Oil on canvas 35 × 44 (89 × 111·5)
Berlin, Staatliche Museen

253 JOSEPH MALLORD WILLIAM TURNER
1775–1851
The Evening Star (unfinished). Before 1840
Oil on canvas 36¼ × 48¼ (92·5 × 123)
London, by courtesy of the Trustees of the
National Gallery
Photo National Gallery

254 JEAN-BAPTISTE-CAMILLE COROT
1796–1875
Pont de Narni 1826/7
Oil on canvas 16½ × 24⅜ (42 × 62)
Paris, Louvre
Photo Giraudon

255 THÉODORE GÉRICAULT 1791–1824
Raft of the 'Medusa' 1819
Oil on canvas 193¼ × 282½ (491 × 717)
Paris, Louvre
Photo Bulloz

256 EUGÉNE DELACROIX 1798–1863
Massacre de Scio 1824
Canvas 164½ × 128⅜ (417 × 354)
Paris, Louvre
Photo Giraudon

257 PAUL-HIPPOLYTE DELAROCHE 1797–
1856
Little Princes in the Tower 1831
Oil on canvas 16⅞ × 19¾ (42 × 50)
London, reproduced by permission of the
Trustees of the Wallace Collection
Photo Wallace Collection, Crown copyright

258 JEAN-AUGUSTE-DOMINIQUE INGRES
1780–1867
Madame Moitessier 1844/56
Oil on canvas 47¼ × 36¼ (120 × 92)
London, by courtesy of the Trustees of the
National Gallery
Photo National Gallery

259 FORD MADOX BROWN 1821–93
Work 1852–65
Oil on canvas 53 × 77⅛ (134·5 × 196)
Manchester City Art Gallery

260 HONORÉ DAUMIER 1808–79
Third Class Carriage 1863/5
Oil on canvas 26⅜ × 36¼ (67 × 92)
Ottawa, National Gallery of Canada
Photo National Gallery of Canada

261 ÉDOUARD MANET 1832–83
Déjeuner sur l'Herbe 1863
Oil on canvas 83⅛ × 106¼ (211 × 270)
Paris, Louvre

284 ÉDOUARD VUILLARD 1868–1940
Interior 1893
Oil on cardboard 20½ × 31⅓ (52 × 79)
Leningrad, Hermitage

285 HENRI MATISSE 1869–1954
The Dinner Table 1908
Oil on canvas 71¼ × 96⅞ (181 × 220)
Leningrad, Hermitage

286 MATISSE
Negro Boxer 1947
Gouache cut-out 12⅝ × 10 (32 × 25·5)
Paris, Musée National d'Art Moderne

287 ERNST LUDWIG KIRCHNER 1880–1938
Potsdamer Platz 1913–14
Oil on canvas 78¾ × 59 (200 × 150)
Private collection

288 EMIL NOLDE 1867–1956
Red and Yellow Poppies
Watercolour 13½ × 18½ (34 × 47)
Seebull, Ada and Emil Nolde Foundation

289 WASSILY KANDINSKY 1866–1944
Composition IV 1911
Oil on canvas 63 × 78¾ (160 × 200)
Paris, Collection Nina Kandinsky

290 PAUL KLEE 1879–1940
Flagged Town 1927
Watercolour on paper, black background
11⅝ × 8½ (30 × 21·5)
Berne, Private collection

291 MARCEL DUCHAMP b. 1887
Nude descending a Staircase No. 2 1912
Oil on canvas 58 × 35 (148 × 89)
Philadelphia Museum of Art, Louise and
Walter Arensberg Collection

292 PABLO PICASSO b. 1881
Les Demoiselles d'Avignon 1907
Oil on canvas 96 × 92 (244 × 234)
New York, Museum of Modern Art

293 GEORGES BRAQUE 1882–1963
Young Girl with Guitar
Oil on canvas 51⅛ × 29⅛ (130 × 74)
Paris, Musée National d'Art Moderne

294 PABLO PICASSO b. 1881
Vollard 1909–10
Oil on canvas 36¼ × 25⅝ (92 × 65)
Moscow, Pushkin Museum

295 KURT SCHWITTERS 1887–1948
Opened by Customs c. 1937–9
Collage 13 × 10 (33·1 × 25·4)
London, The Tate Gallery
Photo Tate Gallery

296 MAX ERNST b. 1891
Grey Forest 1927
Oil on canvas 31⅞ × 39⅜ (81 × 100)
Private collection

297 WALTER GROPIUS b. 1883
Bauhaus, Dessau 1925–6
Photo Dr F. Stoedtner

298 LE CORBUSIER (CHARLES ÉDOUARD
JEANNERET) 1887–1967
L'Unité d'Habitation, Marseilles 1946–52

299 FRANK LLOYD WRIGHT 1867–1957
'Falling Water', Bear Run, Pennsylvania 1936

300 DENYS LASDUN b. 1914
Royal College of Physicians, London 1964
Photo Copyright Lasdun, Behr Photography

301 LUDWIG MIES VAN DER ROHE b. 1886
and PHILIP JOHNSON b. 1906
Seagram Building, New York 1958
Photo U.S.I.S.

302 CONSTANTIN BRANCUSI 1876–1957
Bird in Space 1919
Bronze h. 54 (137)
New York, The Museum of Modern Art
Photo The Museum of Modern Art, New York

303 PABLO PICASSO b. 1881
Woman Reading 1952–3
Painted bronze 6⅛ × 14 (15·5 × 36)
Private collection
*Photo Copyright Arts Council of Great Britain
John Webb, Brompton Studio*

304 HENRY MOORE b. 1898
Reclining Figure 1929
Brown Horton stone l. 33 (84)
Leeds, City Art Gallery

305 UMBERTO BOCCIONI 1882–1916
Development of a Bottle in Space 1912
Bronze h. 15 (38)
New York, The Museum of Modern Art,
Aristide Maillol Fund

306 ALBERTO GIACOMETTI 1901–66
Man Pointing 1947
Height including base 70 (178)
London, The Tate Gallery
Photo Tate Gallery

307 NAUM GABO b. 1890
Spheric Theme 1951
Version of 1937 original. Plastic h. 22⅜ (57)
New York, The Solomon R. Guggenheim
Museum
Photo The Solomon R. Guggenheim Museum

355

308 FRANK STELLA b. 1936
Bampur 1966
Alkyd 89 × 108¼ (226 × 275)
Zürich, Gallerie Bischofberger

309 ANTHONY CARO b. 1924
Reel 1964
Steel painted red 34 × 40 × 105 (86 × 102 × 267)
Collection Alan Bower
Photo Kasmin Gallery

310 DAVID SMITH 1906–65
Cubi XVIII 1964

Stainless steel h. 115¾ (294)
New York, Marlborough-Gerson Inc.

311 JACKSON POLLOCK 1912–56
Europe 1950
Duco on canvas 106 × 108 (269 × 274)
Collection Lee Krasner Pollock

312 FRANCIS BACON b. 1910
Study of the Nurse from the film 'Battleship Potemkin' 1957
Oil on canvas 78 × 56 (198 × 142)
Collection Mr and Mrs A.M. Burden, New York
Photo Marlborough Gallery

Index